THE BATTLES FOR
CASSINO

Battle Standards Military Paperbacks
from David & Charles

ASSAULT FROM THE SKY: A HISTORY OF AIRBORNE WARFARE
John Weeks

BATTLEFIELD BERLIN: SIEGE, SURRENDER AND OCCUPATION
Peter Slowe and Richard Woods

THE BATTLES FOR CASSINO
E. D. Smith

CHURCHILL AND THE GENERALS
Barrie Pitt

CAEN: THE BRUTAL BATTLE AND BREAKOUT FROM NORMANDY
Henry Maule

COMMANDOS AND RANGERS OF WORLD WAR II
James Ladd

DEVILS, NOT MEN: THE HISTORY OF THE FRENCH FOREIGN LEGION
Roy C. Anderson

DUNKIRK
John Harris

JACKBOOT: THE STORY OF THE GERMAN SOLDIER
John Laffin

LEADERSHIP IN WAR 1939–1945
Sir John Smyth VC

MEN OF GALLIPOLI: THE DARDANELLES AND GALLIPOLI EXPERIENCE
Peter Liddle

OPERATION MILLENIUM BOMBER HARRIS'S RAID ON COLOGNE
Eric Taylor

PEOPLE AT WAR 1914–1918
Edited by Michael Moynihan

PEOPLE AT WAR 1939–1945
Edited by Michael Moynihan

P.O.W.
Richard Garrett

THE LIFE AND DEATH OF HERMANN GOERING
Ewan Butler and Gordon Young

PRISONERS OF SANTO TOMAS
Celia Lucas

THE RAIDERS: THE WORLD'S ELITE STRIKE FORCES
Richard Garrett

THE RESCUERS: THE WORLD'S TOP ANTI-TERRORIST UNITS
Leroy Thompson

THE RETREAT FROM BURMA 1941–2
James Lunt

SECRET WARFARE: THE BATTLE OF CODES AND CIPHERS
Bruce Norman

THE ZULU WAR
David Clammer

BATTLE STANDARDS

THE BATTLES FOR
CASSINO

E. D. SMITH

A DAVID & CHARLES MILITARY BOOK

British Library Cataloguing in Publication Data

Smith, E. D. (Eric David), *1923–*
    Battles for Cassino.
    Battles for Cassino.
    1. World War 2.   Battle of Cassino
    I. Title
    940.54'21

ISBN 0–7153–9421–5

First published 1975 in hardback by
Ian Allan Ltd. This paperback edition
published 1989 by David & Charles Publishers plc
and printed in Great Britain by
Redwood Burn Limited, Trowbridge, Wiltshire
for David & Charles Publishers plc
Brunel House   Newton Abbot   Devon
Distributed in the U.S. by Sterling Publishing
Co. Inc., 2 Park Avenue, New York, NY 10016

Distributed in the United States by
Sterling Publishing Co. Inc,
2, Park Avenue, New York, NY 10016

Cover photographs
Front: A view of the Monastery on Monastery Hill, Cassino, after
        its capture by the Allied troops in May 1944. (*Imperial
        War Museum, London*)
Back: The Monastery *before 15 February 1944. (Imperial War
        Museum, London*)

Contents

Preface 6

Bibliography 7

1 Prologue 9

2 The Germans Come to Cassino 12

3 The Allies Come to Cassino—and Anzio 22

4 The First Battle—The Leaders and the Men Who Followed 34

5 The First Battle—The Monastery 42

6 The First Battle—The Rapido Fiasco 47

7 The First Battle—The Americans and the French Try Again 62

8 The Second Battle—Freyberg's Plan for Victory 77

9 The Second Battle Begins 92

10 The Second Battle Ends 102

11 The Third Battle—Freyberg Plans Again 108

12 The Third Battle is Launched 118

13 The Third Battle—The Climax 135

14 The Third Battle in Retrospect 159

15 The Fourth Battle: Operation Diadem 164

16 The Poles Come to Cassino 174

17 The Fourth Battle: Victory Unfolds 179

18 Rome and the Last Victory 192

19 Judgement 200

Epilogue 208

Index 211

Neither Victory Nor Defeat

"It is not the critic who counts, nor the man who points out how the strong man stumbled, or where the doer of deeds could have done them better. The credit belongs to the man who is actually in the arena; whose face is marred by dust and sweat and blood; who knows the great enthusiasms, the great devotions, and spends himself in a worthy cause; who, at the best, knows in the end the triumph of high achievement; and who, at the worst, if he fails at least fails while daring greatly so that his place shall never be with those cold and timid souls who know neither victory nor defeat." THEODORE ROOSEVELT

As a young man of twenty I played a minor and insignificant role in two of the Cassino battles. I had no real responsibility on my shoulders so that any mistake I made had little, if any, influence on events. I had two personal ambitions: the first was not to let my Gurkha soldiers down in any crisis; the second was to escape death and disablement if God so allowed. In no spirit of pride do I claim that I achieved both these aspirations.

One evening I scribbled in my diary the words: 'If I survive then, one day, I will write a book about all this. Surely it is pointless to keep on attacking the Monastery defences?' The diary is still in my possession; the date when I wrote those words was 19th March 1944; the place, Castle Hill. Twenty-five years later I found the diary and rediscovered a strong latent desire to write my version of the Cassino battles. By that time, however, it would have been impossible to rely on a fading memory and write an 'I was there' book or novel—I was tempted, but I am sure that such works must be written, if not during a lull in the fighting, then at least within hours of the actual events. Such an account will thus bear the tang of the battle-field and describe the brutal degradation of men at war—but its value as history will be doubtful.

Rightly or wrongly I decided to write a factual book on Cassino, although well aware that others have trodden this path before. I have consulted all the sources shown in the bibliography, in addition to the many personal, regimental and other records, official and unofficial, that have been made available to me by so many people.

The most rewarding aspect of writing a book like this has been the number of friends I have made in England, Europe and in the United States of America. I have received personal kindnesses from so many people that it would be difficult to list them all. It is surely a measure of the fascination of the Cassino battles that makes the survivors of whatever rank, walk of life or nationality, give so much assistance so readily and so courteously.

It is to them, men who fought at Cassino, that I dedicate this book.

'Life is eternal and love is immortal and death is only a horizon, and a horizon is nothing save the limit of our sight.'

Bibliography

I readily acknowledge my indebtedness to the following which were my main sources; some of these I milked unashamedly but have marked such passages by quotation marks!

The Alexander Memoirs by Field Marshal The Viscount Alexander of Tunis. Edited by John North   (Cassell)

The Allied Armies in Italy from 3 September 1943 to 12 December 1944 by Field Marshal The Viscount Alexander of Tunis (London) *Gazette* Supplement, 12th June 1950)

History of the Second World War, Vol V by Winston S. Churchill (Cassell)

Calculated Risks by General M. W. Clark   (Harper)

Command Missions by Lt. Gen. L. K. Truscott   (Boulton)

The General's Journal by Maj. Gen. Fred L. Walker   (Taylor Publishing Company)

Infantry Brigadier by Sir H. Kippenberger   (Oxford)

General Lord Freyberg VC by B. Singleton Gates   (Michael Joseph)

The Campaign in Italy by Eric Linklater   (HMSO)

An Army in Exile by General W. Anders   (Macmillan)

Report of the Supreme Allied Commander Mediterranean to the Combined Chiefs of Staff on the Italian Campaign   (HMSO)

Neither Fear nor Hope by General F. von Senger und Etterlin (Macdonald)

Monte Cassino by Charles Connell   (Elek Books)

Monte Cassino by R. Böhmler   (Cassell)

Cassino—Portrait of a Battle by F. Majdalany   (Longman Green)

The Monastery by F. Majdalany   (John Lane)

Return to Cassino by Harold L. Bond   (Dent)

Memoirs of/by Field Marshal Kesselring   (William Kimber)

Battle for Rome by General W. G. H. Jackson   (Batsford)

Campaign in Italy by General W. G. H. Jackson   (Batsford)

Anzio—the gamble that failed by M. Blumenson   (Weidenfeld & Nicolson)

Anzio—an epic of Bravery by F. Sheehen   (University of Oklahoma Press)

Salerno to the Alps by C. G. Starr   (Infantry Journal Press Washington)

The Sangro to Cassino by N. C. Phillips (Vol 1 of Official History of New Zealand in Second World War, Italian Campaign) (Owen Wellington)

The Road to Rome by Christopher Buckley   (Hodder and Stoughton)

Fourth Indian Division by Lt. Col. G. R. Stevens   (McLaren and Sons)

The Tiger Triumphs by Lt. Col. G. R. Stevens   (HMSO)

The Italian Campaign (1943 to 1945) by Shepperd   (Arthur Barker Limited)

The Battles of Cassino (HQ Scotland, 1971 Battle tour) by Col. J. H. Green   (HMSO)

Monte Cassino by Donald Hapgood and David Richardson (Augus and Robertson)

I obtained a lot of help and guidance from Regimental History of the following:

The Essex Regt (1929–1950)

The Royal Sussex Regt (1701–1955)

The Second Goorkha Rifles (Vol III)

The Ninth Gurkha Rifles

The Rajputana Rifles

The only time I have ever kept a diary, in adulthood, coincided with our ordeals in Cassino; the scribbled entries have been invaluable when compiling this book. Needless to say that little brown diary has been the source of quotations by 'a young British officer'. I trust that these have not been overdone.

Soldiers of many nations came to Cassino by sea and air and by many different land routes. Tens of thousands fought under the shadow of the Monastery, perched on the mountain above the ruined little town of Cassino and thousands were to die: rows of headstones in the War Cemeteries bear witness to the bitter struggle and the sacrifice of life made in the battles which raged during the early months of 1944. Today tourists come to visit the newly built Cassino town and drive up the mountain road to the beautiful Monastery, rebuilt and refurbished with such loving care on the ruins that remained after the battles for its possession were over. Visitors from many lands enter the Abbey where the word *PAX* is prominently displayed and gaze down at the countryside below, countryside which saw no peace and witnessed so much destruction between January and May 1944. To the younger generation it is already history, as dead as the soldiers in the cemeteries at the foot of the mountain. For the old and middle-aged, events have dimmed and they too wonder why so many men from different lands came to fight, and some to die, on Italian soil; from Great Britain, Germany and Austria, America and Canada, Poland and India, France and Nepal—and there were soldiers from other nations, too.

Events that brought the opposing armies to confront with each other at Cassino are covered in outline in the first two chapters and these are logical and easy to understand. Of much more complexity are the reasons and circumstances which brought the Allies to Italy to fight a campaign that no one wanted, and one that General Fuller was to describe as being: "Tactically the most absurd and strategically the most senseless campaign in the whole War". Several American writers have made similar comments and German historians tend to side with them. A different opinion was held by Winston Churchill who was consistent in his determination to carry the war to the Italian mainland, to destroy "The Fascist jackal" Mussolini, and thereafter, to attract the German forces "and keep the flame of War burning continually upon the Italian front". It is easy to declare that Churchill was the Allied leader who should take most of the responsibility—and blame, if there is any—for the Italian campaign but the chapter of events that eventually led to the Eighth Army crossing into Calabria on 3rd September 1943, and the Fifth Army convoys leaving for the Salerno beaches five days later, is a long and complicated one. It is part of the story of the whole campaign rather than the battles for Cassino. Suffice to say that in September 1943 no one on the Allied side expected a long drawn out slogging match which would take place from the toe of Italy to the Po valley, but then few expected that Adolf Hitler would decide that no territory was to be given up without a struggle. The British and Americans had different ideas and policies on how the war in Italy was to be waged and their misunderstandings helped the Germans to obey the 'do or die' order of their Fuehrer.

A glance at any atlas will soon show why a war in Italy can be called 'tactically absurd'—the long narrow one thousand mile peninsula; the mountains running down the middle like a fish-bone with peaks that reach 6,000 feet. The coastal plains on both flanks are intersected by fast flowing rivers in deep valleys, all subject to flooding and difficult to cross. All the requisites for a series of good defensive positions are available in Italy and any attacking army requires a considerable superiority in supporting fire by guns and from the air if it is to make any progress by land or, alternatively, complete supremacy at sea and in the air if amphibious forces are to prise open defences by landing in the rear of the defenders. Tactical problems can be resolved if a strategical policy is adopted which employs, to the hilt, a complete superiority in guns, ships and planes. One strategy which must be avoided is a slow and painful land battle from one end of the country to the other. In 1944 the Allies had the overall resources of men, ships and material in the Mediterranean to have adopted a strategy that could have won the campaign in a reasonably short period of time.

That they did not do so was caused by a deep disagreement between the British and Americans on how the war in Italy was to be fought. The British thought it was an ideal chance to take the fight to the border of Germany, a Third Front which would be "a great holding attack" (General Alexander) to draw away as many Germans as possible from Russia and from Occupied France. Before the landings in France began in June 1944, the Americans considered Italy to be a sideshow and viewed the campaign with suspicion: something that might well cause a postponement of 'Overlord' by taking away some of the men and materials of war which were being assembled in the UK, in preparation for the invasion of France. The Americans gave a higher priority to a projected landing in Southern France and, in their eyes, this continued to be more important, even after the German defences in Central Italy had begun to collapse in May 1944. The diverse policies of the British and Americans was the rock on which the campaign floundered—and which led to General Fuller's stricture that "Strategically it was the most senseless campaign in the War".

There were several changes in the overall strategy during the campaign in Italy. The Forces of General Alexander fought in a straitjacket created by the suspicions of the American Chiefs of Staff, who jealously guarded the 'Overlord' invasion plans from any sideshows that would weaken the enterprise. Alexander was not given enough men or sufficient landing craft to continue mounting amphibious operations, which would have been less costly than the grim series of battles his two armies had to fight from Salerno up to the north of Italy. On one or two occasions when Alexander out manoeuvred his opposite number, Kesselring, and seemed to be on the brink of a major victory, his wings were clipped by the withdrawal of precious infantry divisions and the even more precious landing craft to other theatres of war. And so, slowly, painfully, the Allied armies had to thrust their way to the north, winning gains at a terrible price. The campaign deteriorated into a slogging match between an experienced defending force, utilising all the natural topographical features to the utmost, and the invaders with their superiority in machines and sophisticated weapons of war.

Early in October 1943, Adolf Hitler announced his firm decision that nothing to the south of Rome was to be given up without a struggle. Thereafter, the unplanned campaign in Italy developed into a bitter and unrelenting struggle that eventually cost the Allies over 300,000 casualties. Many of the victims were to fall at Cassino during one of the four major battles that were fought there, battles which still excite controversial opinions from historians and old soldiers, more than thirty years after the events took place.

2

The Germans Come to Cassino

In September 1943 the Italian people greeted the news that Italy had capitulated with scenes of great jubilation and rejoicing. For a few hours the whole nation behaved as if a glorious victory had been achieved. Amidst this excited turmoil the Germans kept their heads and swiftly, efficiently moved units into Rome, and other key centres elsewhere, to disarm and disband their erstwhile comrades in the Italian Army. That there were so few incidents can be attributed to two reasons: firstly, the carefully prepared and brilliantly executed plans of the Germans, and secondly, the overwhelming desire of most of the Italian servicemen to celebrate peace and, if possible, to slip away quietly to their homes.

Rome, where an Allied landing either by sea or from the air, or both, was expected from day to day, was soon securely under German control. The prize for such an attempt was a glittering one, but Eisenhower and his staff had adjudged the risks too great. Fighter cover and support could not have been given to such a force while Rommel's divisions in North Italy were close at hand and would have played a quick and decisive part in the early stages of the battle. Nevertheless, even after the Fifth Army had landed at Salerno on the night of 8/9 September, the German High Command still believed that another Allied invasion was possible so that the Commander-in-Chief South, Field Marshal Kesselring, was left to deal with the Salerno landings, using only those divisions under his direct command. While the Tenth Army in the South desperately strove to throw Mark Clark's army back into the sea, Rommel's Army Group in upper Italy was still disarming Italian troops.

For Mark Clark and his Fifth Army, Salerno was saved from the brink of disaster by some tough fighting, by the guns of the Allied Navies and, not least, by the mysterious decision of Hitler to allow General Von Vietinghoff's small Tenth Army to fight unaided against both the advancing Eighth Army and the invaders at Salerno. Eventually after nine days of bitter struggle the crisis passed, Kesselring had been unable to seize a glorious opportunity and his thoughts could but turn to the possibility of denying to his opponents the early capture of Rome.

Rome was the prize dangled before the Allied generals and Churchill telegraphed his thoughts to Alexander that the end of October "might well see us in Rome". Such an objective was never formally presented to Eisenhower or Alexander by the Chiefs of Staff, but the words of Churchill were soon to be echoed by the soldiers of the many nations, already fighting in the Fifth and Eighth Armies in South Italy: "We will be in Rome by Christmas".

The cold hard facts of the situation in early October 1943 certainly did not indicate that another nine months would elapse before Rome was to fall or that fighting of the fiercest nature was going to make the world remember the names of Cassino, and, to a lesser extent, Anzio, for years to come. But the hesitant advance of the Allies from Calabria, added to the successful actions fought by the German Tenth Army, now caused one man to change his mind: Adolf Hitler.

Hitler had been wavering between the advice given by his distinguished Field Marshals, Rommel in the North and Kesselring as Commander-in-Chief South. Rommel saw little merit in denying the enemy possession of south or central Italy, he was not swayed by political and prestige reasons into defending Rome, and he feared the long vulnerable coast line. The German Reich should be defended, he maintained, from prepared positions in the Alps. Kesselring felt that the enemy should be held as far away from Germany as possible and thereafter made to fight for possession of a series of defensive lines. As an airman he was loth to abandon a succession of airfields that lay closer and closer to the heart of Germany: as a strategist, he felt that an upper Italy in enemy hands would be a dangerous base for other operations against his country.

Having originally abandoned Kesselring to his fate at Salerno and wasted valuable time in alternating between the two policies advocated by his Field Marshals, Hitler finally decided to appoint Kesselring as Commander-in-Chief in Italy and move Rommel to France. Belatedly, the earlier plans of Kesselring were given full support and backing: Rome was to remain in German hands as long as possible and to this end a 'Winter Line', south of the city, was to be defended at all costs.

Field Marshal Kesselring's handling of the subsequent campaign in Italy was to repay fully the trust of his Fuehrer. His choice of defensive positions skilfully slowed down the Allies and he kept their bombers at the maximum range possible from the Po valley and Southern Germany. Kesselring had an optimistic, bold approach to life which, coupled with his professional ability, soon began to influence Hitler into changing his previous orders and sending him more reinforcements. The Gustav Line, with one of its pivots at Monte Cassino, was "to be defended in strength". The Germans were coming to Cassino, to stay and to fight.

One of Kesselring's selected positions, the Gustav Line, was at the narrowest point of the Italian peninsula. During the autumn, military engineers, the Todt organisation and labour battalions had begun transforming an area well suited for defence into an extensive network of strong outposts. The villages and mountains reverberated to the sound of explosions and the hammer of pneumatic drills. Minefields were laid and rivers such as the Rapido and Garigliano were dammed in order to flood their valleys. The Gustav Line was one of three lines selected and strengthened: it was by far the most formidable and was to resist the assaults of the finest Allied divisions until May 1944.

To complete such elaborate defences required time, and this Kesselring obtained by a stubborn resistance across the whole front. On the east coast, the Eighth Army sector along the River Sangro, and on the Fifth Army near the rain-swollen River Volturno, Napoleon's fifth element—mud—began to slow down the highly mechanised British and American armies. For days on end rain poured down in torrents, turning the streams into rivers and the rivers into floods that covered the surrounding fields with a sea of mud. Operations were not impossible but the great power of the Allied Air Forces was severely restricted, the armoured formations could not be used and the outcome of battles was thus decided by the infantry with their closely-knit artillery and mortar support. The Germans therefore were fighting with more advantages than they could have expected: already their opponents' hopes were dying in the rain and mud. By the middle of November the one thing that was certain was Rome would remain in German hands until early 1944.

These outposts to the 'Winter Line' continued to exact a dreadful toll on the armies advancing up both coasts of Italy. Small German forces, skilfully handled and led by competent commanders, held up superior numbers by tactics that became all too familiar with the men of the Fifth and Eighth Armies. A firm stand on a hill or mountain, a fierce counter-attack at the moment when a British or American victory seemed assured, a quick German withdrawal to yet another feature, often behind a river; then the same process repeated again and again. Days passed, weeks went by, and it was becoming clear that Kesselring had the initiative although fighting a withdrawal. His forces were deciding where and when to fight and slowly, almost imperceptibly, the land campaign dreaded by the Americans was beginning to unfold itself.

As Christmas 1943 approached, Kesselring must have been well satisfied with the way events had gone. Naturally, too, he had regrets; for instance, the unfortunate dual command that had hampered his counter-measures at Salerno and allowed the enemy to seize the important airfields at Foggia at an early stage in the struggle. However, it was not in his nature to brood over the past, and the battles for the 'Winter Line' outposts were enough to keep his forces fully occupied.

This is not a history of a campaign but to understand the background to Cassino, and equally important, to Anzio, it is necessary to realise how bitterly contested these outpost battles were. The Germans had no intention of holding such positions for long although they were determined to make their opponents pay dearly for each and every gain. In their rear the preparations along the Gustav Line, and in particular around its pivot at Monte Cassino, went on apace. A skilfully fought delaying action in the mud and icy rain had already made a great contribution to the fiercer battles that were to follow.

For the men of the Fifth Army who fought and survived until the end of 1943, the advance forward became a series of bloody engagements. The crossing of the Volturno, the struggle for the Mignano Gap, the fighting for Monte Lungo and for the desperately contested Monte Camino—these and other names slowed down General Clark's Army with ever-mounting casualties in battles, from sickness, and from exhaustion. The progress of Montgomery and his Eighth Army was no more encouraging: Termoli fell in early October but first the River Sangro in November, and then desperate fighting at Ortona during Christmas 1943, brought the advance to a standstill by the New Year.

As the Allies knocked at the outer door of the Gustav Line it was time for Hitler to encourage his soldiers with exhortations like: "The Fuehrer expects the bitterest struggle for every yard". This they had obeyed and now in carefully planned defences under a very able corps commander, General von Senger und Etterlin, they awaited the tired Fifth Army with quiet confidence. Unless fresh American or British troops could be sent to Italy or another landing made behind the German defences, Alexander's armies would be bled white before they ever reached Rome.

Thus the German resistance in the closing weeks of 1943 had made another landing inevitable unless the campaign was to be allowed to fizzle out completely. To forego the capture of Rome, would, in Churchill's words, "have been regarded on all sides as a crushing blow"—and the old warrior statesman probably added "over my dead body" in a stentorian whisper. The problems of arranging such a landing were beset with political and strategical considerations. All Churchill's eloquence, determination and bargaining powers were to be needed in full measure before the seeds of Anzio finally came to fruition. Anzio was launched to save Cassino, or more accurately to open the road to Rome, and soon, as will be seen, attacks at Cassino had to be pressed hard in order to relieve the dangerous situation in the small bridgehead at Anzio.

For the Germans the task at Cassino and along the Gustav Line was clear-cut and simple to define, to hold on at all costs. The struggle in South Italy would continue to be the responsibility of the Tenth Army under General Von Vietinghoff, while further back Field Marshal Kesselring held reserves to counter another landing which he still deemed to be inevitable. For the Allies to continue to inch their way forward when the sea was theirs and the Luftwaffe was but an occasional marauder in the skies, seemed quite inconceivable to an air force general like Kesselring. It was also very understandable that the German High Command invariably underestimated the complex problems of any invasion by sea—and thus expected and feared frequent amphibious landings, not only in Italy, but at other points in Occupied Europe. Their expertise gained from two wars fought on land against most of Europe did not include any knowledge of seaborne invasions.

In contrast, their opponent had been learning valuable lessons about amphibious operations, firstly in North Africa, then in Sicily and recently at Salerno. The maritime nations of Britain and America had begun to appreciate the true benefits and to understand the real weaknesses of this mode of warfare. Salerno had taught them that the problems and risks must never be discounted or underestimated. Kesselring and his staff correctly appreciated that the deadlock in Italy would force the Allies into making another landing. What they did not realise was that such a decision was to be made only after intense negotiations, many conferences and deeply divided counsel. In all these deliberations shone the stubborn will and determination of one man, Winston Churchill: in the end his perseverance won the day, but his victory was one that was made and remained under the shadow of that tyrant, 'Overlord'.

Before an examination is made of the Allied discussions that were to have such far reaching effects early in 1944, let us now see why the Germans selected Cassino as the hard core of their Gustav Line. The most important fact was not its natural strength, which was considerable, but that it barred the Liri valley, the road to Rome. If there were alternative routes up the Italian peninsula during the winter months then obviously the Anglo-American forces would have taken them rather than bludgeon their way against a position reputed to be impregnable. What were the factors that led both sides to the same conclusion about the importance of Cassino?

There is no better or more lucid description than Field Marshal Alexander's words in the London *Gazette* of 1950: "I have already described the Liri valley as the gateway to Rome and alluded to the strength of the defences of the gate. A description of the terrain now facing us will make clear the reasons why this one sector was the only place where we could hope to develop an advance in strength and why I was obliged to transfer there ever-increasing forces until by next May the bulk of my Armies was disposed in the Tyrrhenian sector. The Adriatic coastal plain in which the Eighth Army had been operating leads nowhere except eventually to Ancona. The centre of the peninsula is filled by the Apennines which here reach their greatest height: they were now under deep snow and even in summer are quite impracticable for the movement of large forces. The west coast rises steeply into the trackless Aurunci and Lepini mountains and the coastal road runs close to the seashore, except for a short stretch in the plains of Fondi until it debouches into the Pontine Marshes which the Germans had flooded. The Aurunci and Lepini mountains are separated from the main Apennine range, however, by the valley of the Liri. The gap thereby formed through which runs Route 6, the Via Casilina, varies in width from four to seven miles".

Thus the only practicable road to Rome during the winter months was the Via Casilina which runs through a gap to the entrance of the main Liri valley—the Liri valley which could allow the Allies in dry weather to use their great superiority in armour for the first time in Italy. If there had to be an assault on the Gustav Line before the spring weather opened up other possibilities, then it had to be one along Route 6 into the Liri valley—and thence to Rome. Without any political or strategic considerations and blessed with the benefits of hindsight, the best tactical solution would have been an acceptance of a stalemate until April 1944. Such a situation did develop in the Eighth Army sector where both sides held their respective sectors on the Adriatic coastal plain behind strongpoints, covered and aided by the probing of patrols and screened by a defensive curtain of minefields and artillery fire. But to understand the story of Cassino, of Anzio, and indeed of the whole Italian campaign, is to realise that the tactical considerations on the battle field were always subject to the larger issues that faced the Allied leaders in their war against Germany and Japan.

The commander of the German XIV Panzer Corps, General von Senger und Etterlin, was equally convinced that the lure of the Liri valley would attract the main Allied thrust against the gate to the valley itself, the key of which could only be turned by the capture of Monte Cassino. At this gateway to Rome, many armies in past centuries had found the position at Cassino ideal for defence. In the past, the Italian Military College had cited it as being a model of impregnable terrain. If there were a few chinks in 'the titanic setting, noble and theatrical' (Christopher Buckley) then von Senger had time to seal these off before the main battles began.

Monte Cassino—Monastery Hill, as it became known to the men of the many nations who fought under its shadow for so many weeks—completely controlled both the valley that lay before it and also the Liri river to the north-west. Route 6 runs up to, then around the foot of the southern flank of Monastery Hill, having passed through the little town of Cassino which itself snuggles under the haunches of the 1600 foot hill. From the summit of Monte Cassino, an observer could watch any movement in both the valleys, and by artillery and mortar fire seal off the vital artery to Rome, Route 6.

Nature had granted one more advantage to the defenders on Monte Cassino and on the adjacent heights to the north, the heights that culminate at the crest of Monte Caira, a huge cone rising some five thousand feet above the valley of the Rapido. For if the Monte Cassino feature can be likened to a mediaeval castle, then the river Rapido is like a moat which has to be crossed before the ramparts can be attacked. The Rapido, as the name implies, is a fast-flowing river but equally relevant it rushes through a low-lying valley which can be flooded with ease if men so desire. The Germans not only desired; they had the time and the incentive to improve natural defensive barriers with all the means at their disposal.

To the north of the town of Cassino, German engineers dammed the river so that much of the valley was turned into a sea of mud and swamp. Following the river down, both banks were heavily mined, with trip wires laid on all the likely crossing places and approaches, and existing farm buildings and outhouses were strengthened or converted for defensive purposes.

All the civilians had been moved from the town which, in turn, became heavily fortified. Concrete reinforced buildings were transformed into strongpoints designed to withstand bomb and shell. A few tanks were concealed inside some of the larger houses, tanks so placed that no one could pass them while their crews lived to man the guns or shells remained to be fired at the enemy. Cellars and bunkers were constructed on all possible routes into the town.

Above the town, the work continued in a similar fashion on the face of Monte Cassino itself. Caves were created or enlarged so that guns could be hidden and gun-crews housed. Machine-gun emplacements were made, strengthened and camouflaged. In the deep valleys and ravines mortar emplacements were sited and the guns were ranged on to meticulously plotted targets. And wherever the gorse thickets grew on the mountainside, mines, booby traps and wire were hidden with all the ingenuity of an experienced defender.

Day by day the work went on under the vigilant supervision of

General von Senger und Etterlin. If any further incentive was needed to the stirring battle orders received from Adolf Hitler, then the ever-increasing background noise of the Allied guns acted as a spur to the men who laboured at creating a barrier that would cause the Allies to remember the name of Cassino for many months to come.

In January 1944 the German Tenth Army finally moved back to occupy the Gustav Line: there was little time to spare if they were to get there before the Fifth Army because on the 15th January, the last outpost, Monte Trocchio, barely one and a half miles from Cassino, was taken by the Americans. From that moment on, the hill would serve as the forward observation post for, first, the Fifth Army and later in the Spring of 1944, the Eighth Army as their soldiers battled for possession of Monte Cassino.

Field Marshal Kesselring paid a well deserved tribute to his soldiers who had come to Cassino, under pressure and step by step, from the battles of Salerno and the South. He said, amongst other things: "Eisenhower's and Montgomery's hopes have been thwarted because we have survived all the hardships of mountain warfare and have risen superior to both the physical and moral effects of the heaviest possible artillery bombardments and air attacks". At about that time Eisenhower and Montgomery left Italy to take over new responsibilities in connection with the projected Second Front so that Kesselring's words meant little to them personally. But for Alexander, for Mark Clark and the new Eighth Army commander Oliver Leese, the statement to his German soldiers ended with a prophetic truth: "Your soldierly bearing in battle, the steadiness of your morale, and the skill of your leaders will continue to thwart every enemy attempt to destroy us".

Cassino and Anzio are names that bear witness to the truth of Kesselring's Order of the Day. It is also an appropriate moment to pay a tribute to the German divisions who had fought this long rearguard action south of the Gustav Line: 9th Division, 29 Panzer Grenadier Division, 15 Panzer Division, The Hermann Goering Division, 5 Mountain Division. Much was to be made of the true fact that the American Fifth Army began the first Cassino battle in an exhausted state after weeks of searing struggle against the elements as well as the Germans. However, at the same time, it must be remembered that the German divisions which first occupied Cassino and the surrounding mountains contained few fresh or rested soldiers.

If anything, for them the struggle had been harder because, always lacking the resources of their enemy, the Germans had fought under a sky completely ruled by the Allied air forces. Every move by day had invited the attention of British and American pilots and even at night the supply lines to the rear were under heavy attack. The German Tenth Army was continually forced to plug the gaps in the front by moving formations from one crisis point to another. Only one Division, 94 Infantry Division, was rested and at full strength when the struggle for Cassino began. All the others were under strength and physically exhausted, but morale even after a succession of withdrawals was still at a strikingly high level. The German soldiers were fighting each battle just as toughly and bravely as the one before. Now at Cassino, behind fortifications carefully planned and prepared, there were to be no more retreats without the bitterest struggle; every yard was to be contested on the express order of the Fuehrer himself.

These soldiers of Germany obeyed the order to the very letter.

3

The Allies Come to Cassino—and Anzio

For the Allied planners the hopes of autumn slowly died. As the winter approached, the weather conspired to make the terrain as hostile as the German defenders themselves. No longer could optimistic intelligence officers talk about weakened German forces when all the evidence showed that fresh troops were available in upper Italy and that the Gustav Line was going to be defended to the death.

Now, for the first time, the long term implications of this campaign had to be faced with realism. The most unpalatable fact was that in Italy itself there were approximately twenty enemy divisions—the word 'approximately' is used advisedly as the number was not always a constant one. Although only eight of these were south of Rome, others could be moved down from upper Italy either to relieve tired comrades or to be used for any particular operational role.

The Allied commanders in Italy appreciated that their primary task was to draw German divisions away from north-west Europe and Russia: to draw and keep them away implied offensive action being continued throughout the winter. Within the directive that had been given them there was no alternative and to effect it meant ceaseless aggression "to keep the Germans on their heels", as Alexander put it. But equally obvious was that such a policy of unrelenting pressure would have to be carried out in the heart of winter when Allied superiority in the air, in tanks, armour and in vehicles, would be nullified by the weather, the mud, impassable roads and swollen rivers.

The drive towards Rome and a series of all out attacks on the German Army could only take place if fresh forces and infantry in particular, could be made available, not only to keep up the pressure on the existing fronts but to land behind the heavily fortified German defensive lines. Reserve divisions were required, logistic support had to be assured, and assault-shipping in sufficient numbers both to mount and maintain amphibious operations, were vital requisites if offensive action were to continue. But hanging over the Allied planners in Italy were decisions that had been taken during the Trident conference at Washington in May 1943, before Sicily had been invaded or Italy had capitulated. For example, seven divisions—four American and three British—were to be ready to move to Britain by November 1943. In addition a large proportion of naval forces and landing craft were either earmarked for 'Overlord' or, to Churchill's great dismay, for operations in the Far East.

At the time the Trident decisions were made, and agreed to with reluctance by the British, no definite instruction had been issued to withdraw vital troops, ships and stores from Italy. After the Sicilian campaign had ended such a proviso was insisted on by the US Chiefs of Staff and thereafter remained inviolate in their eyes, although subject to ever-increasing oral attacks by Churchill and his service advisers.

By late October 1943, one American commander was beginning to realise how the shackles had been thrown around the forces under his overall command. General Eisenhower, with three months still to go before handing over his responsibilities in the Mediterranean, increasingly found himself restricted by the policies of his President and the way his wings were being clipped by the withdrawal of vital forces from Italy. At a time when the advance on both coasts was faltering, it was clear that another reappraisal would have to be made. Churchill sent a series of telegrams urging action to Roosevelt, to Eisenhower and to Alexander, but no radical change in policy could be made until the fourth Allied conference was held in Cairo and Teheran, between the 22nd of November and the 7th of December 1943.

It was in Cairo that Churchill made the remark that explained the British viewpoint in a sentence: "Overlord remains top of the activity in the Mediterranean". He was not attempting to detract from or reduce the scope of the Second Front invasion, but he was determined and keen to exploit the German problems in the Mediterranean—in Churchill's eyes the whole area was then a theatre of exciting possibilities. The Aegean Islands, Tito's Partisans in Yugoslavia, the South of France, all these were prospects that might bear rich fruit. But apart from the troops required, any further amphibious operations would need more and more landing

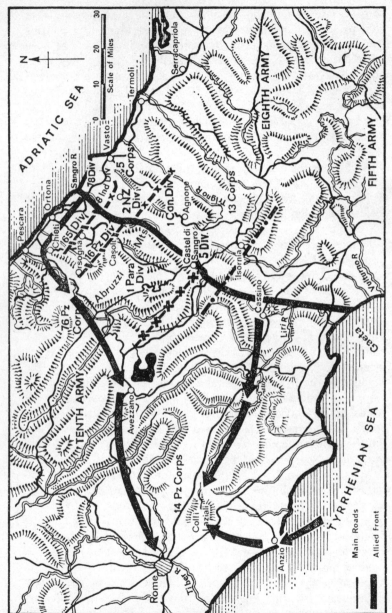

Map 1: General Alexander's plan of the Central Italian Battlefield (dispositions as on 14th November 1943).

craft—and it was planned that 68 of these precious ships would sail to England for repair and refitting, prior to Overlord or for use in amphibious operations in South East Asia.

Although initially the main opposition to the British plans came from the United States Chiefs of Staff, it was Stalin who was determined to keep his Allies away from the Balkans and the Eastern Mediterranean. For his own political reasons he strongly urged that, on military grounds, the Italian campaign should be of a low priority, with its sole purpose being to act as a springboard for the invasion of Southern France in support of the Second Front. Stalin's views were welcomed by the Americans and the British were forced to compromise and seek another solution.

The wrangling between the Allies at the Cairo and Teheran conferences eventually produced decisions that gave the British a little but, as it transpired, too little for the success of the campaign in Italy. Overlord, quite rightly, remained untouched—and an invasion of South France, 'Anvil', was given next priority. For the first time, the immediate aim of capturing Rome was officially acknowledged, with a subsequent advance to the Pisa-Rimini Line being authorised; and it was stressed that pressure was to be maintained on the German Army in Italy only as far as the detachment of forces for Anvil would allow.

Finally, the complex question of landing craft was temporarily resolved; 68 LSTs, which were due to sail from Italy on 5th December, could be retained until mid-January 1944. Thus it appeared that another landing on the coast of Italy could be made even if, of necessity, its scope would be limited. Moreover it would have to be launched in January irrespective of what progress was being made by Fifth Army, south of the Gustav Line. Churchill had obtained these concessions with great skill and patience; thereafter he awaited detailed plans from Alexander's Army Group to see how his efforts at the conference table could lead to the fall of Rome and a revitalised campaign in Italy.

To Churchill's dismay the plans provided little encouragement, chiefly because by this time both the Fifth and Eighth Armies were painfully edging their way forward at a great cost. If a landing was to be made south of Rome then it was essential that the main Fifth Army was capable of joining up quickly with the amphibious force, which itself needed to be strong enough to stand on its own as well as being capable of "clawing the Germans down from the rear". In mid-December 1943 it was clear to the Commander of the Fifth Army, General Mark Clark, that there was little chance of any immediate break through to link up with such a beach-head unless the landing force posed such a threat and caused the German Tenth Army to abandon the Gustav Line. Only if the assaulting forces achieved complete surprise, and acted in an aggressive manner, was it just possible that the Germans might panic and withdraw to the north of Rome.

The precious landing craft had to be used before the deadline date for their return to England, which meant that an initial striking force of two divisions would have to be mounted, subsequently landed, quickly reinforced and maintained through the beach-head. All this had to be accomplished if the chance was to be taken to end the costly deadlock into which the Italian campaign had been drifting since September 1943. Once again, Mr Winston Churchill was galvanised into action: signals flew in all directions; staff officers in London and in the Mediterranean were asked to re-examine the means of obtaining more shipping or retaining existing landing craft; the American President was asked, once again, to agree to the precious assault ships being held until February 1944, a further postponement which meant a delay of a few more weeks.

The eloquence, energy and the strong determination of the British Prime Minister overcame all these obstacles, swayed those of his colleagues who had doubts, and for the moment scorned the sceptics into silence. Anzio was, in truth, a Churchillian enterprise and his delight at the President's acceptance of the plan for the landing caused him to signal: "I thank God for this fine decision which engages us once again in wholehearted unity for a great enterprise".

Planning time for such a complicated operation was short, woefully short especially as the President's decision to release the landing craft was only received on the 28th December. The landing code name 'Shingle', was to take place as near to the 20th January 1944 as possible—this date would take advantage of the best landing conditions and allow the assault shipping to be released in early February. The Fifth Army planning team for 'Shingle' had to work under severe pressure. They selected a beach for the landing near the small port of Anzio and decided that the force, under the command of the American General Lucas, was to consist of four divisions, some commandos, a ranger battalion and a US para-chute regiment.

The detailed plans for Anzio, and indeed the story of the land-ing itself, are not within the scope of this work except so far as they influenced the battles of Cassino, soon to begin. Such an influence was felt from the beginning because Alexander could now plan his strategy on the main front. The first move would find the bulk of the Fifth Army striking at the Gustav Line to draw Kesselring's reserves southwards towards the Liri valley. Then, the 'Shingle' force under General Lucas would land and force the Ger-mans to shift their balance yet again. Such a situation, with a large and, Churchill hoped, aggressive force in their rear, would unsettle the Germans so as to cause them to withdraw to the north of Rome. On paper the whole plan seemed to promise success be-cause the aim was clear and hopes were high that this was to be 'The Battle for Rome', as HQ 15 Army Group optimistically called the Operational Instruction.

There is little doubt that Allied Intelligence assessments had helped to build up a spirit of optimism by painting a picture of an exhausted German Army, its morale at cracking point and with few available reserves. Such an attitude was reflected in the Fifth Army Intelligence Summary dated 16th January which ended by saying: "It would appear doubtful if the enemy can hold the or-ganised defensive line through Cassino against a co-ordinated army attack. Since this is to be launched before Shingle it is con-sidered likely that this additional threat will cause him to withdraw from his defensive position once he has appreciated the magnitude of that operation".

Fred Majdalany, after quoting that intelligence summary, con-sidered that it must surely take a prize as one of the most remarka-ble pieces of wishful deduction in the war. Just wanting something to happen was not enough especially when faced by adversaries like the Germans. Wishing will not win battles or, in the words of the song, make it so. The Allied generals were soon to find out that the hard facts of life in early 1944 continued to be a resolute enemy, a wet, bitter winter and a hostile terrain, all of which proved to be more difficult to conquer than the string of outposts the Fifth Army had captured between Salerno and Cassino.

While detailed planning for the Shingle operation continued against the clock but with relative smoothness, Fifth Army was engaged in closing up to the entrance of the Liri valley, guarded by the River Rapido. Monte Trocchio fell on the 15th January to the soldiers of II (US) Corps, only five days before the same men were due to begin their part in the next winter offensive. The time factor here was to be even more limiting and crippling than the three weeks' grace given to the planning staff for Shingle because the overall plan demanded that the whole of the Cassino front should be ablaze before the first soldiers landed at Anzio on 22nd January.

Alexander's formal directive to Mark Clark had ordered him "to make as strong a thrust towards Cassino and Frosinone shortly prior to the assault landing to draw in enemy reserves which might be employed against the landing forces: and then create a breach in his front through which every opportunity will be taken to link up rapidly with the seaborne operation".

Without doubt, General Clark's plan to implement this directive was based on the trump card being played at Anzio. General Truscott, later destined to play a vital role at Anzio, mentions in his memoirs ('Command Mission') that Clark believed that provided the beach-head held firm, then it would cause the Germans so much concern that they would withdraw from the southern front. Such an assessment by Clark influenced the way in which the Anzio beach-head was established and the initial moves made by Fifth Army against the Gustav Line.

As far as Churchill was concerned, his concept for Anzio did not visualise a beach-head being established, merely to be held until it was sealed off by the Germans. Such tactics at Salerno had nearly led to disaster. In Churchill's mind the Anzio landing was a calculated risk which would gain the prize of Rome and justify the importance attached to the Italian campaign by the British Government. Alexander, too, hoped that if complete surprise were obtained, then the invaders would move inland to seize the Alban Hills and thus cut off the German Tenth Army operating in the south. Be that as it may, Mark Clark's orders to General Lucas did not reflect the aggressive wishes of the British Prime Minister: Lucas was "to seize and secure a beach-head in the vicinity of Anzio . . ." when he was "to advance to the Alban Hills". But there was no reference to speed or rapid exploitation. Without doubt, General Clark's instructions were based on the optimistic intelligence forecast that the mere presence of such a beach-head would cause the Germans to panic and pull back. In addition, Clark's experiences during the tough battle of Salerno made him treat the projected landings at Anzio with caution and care.

To the prematurely old and battle-weary General Lucas, Clark's instructions meant but one thing; a strong, secure beach-head would have to be built up before any aggressive action could even be contemplated. Basically he had little faith in the enterprise anyway. While Churchill wrote that "it was with tense, but, I trust, suppressed excitement that I awaited the outcome of this considerable stroke", the commander in whom he put such trust was writing that the Anzio enterprise "bore the strong odour of Gallipoli and apparently the same amateur was still on the coach's bench". The story of Anzio, like Gallipoli, might have been very different if the 'amateur' himself had been a commander in the beach-head instead of a statesman, tense with excitement, back in London.

Provided that the Germans reacted in confusion to the new and surprise threat to Rome, in the way Clark hoped they would, the last part of Alexander's directive, the creation of a breach in the main front, might be brought about without too much fighting and when the Liri valley would be open to a rapid thrust forward by the Allied armour. General Clark did not plan such a breach in any detail but concentrated on a show of force along the whole front which, he hoped, would draw away German reserves from the Rome area and pin them down on the main front before the assault boats touched the beaches of Anzio. These preliminary attacks were not really capable of breaking the Gustav Line because the plan of making three Corps probe forward over a wide front meant that any local success obtained could not be exploited and turned into a major breakthrough. There was nothing readily available to be quickly pushed through any gaps made in the German defences.

On the extreme left, on the 17th January, the British 10 Corps began to force a crossing over the River Garigliano near the coast, a none-too-easy task across a large fast-flowing river in winter under the eyes of vigilant German defenders. Initially, this well planned attack was successful, bridge heads were established, the town of Castelforte was threatened and the German 94 Division was in a lot of trouble. Indeed it could be said that the left flank of the Gustav Line had been dented; certainly the Corps commander,

General von Senger, was so alarmed by events as to ask for reinforcements from Field Marshal Kesselring.

If General Mark Clark did not recognise this as promising to lead to an important success, Field Marshal Kesselring did. Although he believed that an Allied landing south of Rome was imminent if not overdue, Kesselring showed great courage and decisiveness in dealing with the crisis near Castelforte. The 29th and 90th Panzer Divisions were sent from the Rome area and by the 21st January were counter-attacking 10 Corps. The first, and best chance of turning the Gustav Line ended in a victory for the Germans—but only just. On its own, 10 Corps lacked reserves when the early breach had been opened but its three divisions made Anzio possible by drawing the two German reserve divisions away from Rome; this is an important fact to be remembered when the story of the first Cassino battle is told and an assessment is made as to whether the heavy losses of the American 36 Division were warranted or had any strategic or tactical significance whatever.

Before we leave the attack by 10 Corps certain questions must be posed and answered: the early gains, won near the coast by British Corps, could these have been pressed home? From where could troops have been obtained to reinforce their bridge-heads over the Garigliano? Could extra troops have been in battle before the German divisions arrived from Rome?

The answers must surely be that although the original Fifth Army plan of attacking over a wide front was an indifferent one, there was still time to have cancelled or altered the projected II Corps assault across the Rapido, and to have moved one or both American Divisions across to exploit the British thrust over the Garigliano. Time was short but many of the American troops could have been in action at least three days before the two Panzer Grenadier Divisions made their presence felt. The entrance to the Liri valley might have been outflanked if this opportunity had been recognised and thereafter exploited.

Only the Germans recognised how near to disaster the south end of the Gustav Line was until their reserve divisions arrived and, with little time to spare, were able to plug the gap. The three British divisions of 10 Corps had shown that there was a way over the Garigliano and up the Ausente, following the axis of Route 7. It is true that later Route 7 "became involved with the Aurunci

Mountains", (Alexander's words and misgivings), but eventually in May 1944, the thrust of some seven divisions through these hills prised open the Gustav Line. It is also true that seven divisions were not available in January but less might have won the day at a time when the German 94 Division was completely surprised between the 17th and 19th January by 10 Corps' attack.

Thereafter the Fifth Army plan of piecemeal attacks continued as arranged. On the extreme right another attempt to outflank the Cassino bastion was made by the French Corps under General Juin. This began on the 12th of January and like 10 Corps the French had an encouraging start. The Moroccan and Algerian Colonial troops were experienced in mountain warfare, were well led by the best of French officers, and in Juin they had a commander of great ability. Juin was convinced that his plan of thrusting into the Liri valley via the Atina basin was possible provided that logistic support over the mountains was assured and an extra division was made available to keep up the pressure. Unfortunately Juin's great personal charm, loyal spirit and co-operative manner never commanded a lot of influence in the Anglo-American councils of war in Italy and his pleas were disregarded by his superiors.

If an extra division had been sought to help Juin then it might have come from Eighth Army resources. Already, there was discussion about bringing two experienced divisions across from the Adriatic Coast. One of these, the Fourth Indian, had considerable experience in mountain warfare with its newly joined II Brigade having recently undergone extensive training in the Lebanese mountains. General Tuker, the Fourth Indian Division commander, whose part in the Cassino battle was to be sadly curtailed by a severe illness, later maintained that Juin's Corps, aided by his Division, could have opened the Liri valley from the north.

The fascination of the Cassino battles and indeed, of the early probes against the Gustav Line itself, lies in the perennial question 'If this had been done would the result have been different?' Historians may surmise and then assess chances but even with the comfort of hindsight it is impossible to claim a particular outcome with any degree of assurance. Battles are fought by men, and the result of any day's fighting may depend on some relatively minor mistake made by a junior officer. Brilliant plans on paper can only be adjudged by results after the operation is over. In every battle it will be found that some plans go awry because Man is unpredictable and an enemy rarely reacts in quite the way his opponent antici-pates.

Juin, with the support of Tuker's Fourth Indian Division, might have opened the northern flank. It is equally possible that the se-vere winter of February and March 1944 might have made the lo-gistic support of such a force far too difficult a venture. No verdict can be given except to note that General Senger was to remain concerned about his northern flank until early February when the divisions of the French Corps had shot their bolt. By that time they had become involved in the first battle for Cassino and some of their story will follow in another chapter.

The two attempts to turn the flanks of the Gustav Line had given encouragement to the Allies and had caused the Germans a lot of worry but both attacks failed because nothing could be done to exploit their early successes. The German Corps commander, General von Senger und Etterlin, albeit with the aid of the two di-visions from Rome, was able to move his reserves to the right places at the crucial moments. He was able to do this without at any time weakening the key stronghold at Cassino because the thrusts against his flanks were not strong enough and dissipated over too wide a front. He sensed that these moves were but the overture to an impending main thrust, aimed at the Liri valley and made in the most direct manner—across the River Rapido, astride Route 6 into the town of Cassino, and against its guardian feature, Monte Cassino.

Fifth Army's next step, the attack in the centre across the Rapido was due to begin on the 20th January, two days before General Lucas' force landed at Anzio. The strength of the all but impregnable Cassino defences were about to be tested by a mod-ern army, aided by the weapons available to its soldiers after five years of war.

The main battles for Cassino were about to begin. For the American II Corps and 36th (Texas) Division in particular, the experience was to be one which would never be forgotten by those who survived.

National differences in the political and strategical waging of the war in Italy had led the Allies to this situation—the launching of a hurried attack on Cassino in order to assist a landing at Anzio which had to take place before the extra assault ships were with-drawn from the Mediterranean. Anzio, which was seized to curtail a long struggle at Cassino, was soon to require unrelenting pressure by the troops at Cassino in order that the pitifully small beach-head could survive.

The opposing armies at Cassino were separated by the small but swollen River Rapido as the prologue to the first battle came to a close. The senior commanders on both sides were about to be tested and the outcome of each of the four battles was influenced, to varying degrees, by the personalities of the leading figures in the tragedy of Cassino: Generals Alexander, Clark and Freyberg, Walker and Ryder, von Senger, Heidrich and Baade, and in the final stages, General Anders of Poland. Each and every one of these Generals was to taste the bitterness of defeat as well as savouring moments of triumph.

4

The First Battle—The Leaders and the Men Who Followed

The battles at Cassino were never directly controlled by the two opposing Commanders-in-Chief, Alexander and Kesselring, but their strategy had brought the armies face to face near the banks of the River Rapido by the middle of January 1944. Alexander had to keep the pressure on the Germans throughout the winter in order to carry out the directive given him by his political and military masters, a directive which now included the early capture of Rome. By his successful dogged defence of Southern Italy, Kesselring too had been given a directive by his Supreme Commander, to fight for every yard and not to give up anything without a struggle.

Both commanders were to suffer from these directives. Alexander found that he was forced to attack, and to keep attacking, at a time when the climatic conditions combined with the unfriendly terrain indicated a period of relative inactivity. On the other hand, although initially Kesselring was sustained by the fiery messages of defiance sent by Adolf Hitler, later in the campaign when a quick withdrawal might have saved a particular situation, he was made to justify such a measure before permission was given and on one or two occasions he was urged to hold on until the position became untenable.

Fortunately both men were of such a temperament that they could withstand the pressures imposed on them from above, and still retain the trust of superiors and subordinates alike. Alexander and Kesselring were outstanding commanders—dissimilar in physique with different service careers and experiences, their achievements and qualities made them worthy opponents who were evenly matched. While Alexander was given superiority in resources and virtual control of the seas and the air, Kesselring was favoured by the terrain of Italy which enabled his army to remain on even terms while fighting one defensive battle after another during the long withdrawal from south to north.

General Sir Harold Alexander, as he was in January 1944, had become one of the most experienced generals in the War. He had faced early disasters in France and Burma in a calm steadfast manner and he had experienced triumphs in North Africa and Sicily in the same quiet, dignified and unassuming way. Alexander was a charming officer and gentleman but, more than that, he was a magnificent soldier who did not need a public-relations machine to project his image. His neat and well turned out presence, his cool judgment and complete disregard of danger earned him the respect of the Americans as well as the British.

On many occasions during the Italian campaign, soldiers in the front line were inspired by the presence of their immaculately dressed Commander-in-Chief as he arrived, without fuss or bother, to examine key positions and see for himself how his soldiers were faring. He was welcomed and admired without reservation by the polyglot army that fought under his command: by the British, Americans, French, Indians, New Zealanders, Poles—and even then the list is incomplete. Perhaps there is no better way of conveying the respect and esteem in which this modest soldier was held than by quoting an American General, Truscott, who wrote: "He had all the personality and drive of Patton and Montgomery without any of their flamboyance. He had the intellect and astute diplomatic skill of Eisenhower; he was outstanding among the Allied leaders".

It is completely in the character of such a man that unlike his wartime colleagues, nearly twenty years were to elapse before he allowed his memoirs to be published, memoirs that contain neither excuses nor recriminations against superior or subordinate, but are full of praise for the men he led to final victory.

Alexander's great popularity was achieved without any conscious efforts being made to appeal to those working with him in the Allied armies in Italy. Nevertheless, although he was able to weld together the diverse, and often strong personalities of the Allied leaders under his command, the seeds of a weakness were to some extent hidden by Alexander's easy-going and somewhat detached attitude to life. Firm directives were not always forthcoming when these were required in a crisis and Alexander was sometimes inclined to allow subordinate commanders a little too much scope when it was clear that their handling of a particular battle was at fault. History will have to decide to what extent such an attitude was forced on Alexander by his role as co-ordinator, at the head of a multi-racial army group, as opposed to his own reluctance to tackle unpleasant details. Whatever the verdict, there is little doubt that Alexander's character was an important factor in the battles of Cassino, with his triumph being obtained when the Gustav Line was shattered in May 1944.

Throughout the Italian campaign Alexander was continually seeking to outwit his opponent and on several occasions he obtained complete surprise by the timing and direction of a major thrust and by the unexpected strength of an offensive. A lesser man than Kesselring would have been hard put to retrieve and redress such situations. But, like a skilled boxer, the German Commander-in-Chief was always quick to regain his balance, to nullify the body blow, and to ride the possible knock-out punch so that his army lived to fight in yet another hard-fought battle.

Kesselring, too, dispensed with showmanship and eschewed anything flamboyant. He was an airman who had not always basked in the favour of his Fuehrer although he had never taken any interest in German politics. Hitler knew that Kesselring had considerable affection for the people of Italy and suspected that the Field Marshal had been hoodwinked in 1943 by the Italian conspirators who had overthrown Mussolini. That was one of the reasons which had caused Hitler to hesitate and vacillate before entrusting Kesselring with the defence of Italy. Kesselring accepted his initial eclipse, and then his subsequent reinstatement, with complete loyalty and equanimity. Writing his memoirs retrospectively after the War, he did not reveal any bitter thoughts or words about these episodes.

Kesselring convinced the German High Command that it was not only possible to hold the Allies south of Rome but that there were distinct advantages in doing so. As stated, he did not favour a strategy which allowed the Allies, and their air fleets, to close up to the southern border of Germany without exacting the maximum penalties in men, machines and time. After Hitler had given him full support Kesselring was able to fight such a delaying action with somewhat limited resources but with considerable skill—even though the all-important airfields around Foggia had already been lost to the Allies before his strategy had gained the Fuehrer's approval.

Field Marshal Kesselring, a man of simple tastes, was a hard worker who radiated optimism and faith even when ill-tidings and gloomy prospects were constant visitors to his headquarters. Subordinate commanders respected his judgement, admired his self confidence and enjoyed a great measure of independence within their own commands. If he interfered then it was at some crisis when he would make firm decisions without recrimination or delay. It is one of the ironies of the Italian campaign that this airman fought a land campaign against an enemy, invariably superior in numbers and always in materials, with his own air force completely outnumbered and outclassed. As the campaign unfolded so did Hitler's trust increase and after the War was over, Kesselring summed up his position vis-à-vis Adolf Hitler: "I always succeeded in persuading Hitler to agree to my suggestions and in extricating my troops from the most difficult situations without total loss, I had won Hitler's unreserved confidence. He knew I had no axe to grind".

Alexander and Kesselring were indeed well matched and both were worthy of the trust placed in them by their armies.

The two Corps that confronted each other during the First battle of Cassino were the Second American and Fourteenth (German) Panzer Corps respectively. The latter formation was responsible for the southern half of the Gustav Line and was thus stretched to the limit: five divisions were in the line without any immediate reserves when the first Allied attacks were launched by the Fifth Army. The American II Corps consisted of only two divisions, the 34th (Red Bulls) and the 36th (Texas) Divisions but it was intended that their thrust towards the Liri valley would be exploited subsequently by tanks of I Armoured Division if the initial crossings over the Rapido had been as successful as the planners had hoped.

The overall responsibility for the defence of the Cassino area was on the shoulders of General von Senger und Etterlin, Commander of the XIV Panzer Corps. The title of the book he wrote after the War, 'Neither Fear nor Hope', gives an insight into the character of this able officer. General Senger was a devout Roman Catholic; indeed he was a lay member of the Benedictine Order, many of whose members in early January 1944 were still in the ancient Abbey at Cassino. He was a sensitive and well-educated man who had little faith in the Nazis and detested their doctrines. The German Corps commander was an Anglophile stemming from the days of his youth spent as a Rhodes Scholar at Oxford; in addition he had a genuine affection for the Italian people, for music and for the arts, and he loved the simple beauty of the countryside where now he was fighting for a cause in which he did not believe.

Senger's competence and professional skills had won him a high reputation in the German Army. Although his dislike for Adolf Hitler was reciprocated, in the time of need the Fatherland had to rely on the services of such as General Senger, even if the Fuehrer knew that many officers were opposed to his Nazi regime. For von Senger his duty was clear even if his sensitive soul recoiled from the dilemma he was in. Every day that his Corps held up the Allies around Cassino enabled the detested Nazis to continue to rule in his beloved country and to resist those devoted to their destruction, from outside and from within Germany itself. He was buying time for men he hated but fighting for the country he loved—and he fought without fear or hope.

On the south of the Rapido valley General Senger's opposite number was the commander of the US II Corps, Major General Geoffrey Keyes. In reality, however, the German XIV Panzer Corps' boundaries coincided with those of the Anglo-American Fifth Army so that it is more accurate to treat General Mark Clark as the officer who had overall control during the first battle of Cassino. Later, as the agony and anxieties of Anzio increased during February, so did Clark's personal direction of the subsequent struggle at Cassino decrease until the major crisis had passed.

The story of the first abortive crossings over the Rapido river shows that Major General Geoffrey Keyes was very much an intermediary between the unfortunate 36th Division and Mark Clark himself. Little is recorded about Keyes apart from the fact that he was reported as being a quiet competent man, neat in appearance and invariably well dressed, with a likeable personality. Like several other American Generals at this stage in the war, Keyes lacked practical experience as a commander; a subordinate divisional commander, Major General Fred L. Walker stated that Keyes had many ideas of academic rather than practical value.

When the bitter survivors of the Rapido crossing decided to petition Congress for an investigation, the general whom they named as being inefficient and inexperienced was not Geoffrey Keyes, but General Mark Clark. (General Mark Clark's Fifth Army was the

ing movements through field glasses and then bringing down devastating artillery fire on the Allied soldiers. During the first battle the Monastery was granted immunity and still presented a noble sight with the pale winter sun shining on the glass of its windows and the great towers and dome outlined against the grey sky. But slowly it became obvious to the men fighting on the steep slopes below the Abbey or dying on the banks of the Rapido or attacking on the fringes of the already battered town of Cassino that the Monastery and Monte Cassino, the building and the mountain, were one integral part, the key part, of the German defences. If Monte Cassino had to be taken then the Monastery could not escape; the Benedictine Brothers could not remain in their beautiful building as spectators while men fought to the death around them. The devout Roman Catholic General Senger could not protect a building by proclaiming a neutral zone of three hundred metres around it, because he and his superiors had condemned the Monastery to destruction by selecting the Cassino area as the lynch pin of the Gustav Line. In war they could but protest when bombs and shells crushed the building into dust. In their hearts could they really have expected anything else?

From September 1943, the Bishop and his monks had given shelter and succour to thousands of civilian refugees. At the foot of the mountain and within the town of Cassino the bottleneck of Route 6 had been an inevitable, clearly defined and oft-bombed target so that the Abbey was like a magnet for frightened fugitives who came from near and far. Even when the ornaments and treasured valuables were removed, many of the refugees remained within the sanctuary of the Monastery as the tide of war swirled across the Rapido river.

Not until the first battle had petered out did the final evacuation of the remaining civilians and monks become a matter of urgent necessity. Until then, while the American commanders peered across the Rapido valley from Mount Trocchio, noting the strength of the defences and the grandeur of the setting chosen by the Germans to conduct their defence of the Liri valley, the future battlefield was dominated by the Monastery, a building that still sheltered people who clung to their faith in God for survival.

In January no one was to know that the Monastery would become the symbol of the four battles of Cassino, the prize sought after by the Allies and stubbornly defended by the Germans.

When it eventually fell there were but the ruins, stones and rubble. One thing alone survived—as it has done throughout the centuries. The tomb of Saint Benedict was later found to be completely untouched and undamaged: miraculously a slab of flat stone was to break in two over the tomb and form a protective roof over it. But thousands of soldiers were to die before the sounds of war left the valley around Cassino.

6

The First Battle—The Rapido Fiasco.

Although there were but five days between the capture of Mount Trocchio and the abortive crossings attempted by the 36th Texan Division, the problem posed by the river had haunted the Fifth Army generals for some time. On Christmas Day 1943, General Clark had gazed across at the Cassino defences in company with his subordinate generals, Keyes and Truscott. At that time there was a chance that Truscott's 3rd Division might have the doubtful honour of leading the advance across the Rapido.

General Truscott was worried that his division would have to establish a bridgehead near the village of San Angelo built on a bluff about forty feet above the river. From their observation point the generals saw the farmland valley with the Rapido river almost inundating the banks as it flowed down from the mountains above Cassino, then meandered across the valley to join with the River Liri—thence to become the Garigliano river over which 10 Corps established their bridgehead during the third week in January. On the enemy side of the Rapido, the ground was far more broken and of a rolling nature, even to the brink of the river whilst on the Americans' side the country was flat, muddy and open to observation from the heights above.

It was obvious that the defenders would have established posts and strong points right down to the river's edge and no men, guns or tanks could cross the river without bridges or assault boats. Truscott was extremely worried that any bridge so erected would be under direct observed fire from the hills above Cassino, opposite the proposed crossing places. If the bridges were destroyed faster than the Americans could build them then the assaulting infantry would be forced to face the enemy without tanks or anti-tank guns in their support. In Truscott's words: "My fine infantry battalions would be eventually whittled away by German armour, artillery and infantry. And 1st Armoured Division would still be south of Rapido".

47

His fears were well founded and unfortunately not heeded by Keyes or Mark Clark so that the prediction came to pass—with 36th Division being hurled into the venture in place of Truscott's 3rd Division. The glitter of Rome, the gamble that 1st Armoured Division might get across and into the Liri Valley still caused Fifth Army Headquarters to wear blinkers even when the facts all added up to a hazardous enterprise against the strongest point in the German Gustav Line.

General Mark Clark did waver once more when, three days after the visit to Mt Lungo, he had another talk with Truscott: although by this time both knew that Truscott and his Division were bound for Anzio and not Cassino. The words used by the generals concerned are quoted in full from Truscott's book, 'Command Missions':

> Clark: "Would you be willing to undertake that Rapido crossing if those heights on either flank were under attack although not actually in our possession?"
>
> Truscott: (after consideration) "Yes, but those attacks should be so powerful that every German gun would be required to oppose them for only two or three concealed '88's would be able to destroy our bridges. I doubt our capacity for such attack".

General Mark Clark agreed: but with his three Corps spread across the Fifth Army front it would only have been possible to mount such a series of attacks around Cassino by abandoning his projected plan to attempt turning both the flanks as well as butting a way across the Rapido. In the end, Truscott's warning was ignored and the two flanking Corps, Tenth British and the French, continued as mentioned in an earlier chapter to launch their assaults without any reserves to thrust into gaps made. The early crossings over the Rapido became as inevitable as the last act of a Greek tragedy.

Meanwhile, General L. Walker of the 36th Texan Division had also been devoting a lot of thought to the problem that was now to be his. The more he pondered the less he liked it. Almost 26 years previously, when in command of a battalion in France, Walker and some 1,200 soldiers had fought a German Division of about 10,000 men who had to cross the River Marne: they had not only defeated the Germans but had slaughtered them. In January 1944 with an unfordable river to cross against an experienced enemy division, Walker's men were facing an infinitely more difficult task than the Germans had attempted in July 1918.

General Walker's fears that history was about to be repeated in reverse were communicated to his superior commanders, Keyes and Mark Clark. They could not, or would not see the difficulties. It is possible that they felt that the bold piecemeal methods which had been used throughout the winter against German delaying positions would again cause the 15 Panzer Division to withdraw. Perhaps, too, before the initial successful crossing by the British Tenth Corps over the Garigliano had been made, there were sufficient reasons for the planning of this crossing as a diversion before the Anzio landing in order to draw German reserves away in case the Tenth Corps assault proved a failure. The planning was justified but the subsequent failure to reorganise and react to the advantages secured by Tenth Corps sounded the death knell for the two assaulting infantry regiments of the 36th Division.

On the German side, General von Senger telephoned Field Marshal Kesselring asking him to send the Army Group reserves as a matter of urgency—to avert the danger that was threatening the whole of the Gustav Line on the lower Garigliano. This was done whilst Fifth Army and 36th Division in particular continued to prepare for their first crossing over the Rapido.

It is important to realise that the German Tenth Army Group reserve divisions—29 and 90 Panzer Grenadiers—had both moved to oppose the British Tenth Corps before 36th Division ever began their attack. The justification for the attack, wrote Mark Clark in his diary a few hours before it started, was 'to hold all the German troops on my front and draw more to it, thereby clearing the way for Shingle (Anzio landing)'. The first few hours of the Anzio landing were devoid of any real opposition: the immediate German reserves had moved south to oppose Fifth Army—but they went not to Cassino or opposite San Angelo but first to halt and then to counter-attack General McCreery's 10 Corps.

Whilst the staff and engineers of 36th Division worked with feverish activity to prepared detailed plans for the crossings near San Angelo, the unhappy General Walker faced a terrible personal dilemma. He, like Truscott, had no confidence in the operation, writing on the 8th January: "I'll swear, I do not see how we can ibly succeed when that stream is in the main line of resistance German position". The term 'stream' was a misnomer for an unfordable river, eight to twelve feet deep, forty to fifty feet wide with steep banks, a swift current, ice-cold water and no bridges. In private, the General wrestled with his doubts and fears without daring to reveal his feelings to subordinates. He even considered asking to be relieved from his command in protest but how was such a thing possible on the eve of battle? Walker had raised, trained and commanded the Texan Division over the previous 2½ years: he knew many of the men and was respected by them. If he deserted his Division at this stage would a new commander conduct the hopeless operation as well as he could? Walker decided to stay with his soldiers praying that if things went wrong then he might be able to prevent further useless attempts and unnecessary sacrifices of life.

In retrospect, the General's decision was the only possible one: he had to lead the Division into this attack, knowing that none of his officers or men could refuse to partake in the forthcoming battles. For soldiers, from the General down to G.I., there was no alternative.

It has been stated by Majdalany that the period of intensive planning between 15 and 20 January provides a striking example of the differences between the American and British methods of command and control at that time. He alleged that the Americans had nothing comparable to the British divisional conferences and discussions. General Walker kept a journal at the time and his entries refute these statements: "General Wilbur, the Division Staff, the Combat Team commanders have been discussing this (Division Field Officer No. 42) since the 16th". Survivors bear out this testimony. Detailed plans for regiments were produced by 36th Divisional Headquarters and detailed orders were produced in an attempt to meet any likely eventuality: it is, however, possible that over-meticulous detail contributed to the confusion when things went wrong from the very start.

The official statement that 'plans were made carefully on the lowest level' was, in many ways, accurate. Great care was taken but some of it was misguided and misdirected. When Howard Kippenberger, commanding the New Zealand 5th Brigade, later saw the operation orders that had been issued to 141 Regiment he commented: "almost everything that should have been done had not been done and few things that should not have been done been attended to". Unfortunately from the historians' po

view, he did not elaborate or explain what things he specifically referred to by such a stricture.

Apart from an allegedly inflexible system of command which may or may not have contributed to much that went wrong, one of the biggest problems that faced General Walker was the open nature of the ground between the positions occupied by the Americans and the river itself. This meant two things: firstly, that there would be a long walk over comparatively uncharted country to the river; and secondly, such a move would have to be done under the cloak of darkness. Neither in planning nor in the execution thereafter did 36 Division solve this problem: even with hindsight and freedom to roam in peaceful conditions on both sides of the river, twenty-five years after the event, it is not easy to suggest with confidence what the correct solution should have been, except to conclude, like General Walker, that it was the height of wishful thinking to expect two lone Infantry Regiments to succeed at this particular sector of the German front.

Great efforts were made to clear the minefields on the American side of the river before the attack began but through lack of time this was not completed. Another problem was that even when mines were lifted or marked, there was nothing to stop German patrols from slipping across the river to lay more mines and booby traps on tracks which their opponents thought they had 'cleared'. Majdalany affirmed that a holding force was required near the river who could have cleared an area and thereafter deterred the Germans from upsetting the assault forces as they moved forward. It might have been difficult to put such a theory into practice in daylight when the whole area was open to observers on the hills around Cassino, and it is debatable if such a force would have 'held' the area at night. However, if this had proved possible and had been done during the night before the attack, i.e., 19th January, then a firm base would have existed for the next phase, the actual crossing of the Rapido. Ideally, the third Regiment of the Division, the 142nd Infantry should have been used in this role but unfortunately, and because the overall difficulties had been greatly underestimated, it was Corps reserve and not made available to Walker.

General Walker decided to begin the crossing three hours after sunset, at 2000 hours. Between then and daylight on the 21st January his six battalions would have about eleven hours of darkness. During this time, they would have to get across, clear the far river bank and seize enough ground so that the engineers could erect their bridges, free from German rifle and, if possible, mortar fire. Then, and only then, could the bridgehead stand a chance of success as tanks, guns and more troops would be able to cross the bridges and prevent the infantry from being whittled away when daylight appeared.

One Regiment, the 141st, was to cross the Rapido north of the village of San Angelo whilst the other, 143rd, had a similar role to the south. All the crossing equipment had to be hand-carried to the river bank by the infantrymen. All in all, the operation called for many hours of careful and skilful planning whereas, in fact, it was conceived in haste, with complicated staff work so rushed that elementary mistakes were made which contributed to chaos even before zero hour—2000 hours on the 20th January, 1944. General Walker wrote on January 20th: "on top of everything else, Army has rushed us into this mission too fast. We should have had ten days to get ready instead of three".

Late in the afternoon General Clark telephoned Walker to wish him success, adding that he was worried. General Walker records that his part of the conversation was not encouraging, with his men tense on a cheerless day, resolved to do their best in an attack on one of the strongest defensive positions the Germans were ever to have in Italy.

A heavy fog, cold and dense, hung over the river that evening with visibility near zero. As the first assault battalion began moving from their assembly area, the artillery on both sides destroyed every illusion that this was to surprise the Germans. Mortar shells crunched down on the Texan soldiers as they tried to follow guides or white tapes carefully placed to mark clear lanes through minefields. The curses of the men mingled with the screams of the wounded as routes were lost, mines exploded and the devastatingly accurate German artillery decimated small groups before they had even reached the river.

Junior commanders struggled to keep some semblance of control: courage and resolution alone kept the momentum of the attacks going over the river itself where the swirling current swept boats and men downstream. Many assault boats were damaged before reaching the river or capsized as men climbed into them. At the 141st Regiment crossing places, a few boatloads had reached the far bank by 2100 hours. Under heavy fire and working with

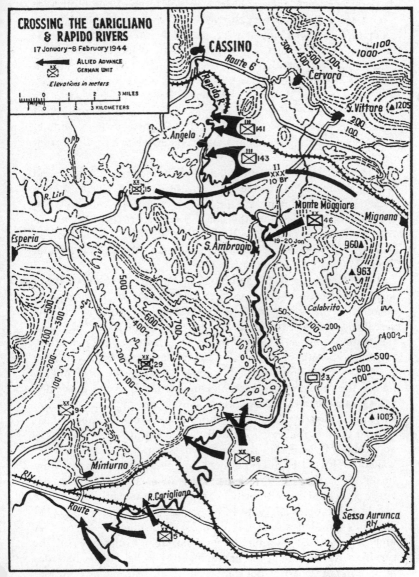

CROSSING THE GARIGLIANO & RAPIDO RIVERS

17 January–8 February 1944

ALLIED ADVANCE
GERMAN UNIT

Elevations in meters

0 1 2 3 MILES
0 1 2 3 KILOMETERS

CASSINO

Route 6

Cervaro

S. Vittore ▲1205

Rapido R.

S. Angela

141

143

11
XXX
10 Br

15

R. Liri

Monte Maggiore

46

Mignano

Esperia

S. Ambrogio

19–20 Jan

960▲

▲963

Calabrito

▲A 400

29

23

94

▲1003

56

Minturno

Rly

Route 7

R. Garigliano

5

Sessa Aurunca
Rly

Map 2: The First Battle of Cassino showing 10 Corps attack and 36 Texas
Division attack.

desperate courage, the engineers managed to erect one footbridge out of four damaged or destroyed ones. Across this bridge, the remainder of two companies scrambled before 0400 hours next morning; then this one link was itself badly damaged. On the far side about four hundred men tried to force their way through barbed wire and mines as well as heavy machine-gun fire but they were soon pinned down near the bank of the river. Forced to dig in, unable to be reinforced or even to communicate by radio these men could not return to the near side and clung to their pitifully small gains, praying that help would soon arrive to save them from death or captivity.

The remainder of the battalion, unable to cross the river and with nowhere to hide as the first signs of daybreak revealed open meadows around them, were quickly and mercifully withdrawn on the orders of the assistant-divisional commander, Brig. Wilbur, to their original jumping-off position. 141st Regiment faced the day with a small group marooned on the German side of the Rapido at the cost of some hundreds of casualties.

143rd Regiment, to the south of San Angelo, also had a night of death and disaster. Their approach march to the river was equally chaotic in the heavy mist with intermittent artillery and the screaming whine of the 'Nebelwerfers' (heavy mortars) adding to the confusion. Nevertheless at the most northerly of the two crossing points one company was able to cross in rubber boats just after 2000 hours, H. hour. Scrambling their way up the high muddy banks, they came under accurate small arms fire from concealed posts, so close that the American guns could not support them. Casualties were high but even more serious, enemy mortars destroyed their rubber boats as well as pinning the company to the very edge of the river. Behind them, the other two companies waited whilst the engineers sought equipment which guides were unable to locate or tried to repair parts damaged by shell fire. Already key leaders were being killed and wounded, men whose presence was especially vital in a comparatively inexperienced Division as the 36th was at this point of its distinguished career. A night that seemed interminable remains in the memories of the survivors: frustration at the delay, inability to help their comrades in peril over the narrow but dangerous river, fear, pain, confusion, these feelings have not been completely erased by the years.

Just when it seemed as if nothing would cross before the first rays of light on the 21st, two footbridges were at last assembled and by 06.00 hours the rest of the battalion crossed under fire even though the bridges were quickly sunk. So much for one of the battalions of the 143rd Regiment: the other, a little to the south, came to grief as they moved down to the river. Some sub-units strayed into a minefield where they were completely unnerved by the sudden explosions and casualties. Another group failed to find their boats or their engineers or both. And all the time the unerring accuracy of German guns and mortars added to the misery, doubts and considerable disorganisation. By day break, on the 21st, not a single man from this battalion had even reached the far bank of the Rapido.

The overall result of a night of terror and loss was two groups in enemy territory, the two companies of 141st Regiment in the north and the one battalion from the 143rd Regiment to the south of San Angelo. The latter tried desperately to drive the Germans away from their immediate perimeter but as their exact position became clearer to the German artillery spotters on Monastery Hill and the adjacent heights, so did the devastatingly accurate and furious weight of shells descend on to the battalion, literally caught in the open. Their commander, Major David Frazior ordered his men to dig in and keep digging but within an hour the Germans began to attack with tanks and self propelled guns in support. In face of complete annihilation Frazior asked permission to withdraw across the river by the one remaining but now damaged bridge. The request was refused but the refusal arrived after the survivors of the battalions had recrossed to the east bank, some by swimming in the cold swirling Rapido or by balancing on the one footbridge still in place under water.

At about 1000 hours that morning, the 21st, an immaculately dressed General Keyes arrived at the 36 Division command post to confront a tired, worried General Walker who was planning a second attempt for the evening, principally to rescue the men who were isolated on the far side, wounded and able-bodied alike. The two men disagreed on the timing; Keyes wanted an all-out attack at once, preferably before noon because, he said, the sun shining in the eyes of the German defenders would make it difficult for them to see. Walker pointed out that this left them with less than two hours to prepare for such an attack. An impossibility when his units were so disorganised. The Corps commander still insisted that the troops were to cross over the Rapido at once—and then left the details to the harassed 36 Divisional Commander.

An unrealistic time of 1400 hours was decided on but the deadline went back and back in spite of impatient prodding by Keyes. He was convinced that the Germans would reinforce the San Angelo area before Walker's infantry started to attack. His fears were not unfounded but it is quite clear that the previous reverse had been far more complete and demoralising than the Corps Commander realised; the two Regiments needed time to reorganise and regain control of themselves whilst to repeat the previous night's attack at the same place in daylight was making the German defenders' task an easy one. It is not surprising that General Rodt of the 15 Panzer Division reported that these forays were 'armed reconnaissance' and only revised his opinion later when the bag of prisoners grew from dozens to hundreds and the dead and wounded soldiers from Texas were collected after the fighting had died down.

The 143rd Regiment were the first to begin the second follow up attack in the late afternoon of the 21st. The air was thick from smoke shells fired by the Americans in an attempt to screen the attack and in particular to protect the engineers with their bridging equipment. The cold weather continued dry with the January sun low in the south and it gave little heat to the infantry soldiers as the leading (3rd Battalion) ferried three companies across by about 6.00 p.m. At first and in spite of spirited defiance by the Germans, things went reasonably well: a footbridge was thrown up, the equivalent of two battalions of the Regiment were across and striving to push the enemy back by midnight. This was to be the height of their success however—the initial gains proved but little and of no value whatever because, once again, no tank bridges could either be assembled or, if erected, remain undamaged; as dawn broke the men of 143rd found Germans everywhere, mortar shells repeatedly causing casualties and as before, they were pinned down in the low wet meadows, utterly naked to enemy observation with no friendly tanks on their side of the river.

The outcome was inevitable; between 9.00 and 10.00 a.m. on the 22nd heavy enemy rocket fire plastered the small bridgehead and made it untenable. By this time, too, one battalion had lost all its senior commanders; inevitably disorganisation crept in. Bridges, boats were sunk and just after midday, the battalions were ordered to move back east of the river, the majority by swimming, leaving dead, wounded and a few isolated groups still in enemy hands.

The two companies from 141st Regiment (First Battalion) to the north of San Angelo remained in isolation on the German side of the Rapido throughout the 21st January but out of radio contact with any friendly headquarters. A follow-up attack was organised to begin at 10.00 p.m. that night. 15 Panzer Division was expecting such a move and the same difficulties were experienced as on the preceding night. The rubber boats were quite useless in the fast flowing water, the pre-constructed footbridges proved to be completely unsatisfactory and, as before, the German gunners harassed them unmercifully. Nevertheless, improvised footbridges were erected so that the assault elements of two battalions had reached the far bank just before the first light on 22nd January. General Walker realised that if this limited success was to survive and flourish during the daylight hours, a Bailey bridge had to be erected so that tanks could cross and protect his infantrymen. He ordered the engineers to press on with this, in spite of the murderous fire and regardless of loss; this was attempted but direct hits on the bridge destroyed a gallant and forlorn attempt.

In spite of the setback, the men of the 141st hacked a way through wire, minefields and defences up to distances of about half a mile before being forced to dig in as the weight of enemy fire increased both in effect and ferocity. The next few hours were hell on earth for these Texan soldiers. The Germans, sensing that this crossing was doomed without American tanks, mounted attack after attack; the number of wounded rose but they could not be evacuated, ammunition reserves dwindled but nothing could be resupplied across the river, communications scanty at first ceased to operate at all as the hours dragged by, as the commanders one by one fell dead or wounded and the survivors fought on until nothing was left to fire and escape or surrender became inevitable. To those who waited and prayed in friendly territory on the east bank, the noise of Americans firing was no longer heard after 10.00 p.m. On the 22nd January, 141st Regiment of the 36 Division had virtually ceased to exist—some forty men finally rejoined either by swimming back or hiding until other opportunities occurred to escape. The units who had striven to cross and put bridges up had suffered nearly a thousand casualties in two nights.

With the deepest bitterness 36 Division was ready to concede the battle to the Germans but Generals Clark and Keyes were not yet convinced that the defeat was a final one. Keyes wanted another attack to be put in by the third Regiment, the 142nd which had been held back as Corps reserve. He claimed that the Germans were groggy, thought their morale was low and believed that they might even be preparing to withdraw. General Walker, quite rightly, considered this to be the height of wishful thinking. The Germans even after the second attack did not fully appreciate the terrible losses they had inflicted on the 6,000 men from the 36th Division who had been thrown against the defences around San Angelo. No call for reserves and assistance had been sent back by General Rodt to his superiors nor had the Divisional reserves taken any active part in the bloody repulse of the Americans. 36 Division soon knew what their opponents thought about the debacle when the Germans released a carrier pigeon they had captured. Back to its loft flew the bird with a message which read: "Herewith a messenger pigeon is returned. We have enough to eat and what's more we look forward with pleasure to your next attempt".

On the morning of the 23rd, General Walker was no longer prepared to send another attack across the Rapido without the strongest representations being made to General Clark himself. Certain plans were made, however, and at one headquarters the senior officer gathered his surviving officers in a room and said goodbye to them. On Clark's orders the projected attack was called off; about noon Clark and Keyes came forward to Walker's command post. "Tell me, what happened up here", Clark said quietly. Walker told him: there were not and could not be any recriminations.

Keyes pointed out that at one time on the 22nd, the maps and reports at the Divisional Command Post, and as transmitted to his headquarters, showed nearly six battalions on the far side of the river. (In fact there were never more than the remnants of four battalions across the river.) On this basis he had pressed for a renewed effort. General Clark whose responsibility also included the troops now ashore at Anzio, turned to Keyes: "It was as much my fault as yours", he said.

He was never to repeat this again. Indeed when the political storm arose after the war, Mark Clark continued to claim that the early Rapido attacks had an importance in the overall strategic plan; the War Department concluded that he, Clark, had exercised sound judgement in planning it and ordering it and thus absolved him completely from any responsibility for the fiasco.

The world may have accepted this verdict but the veterans of the 36th (Texas) Division did not forget the Rapido River crossing. More than 2,100 of their comrades were killed, wounded or missing in a heroic and needless sacrifice. Certain accounts of the catastrophe have even blamed, without justice, the failure on inefficient planning at Divisional level and on the inexperienced infantry soldiers in the two Regiments, 141 and 143.

It has already been said that, because time was short, Divisional planning was misguided and inflexible so that it added to the confusion. As far as inexperience was concerned it is possible that the regrettably heavy casualty list stemmed to some degree from this factor but no other Division, however experienced or battle-scarred, could have succeeded under the conditions that prevailed on January 20th. Later, in the place of this single Division, a complete British Corps was to be required before a bridgehead was seized around San Angelo—and this after severe fighting using vastly superior numbers against the German defenders.

The survivors did not believe that the sacrifice was necessary or even justified. In Texas the bitter feeling grew and grew until Congress was petitioned to investigate the disaster.

A hearing before the Committee on Military Affairs was held in early 1946. The Resolution presented by the Thirty Sixth Association was indeed cast in strong bitter tones: it included such statements as: "Whereas the whole attack and terrifying conditions under which it was ordered have stirred up bitter anger, among men and officers involved in the disaster: and whereas Generals are supposed to save lives of the men . . . whereas General Clark apparently maintained the reverse attitude to such tactics".

The Resolution ended with a petition: "To investigate the Rapido River Fiasco and take necessary steps to correct a military system that will permit an inefficient and inexperienced officer such as General Mark W. Clark in a high command to destroy the young manhood of this country and to prevent future soldiers being sacrificed wastefully and uselessly".

The Hearing was held but not the investigation they wished. At the Hearing, General Fred L. Walker and two other witnesses were allowed to make statements and thereafter were subjected to questions, a few searching ones and several on irrelevant aspects. On at least two occasions, the Chairman made a plea for brevity on the grounds that the Committee had more pressing business to conduct and time was limited. After the Hearing, the War Department officially absolved General Clark, adding that while the casualties were to be greatly regretted, the heroic action and sacrifices of the 36 Division undoubtedly drew the Germans away from the landings at Anzio.

General Fred L. Walker and the Divisional Association have never accepted this verdict. They have since been strongly supported by their erstwhile opponents. Field Marshal Kesselring, several years later, when talking about the Rapido action said that had one of his subordinates ordered a similar attack, he would not have treated him very kindly. General von Senger und Etterlin dismissed it as 'a sideshow', but continued to worry about the British bridgehead over the Garigliano. The Commander of the 15th Panzer Grenadier Division counted 430 American dead and 770 captured, a total of 1,200 of those who had managed to cross the river. Nine hundred others fell dead and wounded on the American side of the Rapido. In comparison the German 15th Division suffered less than 250 casualties, 64 killed and 179 wounded.

The verdict of history must be that the Rapido Fiasco was an unnecessary attack, that the conditions made it impossible for 36 Division to succeed, that the result was not only tragic and inevitable but contributed nothing either to Anzio or the main Fifth Army front. The Germans dismissed it with contempt. All that emerges from the sacrifice of these sons of Texas, as well as those from other States, is the loyalty, courage and devotion with which they followed their Commander, General Walker, into an enterprise which they knew to be hopeless.

The Rapido still flows—a small and comparatively insignificant river which has witnessed a debacle—one an American correspondent called the biggest disaster to American arms since Pearl Harbour. This was an exaggeration but certainly it was an unnecessary sacrifice of young American manhood. General Clark ends his very unconvincing account of this episode by saying: "I salute them for their charge and courage. As for myself, I can only say that in the same circumstances, I would have to do it over again—

and if I am accused of something, thank God I am accused of attacking instead of retreating".

In the context of the Italian front during 1944 the last sentence is both revealing and unfortunate. Far better to have said, perhaps, "Nothing was right except the courage".

7

The First Battle—The Americans and the French Try Again

The 22nd January saw not only the crushing defeat of General Walker's 36th (Texas) Division but the beginning of another Fifth Army enterprise when VI Corps landed at Anzio. Operation Shingle had begun in the most favourable conditions, reflected in the first message sent by the Commander, General Lucas: 'Weather clear, sea calm, little wind, our presence not discovered. Landings in progress. No reports from landings yet'.

His reports continued to indicate that the Germans had been surprised; only about a thousand enemy troops opposed the early landings and the Allied build-up continued throughout the 22nd with men and vehicles pouring ashore in the way the staffs had planned. By the late afternoon everything seemed to be going far better than anticipated. General Mark Clark then decided that pressure had to be maintained on the Cassino-Rapido front to stop German Tenth Army reserves being pulled back from the main battlefield to oppose the Anzio beach-head. It was to be the turn of the American 34th Division to cross the Rapido. The fighting that ensued was to be as bitter as any during the five month struggle at Cassino. The Rapido was fordable at a point about two miles to the north of San Angelo—indeed, General Walker had originally asked if his initial attempt at a crossing could be made there. His request was refused because, optimistically, Headquarters Fifth Army was more concerned with the exploitation of such a crossing, a thrust into the Liri valley by the tanks of I Armoured Division near the village of San Angelo. The bitter experiences of 36 Division now influenced Generals Clark and Keyes into making a methodical and careful attempt to break into the Cassino defences from the north without being swayed by the next stage of a 'break out' into the Liri valley.

The attack was made at what General von Senger considered to be the weakest point of his front, although the German positions were protected by formidable obstacles and, as at San Angelo, the ingenuity of man had created new hazards and added to the ones made by nature. The fordable river was effectively dammed so that the entire plain became an impassable sea of mud where tanks could move only if artificial support was laid for their tracks. Mined ditches and river banks were protected by extensive wiring up to four hundred yards west of the Rapido, from south of Caira village to Cassino town. In the rear, a series of pill-boxes and concrete block houses covered the approaches to the steep slopes of the hills north of Cassino, on the crest of which carefully sited observers could survey and dominate the whole battlefield from their mountain wall.

In spite of these difficulties there were two important factors that favoured General Ryder's attack. The first has already been mentioned—the Rapido could be forded so that rubber boats and foot bridges were not required by the combat infantry—and secondly, the advancing French Corps was near enough on the east flank to distract, harass and divert the attention of the German 44th Infantry Division opposing the American assault troops. Consequently both the French and the Americans chose the same night, the 24th January, to launch their attacks.

Initially General Juin's aim was to capture Monte Cifalco, a feature which overlooked the Secca Valley and the northern end of the Rapido Valley. With great élan forward positions were taken by the Tunisian Regiment but troops of the German 5th Mountain Division clung to positions on the mountain itself—and continued to do so until the end of the Cassino battles. From its slopes their artillery observation officers had a clear view of the flanks and rear of the French and Americans as they advanced southwards. Constant harassment by artillery from this position made the task of resupplying the French forward positions one of ever-increasing difficulty. Juin was convinced that if the momentum of his advance was maintained, then the whole enemy central sector would be threatened and direct attacks on the Cassino bastion would prove to be unnecessary. He continued to plead for more reserves and increased logistic support but Monte Cassino was to exercise a strong magnetic influence on the Allied Corps commanders, Generals Keyes, Freyberg and Anders. One by one they decided to take the bull by its horns by attacking the strongest point in an almost impregnable defence and the losses in the three Corps that fought at Cassino were to pay testimony to the bankruptcy of such tactics.

On the morning of the 25th January, soldiers of the Algerian Division, after bypassing the Monte Cifalco strong point, first captured Monte Belvedere then Colle Abate. During these battles devastating German artillery fire caused heavy losses, and disrupted supplies and the movement forward of reinforcements. Their continued progress very much depended on the outcome of the attack made by the American 34th Division, north of Cassino town. Nevertheless, the spirited audacious penetration of the French caused General von Senger deep anxiety during this period. A breach had been made, he had no one to move into the gap but fortunately for the Germans, General Clark did not, as previously arranged, give Juin the help required to tip the balance. By this time Clark's attention was closely riveted to events at Anzio where German counter-measures were becoming increasingly powerful, coinciding with the initial efforts of General Ryder's Division to cross the Rapido River near Cassino—which were to meet with failure.

Hindsight makes wiseacres of all men, especially historians. There is no doubt that the dual responsibility for the Anzio and Cassino fronts, borne by General Mark Clark during this period, was a heavy burden for one commander to shoulder. It is equally easy to understand why such an arrangement had been made. If as a result of the Anzio landings in their rear the Germans had reacted in the way that the Allied planners wishfully expected them to then there would have been considerable merit in VI Corps at Anzio remaining under General Mark Clark's overall command. If, as had been hoped, the German Tenth Army had been withdrawn in some haste either to meet the threatened landing or to avoid being cut off by General Lucas and his VI Corps, when they struck inland to seize the Alban Hills, then events might have moved with considerable speed and the highest degree of co-ordination, exercised by one headquarters, would have been vital. Hence the decision to leave the overall responsibility of the Nettuno landings on General Mark Clark's shoulders. It transpired that nothing moved at speed anywhere—progress on the Cassino front was soon to become measured in yards at a high cost of life, while the Anzio beach-head changed into a desperate struggle for survival and Churchill's hopes that "it would be a wild cat clawing

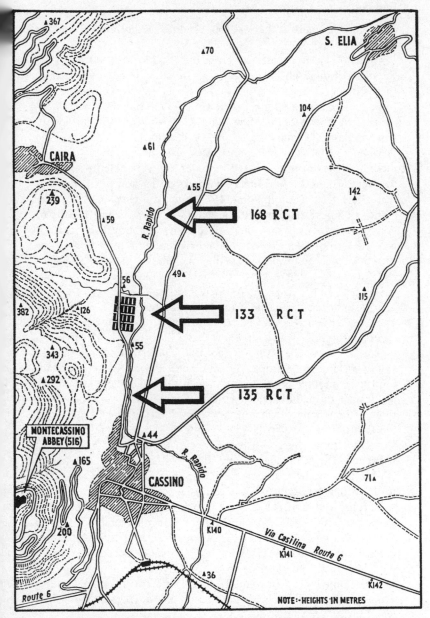

Map 3: The First Battle showing the Rapido River crossing and the US 34th Division's attack on 24th-25th January 1944.

down the Germans in the rear" mocked those fighting with the sea at their backs.

General Ryder decided to cross the Rapido at 2200 hours on the night of the 24th of January. 133 Infantry Regiment moved up to the river covered by thirty minutes of intensive artillery fire from the concentrated guns of II Corps. One battalion was disorganised by a minefield a few hundred yards from its start point. Nevertheless, the guns' fierce, heavy bombardment so shook the German 134 Grenadier Regiment that elements of the two assaulting battalions not only crossed the river but were able to reach the defences around the old Italian barracks at the foot of their immediate objective, a knoll Point 213. With daylight came the Germans' trump card—complete observation of the small groups of American infantry below them on the end of the muddy plain. It was the turn of their gunners and mortar crews to punish these opponents. Accurately spotted shelling mercilessly drove the remaining American soldiers back to where they had started their advance, back to the east bank of the Rapido.

Still smarting from the San Angelo defeat, the Corps Commander General Keyes was determined that 34th Division would secure a foothold which he knew could be held only if American tanks got across the river. In fact, the valley, barely one mile in width, was not to be crossed by an organised force of tanks and infantry for another three days although the Americans never gave up trying throughout this period. The task of 34th Division remained unchanged which was to cross the Rapido and then seize the first objectives, two knolls, Points 56 and 213, and the large, shattered Italian barracks at the foot of the mountains. The next phase was to scale and secure the high ground behind before wheeling to the left: one regiment was to advance along the ridges to the Monastery whilst 135 Regiment moved in a parallel thrust to capture the town of Cassino which lay some two and a half miles down the road, surrounded by a quagmire of mud. It is to the everlasting fame and credit of the 34th 'Red Bulls' that they got to within a hair-breadth of success; sheer exhaustion, dwindling numbers and inspired leadership by German battalion and junior commanders prevented the Americans from succeeding against odds as difficult as any met by the other Allied divisions who fought in the subsequent battles.

The key to this battle lay in the struggle to get tanks across the river and this was not achieved without improvisation and dogged courage; wire matting was laid on the soft mud to support the tank tracks but little could be done in daylight under the eyes of the Germans on the heights above.

On the morning of the 27th January, two battalions of 168 Regiment tried to cross again, this time about one thousand yards to the north of their sister Regiments' tiny foothold. Supported by 756 Tank Regiment a well coordinated attack went in with the artillery firing deception shoots on to other targets. By 0930 hours four lone tanks had managed to cross the river. With the greatest courage this tiny force smashed a way through clusters of anti-personnel mines and coils of thick barbed wire. They were all knocked out before mid-day. In their rear a squadron of tanks tried to follow but the leading tanks got bogged down, near the river, so that no more could get past and across. Nevertheless, the short-lived but gallant support of the original four tanks had enabled 168 Regiment to widen and consolidate its bridgehead. The infantry burrowed into the soft ground to throw up temporary cover while German strong points were pounded by the Air Forces and by the Corps artillery. In the rear, engineers courageously strove to lay another track of wire matting, working without respite under the grimmest conditions possible. Early on the 29th January their resolution and skill was rewarded when more tanks crossed to join 168 Regiment. The immediate crisis was over and skilfully planned and well coordinated attacks by all arms during the night of 29/30th January, led to the capture of the two knolls, Points 56 and 213.

Here the Americans found concrete defences, big enough to house 28 to 30 men, many with bunks and efficient heating arrangements. The Germans had intended to stay and to this end they launched one bitter counter attack on the next day. This was beaten-off and following it up, the village of Caira, containing men from the German 131 Panzer Grenadier Regiment, was captured. Only now could it be claimed that a permanent crossing had been achieved. In retrospect, it was one of the outstanding feats of arms at Cassino. Only dogged perseverance had enabled the 'Red Bulls' to succeed.

Two or three weeks after these events, the author was talking to a haggard, young officer of the Division, standing on a hill above the Rapido valley. "How the Hell your chaps did it, I can't imagine". The American Lieutenant silently considered the remark before saying: "Brother, it was hell. I guess we just wanted to show those Jerries that we peace-loving Yankees were as tough as they were". 34 Division did just that.

A crucial stage in the first battle for Cassino had been reached. The inner short-hook mounted by 34 Division had reached the outer perimeter of the Monte Cassino defences while on their right the French were poised to continue with the wider thrust through the Gustav Line. Both movements stood a reasonable chance of success provided that reserves could be positioned to keep up the forward momentum needed to stretch Von Senger's thinly held defences until they snapped. However, there were no reserves readily available in the whole of the Fifth Army. With the three corps all fighting desperately there was but one Infantry regiment still uncommitted and ready for battle, 142 Regiment from the unfortunate 36th Division. Fate had saved them from the cruel punishment meted out to the other two regiments; now whilst the survivors of the 141st and 143rd still held the sector opposite San Angelo, the 142nd was ordered forward to join General Ryder's 34 Division.

The correct decision to use this regiment was nullified when it was not sent to help the French breakthrough against Terelle and the gateway to Piedmonte but used as a wedge in the more local movement which was wheeling southwards towards Monte Cassino. Juin protested in vain. His Corps with some local assistance from 142 Regiment did recapture Colle Abate which fell to the Algerian Division but snow, ice and bitter weather began to wear down the French Colonial troops. There had been a way over the mountains into the Atina basin but only with more soldiers and far better logistic support would such an advance have been possible or decisive. Although the French continued to fight with gallantry on the right flank, in appalling conditions, their efforts were not and could not be of great importance after the Allied generals had decided that Monte Cassino had to be taken before any major offensive could be attempted elsewhere.

For the men of the 34th, depleted by casualties caused during the crossing of the Rapido valley, as well as by an ever-increasing sick rate from the bitter wintry conditions, there was to be no lull or respite. The Division's task was to force a way up the mountainside and strike towards the Abbey. In the valley, as the month of February began, a battalion of 133 Regiment, together with tanks and air support 'on call', advanced on Cassino town. Although progress was slow, the skilful handling of these battle groups was to gain a foothold in the buildings on the north edge of the already ruined town. As day succeeded day, the air in the outskirts was thick with the stench of decaying mules and human corpses, a smell that is hard to forget. Fighting was bitterly contested with the attackers in the open inevitably losing more men than the defenders did, protected and firing from behind their concrete reinforced strong points. It is, too, fair to say that the Germans did not fight then with the extreme fanaticism that was to be displayed, after the 3rd February, when units of 1 Parachute Division began to make their presence felt.

At the turn of the month, and certainly up to 3rd February, a breakthrough was very nearly achieved. The same factors hampered and crippled both sides; the wintry conditions made existence miserable and exhausting; the unceasing noise of guns and mortars made sleep and rest difficult; the acute problems of resupplying forward positions and equally difficult, evacuating the many sick and wounded were headaches that had to be resolved even when there were lulls in the fighting itself. The German soldiers suffered all these hardships in exactly the same way as the men from 34th Division. Even the iron nerved, cool leadership of General von Senger wavered when, having moved 90 Division back from the Garigliano sector to north of Cassino, he found that the hard fighting was costing his divisions the equivalent of a battalion a day through sickness and battle casualties. Emergency units made up of cooks, drivers and men from other administrative posts proved to be ineffective.

Senger also found that he could not relieve 15 Panzer Division with 71 Infantry Division as previously planned. In his words: "the garrison of Cassino itself and the battalions to the north of the town would have been overthrown if I had not been able to throw in a completely fresh regiment of the newly arrived 71 Infantry Division". Then when units of 34 Division scaled the heights north of Cassino to obtain an unimpeded view of the Via Casilina (Route 6), "I mustered all the weight of my authority to request that the Battle of Cassino should be broken off and that we should occupy a quite new line . . . a position, in fact, north of the Anzio bridgehead". The request was refused at the same time as it became clear to General Senger that his French and American opponents were in no better shape and that no fresh troops were readily available to the Allied Commanders.

34 Division deserved to win Cassino and on occasions, looked like doing so. The margin between defeat and victory was a narrow one and often depended on a handful of resolute defenders as happened during an attack by a battalion of 133 Regiment on the town of Cassino. The stubbornness of the German crew, manning a single SP gun, held up the advancing Americans until resistance in the town had stiffened considerably by the 2nd February. The attack may have been a courageous one but it was, as Christopher Buckley wrote at the time, "A heroic military gesture to attack the town but the Monastery Hill was the key". It was towards there that the other regiments of 34 Division began to fight their way along the hills above the valley.

The fiercest fighting was to take place within an area of six square miles around the Monastery and this was to continue to be the crucial battle ground throughout the subsequent struggle for Cassino. The high ground that runs north from Monastery Hill was ideally suited for defence. There was little in the way of natural cover for the advancing soldiers, the wide valleys and deep ravines were crossed by few but well defined tracks, which were thus mined and covered by defensive fire, while the hard rocky ground did not allow the Americans to dig themselves in to seek a measure of protection from enemy fire. In contrast, the Germans had fully utilised their time before the attacks had begun in blasting holes for weapon pits and constructing deep shelters, all of which were camouflaged with skill and remained invisible to the unsuspecting attackers. A sudden burst of fire was invariably the first indication that the innocent looking scrub and rock contained hidden and resolute defenders.

Even to get up the main track to the forward area around Snakeshead Ridge from the Italian barracks below involved a climb of some two hours. The narrow path, slushy where it occasionally crossed flat patches then rocky and hard when steeply rising, was a particular trial on man and beast, the beast being the mule which took over from the machine, the jeep, confined to the valley below. The Germans had pre-stocked strong points with food, ammunition and water but the Americans—and those who followed them—had to rely on this long resupply route which was continually being shelled and mortared by their opponents. The nearer the infantry got to Monastery Hill, the more difficult and tenuous administrative matters became.

From 1 February onwards names and spot heights of hills and peaks became familiar ones in the minds of those who fought and in the communiques which, in a few crisp words, reported the life and death struggle. In heavy fog on 1 February, 135th Infantry Regiment attacked Mount Castellone and Majula Hill but such features were not easily detected in the mist by the advancing infantry who then edged their way towards Colle San Angelo. The route led along the aptly named feature Snakeshead Ridge, and by 3 February two battalions had closed up to the foot of Point 593, the last but most important bastion by the side of Monastery Hill, barely 1,000 metres away. The Germans deemed this feature to be the key to the Cassino position and fought like tigers for its retention.

As the Americans struggled towards Point 593 the influence of Monastery Hill on their lives, and deaths, with the still undamaged Abbey on its summit, became stronger and stronger. After emerging from a deep valley or steep ravine it meant crossing over open ground in full view of the huge building, when effective mortar or shell fire harassed and struck at them with speed and accuracy. It was not surprising that the Monastery was considered to be as hostile to the Allied cause as the German paratroopers who defended the mountain on which it stood. "Huge and wet in the late afternoon it looked silently across our positions, separated from us only by a deep ravine", wrote H. L. Bond, when units of 36th Division moved up to join and reinforce their compatriots of the 34th Division. After talking to some of the men of the 34th, Bond added that for them Monastery Hill had become the source of all their misery. The fact that the Abbey had been declared inviolate by Allied higher Headquarters was bitterly resented by the combat soldiers who lived under its shadows.

The Germans held Point 593, called by them the Calvary Mount, with men from the Third Battalion 2nd Parachute Regiment. A few days ago this unit had been on the Adriatic sector. The decision to use these high class soldiers in the fight for Cassino was both timely and of the greatest significance. Nevertheless, a battalion of the US 135 Regiment was able to seize most of the Calvary Mount on the 6th February although a few defenders stubbornly refused to give up their posts just below the crest on the far side of the ridge. Only yards separated the German and American soldiers. Point 593 did appear to have been captured by 135 Regiment but unfortunately this key feature was never completely in their possession. It was not to be secured by the Allies until the Diadem offensive in May caused the Germans to pull back and then away from Cassino.

The high-water mark of 34 Division's exploits at Cassino was reached between the 5th and 6th February. A platoon from the 1st Battalion 135 Regiment sneaked up and surprised a German OP on Point 435, capturing fourteen prisoners from a position under the walls of the Monastery. Neither they nor anyone else could have foreseen that that was the nearest to the Monastery any Allied soldiers would reach until the final shots were fired three months later. Apart from a tenuous and disputed hold on Point 593, another thrust, in a straight line for the Abbey, by a battalion of 168 Regiment, took a feature Point 445, less than five hundred metres from the building itself. It seemed as if one more heave would win the day but the expertly sited defences caught the men of the 168 battalion in a deep ravine on the edge of the northern slope of the hill. Murderous crossfire forced them to retire with heavy casualties.

In the north west around Mount Castellone the Americans could now overlook Via Casilina (Route 6) but their advance was checked by the Schultz Battle Group on the very edge of the precipitous slopes down to the valley below. Without prepared positions to fight from, the Schultz Group held on to prevent an American breakthrough which would have cut off the whole of the German defences around Monastery Hill. Later, the keen brain of General Tuker (Fourth Indian Division) was to select this as the weak link in the German defences but his advice was disregarded.

Both sides were quick to appreciate that a most critical time had been reached, at Cassino and at Anzio. From Adolf Hitler came an edict to hold on to Cassino at all costs and to eliminate the Anzio landings. Field Marshal Kesselring was optimistic that such an elimination could be brought about by the Fourteenth Army under General Von Mackenson because they had formed a defensive ring around the beach-head by the end of January. To Mackenson's assistance troops had come from Germany, from France and even from the Occupation army in Yugoslavia. Tanks that could be ill spared were also sent so that Hitler's urgent cry for victory could be realised. After fending off the Allied attacks which had been delayed by General Lucas' caution, the Germans began their first big effort to push back the beach-head into the sea near Anzio on the 7th February. No longer could Winston Churchill expect to see the Alban Hills seized by a coup-de-main, or Rome fall in a matter of days. Sadly he wrote: "We have a great need for continually engaging them and even a battle of attrition is better than standing by and watching the Russians fight".

An even more alarming fact was that the German drive against the Anzio beach-head was made without the assistance of any of Tenth Army from their positions along the Cassino front. On the other hand fresh Allied troops had to be found in order to help 34 Division in their critical struggle and if the 34th failed, to take over when sheer exhaustion and mounting casualties crippled them completely. With the Anzio situation becoming more gloomy from day to day, General Alexander realised that the pressure at Cassino would have to be maintained and even stepped up—despite the bitter wintry weather, the stubborn German resistance and the heavy toll on men.

34 Division badly needed assistance so that the remnants of 36 Division, including its newly joined reinforcements, moved from positions by the river opposite San Angelo up into the hills to take over a sector at Mount Castellone. Into their sector along the Rapido came the New Zealand Division which had been moved across from the Eighth Army's Adriatic sector and now saw Cassino and the Monastery for the first time. The decision to send for the New Zealand and the Fourth Indian Divisions, the most experienced Divisions in Eighth Army, will be touched on in the next Chapter. Let it be said now that their arrival was not welcomed by General Mark Clark without reservations. These fine soldiers took over from the 36th ready to perform two possible roles: the first was to hold the San Angelo sector and familiarise themselves with the Cassino battlefield; the second was to be ready to exploit any breakthrough which the U.S. II Corps might make into the Liri valley.

By 8 February such a breakthrough seemed a possibility though the possession of Point 593 was still being bitterly disputed when first one side then the other would swirl back, with the issue being decided by small groups engaged in close-quarter fighting and by the initiative of junior leaders. On 9 February most of the Calvary Mount was again in American hands although regrettably not for very long and after a heavy toll of lives. The conditions were appalling and digging in the rain and slushy snow was virtually impossible. The air was filled with sound as the guns and mortars on both sides kept up a furious symphony of hate. The valleys and ravines increased the noise of exploding shells and magnified the unearthly whine of the 'screaming mimis' (nebelwerfers) before the bombs disintegrated into great jagged chunks of iron. In such wet, freezing weather, volunteers for stretcher-bearer duties were too easily found. Men of the American Division had been up on these inhospitable hills longer than their opponents; daily the sick and wounded casualties trickled back, while the dead lay in frozen attitudes of despair on the rocks and in the slush. 34 Division could barely hold the ground they had won. With mere handfuls of men they defied the elements and the Germans, but the majority were close to mental and physical exhaustion.

After some hesitation, Alexander agreed to Keyes' request that the men of 34th and 36th should be allowed one more chance to seize the Monastery. Whether Keyes appreciated how near to the end of their tether the soldiers of his Corps were is not certain. In his defence it can be said that his troops had been so near success that the temptation to try once more is easy to understand although the fighting strengths of some of the units were pathetically small. For example, two battalions of the 141st Regiment mustered less than 100 men each out of a normal complement of eight hundred. The remainder combined to fight on as one battalion but even then were pitifully under-manned and were quite unable to carry out a serious attack.

On 11th February the final American assault was launched with hopes set on the capture of the Monastery and of the town of Cassino below. Driving snow and a heavy artillery bombardment heralded and, to an extent, shrouded the assault but the attackers did not get far. The luckless 141st Regiment was held up near Masse Albaneta whilst the 142nd Regiment was severely mauled in trying to recapture Point 593. However the dog fight continued throughout the 11th until the 36th Division's Regiments were forced to give up the attempt because no longer did they have enough men to do anything but cling to their positions.

The Americans were given no rest. The German guns used their precious store of shells for one of the heaviest barrages they were to fire in the whole of the Italian campaign. Alerted to the probability of an enemy assault, 36 Division and its gunner observation officers were ready for the fierce attacks led by Colonel Baron Behr at the head of 200 Panzer Grenadier Regiment. At a critical period in this battle, the American Corps artillery hit, with devastating effect, the Grenadiers who were caught in the open. The Germans lost 150 casualties and had to withdraw, leaving Mount Castellone in the hands of the Texas Division. In this locality both sides had shot their bolt and the dead and dying paid testimony to a fierce struggle which ended in stalemate.

The drive by 168 Infantry Regiment towards Monastery Hill had no better fortune. Little ground was seized and the violent snow and rain storms made it impossible to give observed support from guns or by the Allied Air Forces. The attack petered out and the soldiers prayed for a respite from the conditions which had helped to defeat them after a harrowing three weeks in the front line.

The Commander of the New Zealand 5 Brigade, Brigadier Kippenberger, whilst visiting the American forward position, noticed how tired and exhausted the soldiers were—and asked General Freyberg to mention this at Fifth Army Headquarters. However, the casualty list and the pitifully small battle strengths had told the same story; no troops could have done more and the dogged determination of II Corps from General Keyes downwards had so nearly prevailed in this, the first battle for Cassino. The Americans had battled since January with a gallantry beyond praise but they were fought out and utterly exhausted in mind and body.

Forward came the newly formed New Zealand Corps who were described by H. L. Bond as "clean and spritely, rested and strong. If fresh troops could push the Germans off the ridges behind the Monastery these were the men to do it". Before them the Monastery, still intact, awaited the next act in the battle. Around the building in their defensive positions were the German soldiers of 90 Panzer Grenadier Division under a brilliant leader, General Baade, acclaimed by Senger as being "the victor in the first (and second) Battle of Cassino"; the elite hand-picked parachute regiments and the other units were to enjoy a slight respite after 12 February but it was to be a shortlived one.

In London, Winston Churchill commented that Cassino might

turn into a miniature Stalingrad. Even more aptly Adolf Hitler was to state that Cassino was a battle of the First World War, fought with weapons of the Second. Events were to prove them both right. However, more than ever before the struggles at Cassino were influenced by another encounter in Italy being fought for possession of the beach-head at Anzio.

8

The Second Battle—Freyberg's Plan for Victory

General Freyberg had no illusions about the task given him as Commander of the New Zealand Corps. He had seen the battlefield with its natural beauty and his eye as an experienced soldier in many battles was not beguiled by the stark tangle of the upper Rapido valley and the great battlements of the Cassino massif. When touring the forward areas, Freyberg had seen how gallantly and desperately the Americans had fought against an all but impregnable defence. He was not the sort of man to be downcast or disheartened but his cable to the New Zealand Government was a realistic one: 'We are undoubtedly facing one of the most difficult operations of all our battles'.

The decision to move the 2nd New Zealand, the 78th British and 4th Indian Divisions from the Adriatic sector to form a New Zealand Corps had been taken by General Alexander at the end of January. 78th Division did not arrive on the Cassino front until 17th February and thus did not play a part in the Second battle. The experienced New Zealand and Indian Divisions were to begin a determined effort to capture Monte Cassino and it was hoped that this would deter the Germans from launching a do-or-die counter offensive at Anzio. However, unbeknown to General Alexander, the German High Command had selected the 16th February as the day on which Anzio would be subjected to an all out offensive: by an extraordinary coincidence the same day had been chosen for the attack on Cassino by the New Zealand Corps. Fifth Army sensed that Von Mackenson's attack was imminent without knowing the exact date so that General Freyberg's Corps was given very little time in which to deploy, in which to familiarise itself with the terrain and to find out local conditions by patrolling or even to ensure that its logistic arrangements were ready to cope with the hurried move forward into the American positions. Time was precious and time was at a premium if the German plan to eliminate the beach-head around Anzio was to be forestalled.

Such a situation would have presented the gravest of problems to a full complement of experienced staff officers. However, at such a crucial time, there was no Corps staff available so that an improvised headquarters had to be formed in haste, using many of the key figures from 2 New Zealand Divisional Headquarters. Under the circumstances, there was no alternative but this switching of appointments was psychologically unsound and it caused disruption at a time when smooth planning was vital. What was required was confident, clear-thinking staffwork to make best use of the trump cards held by the New Zealand Corps so that its fine infantry soldiers could start off the battle with a reasonable chance of victory. The detailed coordination before the first bomb dropped, and the first soldier moved forward out of his foxhole, had to be expertly planned and instructions passed down in detail to the men concerned, to the New Zealanders, the Indians and the Gurkha soldiers facing the toughest of the many battles they had already experienced. It was asking a lot for such a high standard of staffwork from a scratch headquarters gathered together in haste.

In addition, the staff officers at Headquarters New Zealand Corps required a lot of understanding and assistance from their overlords in Fifth Army. Relations were not always at a high level of mutual esteem, stemming in part from the fact that General Clark had not been consulted in advance about the future role of the new Corps in his Fifth Army. As a result he was somewhat suspicious and resentful, with these feelings accentuated a little by the fact that he had to deal with an older and much more experienced General, Bernard Freyberg. Clark was subsequently to write about the New Zealand Corps: "I got a definite impression that 15 Army Group and Freyberg were going to tell me what to do".

This sort of feeling at the top spread to subordinates with fault on both sides. Freyberg subsequently clashed with General Keyes, when the latter was still in command at Cassino, which meant that Clark had to intervene and smooth things over. Later in the day he noted ruefully in his diary that his Army had five Corps under command, only two of which were American. 'And thus I was about to agree with Napoleon's conclusion that it is better to fight allies than be one of them'. With the anxieties of Anzio becoming more pressing—and thus taking more of his time—it was inevitable that Clark had to leave the overall coordination of the Second Battle to Freyberg in conjunction with Fifth Army staff at Caserta. It was not always a happy or efficient arrangement.

General Sir Bernard Freyberg brought with him a vast amount of experience and a world-wide reputation as a first class soldier under active service conditions. He was a man who possessed great physical and moral courage, as tough a warrior as any who has ever served the British Crown. Although spending his early years in New Zealand, Freyberg had seen most of his army service with the Brigade of Guards, and only returned to serve with his countrymen after the Second World War had begun. It needed a period of adjustment from his Guards methods to those understood by the citizen army of New Zealand but thereafter Freyberg and the 2nd New Zealand Division became synonymous in a fighting partnership, admired by friend and foe, winning renown in Greece, in Crete and in the Western Desert.

Such was the strength of the man and such were the exploits of the troops he had led with dash and devotion for nearly four years. In two respects, however, Bernard Freyberg was not the best choice to be Corps Commander of a scratch formation and as such, with direct responsibility for the Second and Third battles of Cassino. The first reason was that for the most patriotic of motives this big, burly man had remained at the head of the New Zealand Land Forces, which meant commanding a Division, when many of his prewar contemporaries in the British Army had accepted greater responsibilities so that by 1944 they had gained much experience in handling Corps and even Armies. Freyberg had few opportunities to command anything larger than a Division, and even when he had been given more responsibility, for example as GOC Crete, the venture was short-lived and, through no fault of his, doomed to failure from the start. The second disadvantage from which General Freyberg suffered was that he had direct responsibility to the New Zealand Government for the way his troops were handled and had to be carefully aware of casualties, which his native country, with its small population, could ill afford to suffer. At times this direct political link was of benefit, but there were occasions when it was just another responsibility on his shoulders, broad though they were. It meant that if a situation ever developed into a close struggle, and heavy casualties appeared to be inevitable, then there were definite pressures on Freyberg which made him to hesitate before committing everything available. He

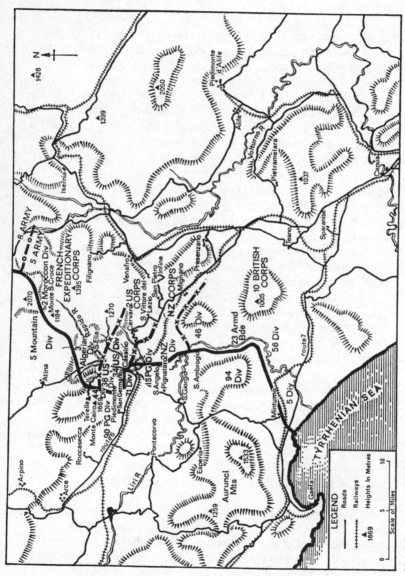

Map 4: The Second Battle, 6th February 1944.

could not ignore such pressures nor was he allowed to do so by the New Zealand Government.

And so, as he contemplated the task set the New Zealand Corps, it is not surprising that Bernard Freyberg accepted the opportunity to harness the offensive on to the chance that the Air Forces might pave the way for his Divisions to achieve a victory without a terrible casualty list. He and his staff were given so little time in which to plan the next attack and the big weapon in the Allies' armoury was their gigantic air fleet of bombers, fighters and fighter-bombers. The logical conclusion was to use the trump card of air superiority against the heart of the Cassino defences, Monastery Hill. General Alexander decided to let the Allied Air Forces take on Cassino in the hope that a massive strike might open the way to Rome and he was reassured by the Commander of 15th Army Group Air Force, General John Channon who said: "If you let me use the whole of our bomber force against Cassino we will whip it out like a dead tooth".

The decision to use heavy and medium bombers to attack the main targets at the very centre of the defences was in itself a gamble. Prior to Cassino, only tactical aircraft had been used in close attacks on targets which were selected by the forward troops. Now it was decided to spare nothing and use the heaviest weapons available, including giant Fortresses and Liberators, against the German divisions. The advantages were obvious because the heavy bombers had the ability to destroy the strongest building and defence works and, moreover, it was assumed that the Germans would be so shaken that their resistance would be half-hearted and spasmodic. One big disadvantage that worried the planners was the safety distance necessary between the Allied soldiers, and the targets under attack by the bombers. If 'own casualties' were to be avoided then inevitably there would have to be a delay in time after the bombing was completed, before opening shots were fired by the Indians and New Zealanders as they pressed home their attacks on the ground.

Freyberg had one other big asset on his side, which was the high quality of the two Divisions in his Corps. The renown and reputation of the New Zealand Division in many past actions has already been mentioned. It is no exaggeration to say that the Fourth Indian Division had built up an equally splendid record in war and the two Divisions were spoken of in the same tone of voice and held in the highest regard by the rest of the Eighth Army. The three Brigades in Fourth Indian Division each had a British, Indian and Gurkha battalion. The Divisional Commander, Major General F. S. (Gertie) Tuker, when serving with and alongside the three nationalities concerned, had recognised that each contributed special qualities to the fighting skill and reputation of the three Brigades in his Division; with the British soldier dogged and imperturbable in defence; the Indian jawan, dashing and bold in attack; and the Gurkha rifleman adept at patrolling and expert in silent night assaults on the enemy. Gertie Tuker had welded all these soldiers into a magnificent Division whose members wore their 'Red Eagle' sign with pride and distinction. General Tuker came to Cassino with a brilliant personal record. In character and temperament he was the complete opposite to Freyberg but, as so often happens, the two men held each other in high regard. Tuker was more akin to General von Senger on the other side of the Cassino Hills, with his clear restless brain which prompted him to explore new methods of training and into experimenting with unconventional tactics and ways of operating in war. Tuker was a man of many parts and had quite a talent for writing and painting. One quality he lacked, which Freyberg possessed in abundance, was that of the common touch, the gift of being able to joke and talk with the soldiers he led and be at ease in their company. Freyberg could slap a subordinate on the back or show displeasure in forcible soldier's language. Tuker was shy and, at times, aloof but no one ever doubted his ability and determination or failed to recognise and admire the high standards he set Fourth Indian Division and himself.

During the campaign in Africa, on more than one occasion, General Tuker had shown moral courage when insisting that the units of his Fourth Indian Division should be used in a way which gave them full scope and exploited their talents. He knew their capabilities and he fought to ensure that his men were given the best chance possible in attack or defence. If ever Tuker's keen brain and natural tactical sense were needed then it was now, from the time the New Zealand Corps went into battle through the days and weeks that followed. Freyberg was his commander but there is little doubt that Tuker's advice could and would have had a considerable influence on the senior General as the drama of the next two battles unfolded.

"After many hours of study of maps and air photographs and of the ground from every possible vantage point and after many discussions, General Freyberg decided on a plan that was in effect a continuation of the Americans"—wrote Howard Kippenberger in his book 'Infantry Brigadier'. He had considered and rejected a repetition of the 36 Division's abortive attempt at crossing the Rapido near San Angelo. He listened to Juin's plea for the attempt to be in support of the French Corps but with the problems of administration across the high mountains now covered in snow, and with the bitter weather which made movement difficult, Freyberg decided that it was too much of a gamble. Tuker thought it a risk worth taking with his men in support of the French because Fourth Indian Division not only contained men trained to fight in the mountains but also boasted three battalions of Gurkhas from the highlands of Nepal. On the 12th February, Tuker made yet another suggestion to General Freyberg which advocated a thrust which would isolate the Monastery. He wrote: "This course I regard to be profitable as the enemy is, I believe, still only in field defences in the mountain areas to the west and south west of Mount Castellone. They're using Mount Castellone and the area now held by the U.S. II Corps has a firm base. We can attack in fast, short jabs to the west and south west of Mount Castellone and cut No. 6 Highway west of Monastery Hill—with the cutting from the north of No. 6 Highway the Monastery Hill will be isolated".

Unfortunately as he was writing this appreciation Tuker was confined to his bed, suffering from a tropical illness, and in his absence, the plea was overlooked and the plan was modified. Instead of the wider thrust across the mountains the attack was to be directed at the heart of the defences, at Monastery Hill itself.

What were the factors that influenced Freyberg into taking this course against the advice of Juin and Tuker? He had noted how the depleted American II Corps had so very nearly reached its goal and only sheer exhaustion appeared to have robbed them of victory. In the place of battle-weary Americans stood fresh battalions of the New Zealand Corps at full strength, all capable of producing extra soldiers at the crucial moments. And, of course, there was the promised air support on a scale far greater than had ever been used before against a small compact defensive area. Even with hindsight and under these conditions who can say that the Second battle was one that did not stand a reasonable chance of victory? If the prize had only been Cassino, with the opportunity to break through the Gustav Line, then there is little doubt that the attack would have been postponed until Spring when the gentle weather would have brought harder ground for the Allied armour and the necessary favourable conditions for a victorious offensive. But VI Corps at Anzio needed help urgently. This was the military reason for the Second battle, and there were political ones as well. Winston Churchill could not begin to contemplate the possibility of Anzio failing after all the difficulties he had experienced in persuading the reluctant Roosevelt and the suspicious American Chiefs of Staff into agreeing to the enterprise. The new Cassino offensive must go in at once; "so Wilson urged Alexander, Alexander urged Clark, Clark urged Freyberg, and Freyberg urged his two Divisions to be ready to attack immediately. Once again there was too little time, everything had to be rushed. Anzio was in serious danger", so wrote Fred Majdalany in his book—and it is an accurate summary of how the Second battle began and the problems that faced the Allied commanders in Italy at that time.

Freyberg therefore accepted the directive which was little more than an elaboration of the plan previously adopted by the Americans, augmented by the promised support of the Air Forces. He decided to use his two Divisions in a giant pincer movement—up on the hills, and attacking through the salient which had been seized and held by 34th Division, Fourth Indian Division would move from the north east to capture Monastery Hill and the Abbey upon it. At the same time, to the south of the town, the New Zealand Division was to secure a bridgehead over the River Rapido and thence join up with the Indians at the foot of Monastery Hill. And then a mobile force, which had been champing at the bit for weeks gone by, would be launched up Route 6 to the succour of VI Corps at Anzio and thence to Rome.

Such a pincer movement relied, to a great extent, on the speed with which the Indian Division was able to capture Monastery Hill after the bombing programme had been completed. The Americans had never been able to launch an attack against the main and final objective. As they struggled forward towards the Monastery, the more stubborn and fanatical the Germans had become behind defences of ever-increasing strength which remained as a barrier to the Abbey itself. The key point, Monastery Hill, which dominated the ridges to the northeast as well as overlooking the town at the foot of the hill and whole valley beyond, had to be so bombarded that infantry soldiers from the Indian Division could get close enough to rush over the last few yards without being cut to pieces by machine guns firing in defence. Such a condition meant but one thing as far as the Allied combat troops were concerned—the Monastery with the German strong points under its walls must be destroyed by any means possible. No matter where the men of the Fifth Army were in the forward area, the building overlooked them, dominating their lives and thoughts, dictating how and when they could move because they all had to answer one question first: 'can I be seen from the Monastery?'

The fighting soldiers hiding behind rocks or crouching in stone shelters had no doubts, or misgivings. Americans in the forward positions had long been convinced that the Abbey was a German strong point and had bitterly resented the embargo on any direct action against the building itself. "You can fight round the Abbey but you can't hit it", one junior officer, H. L. Bond, was told after he had directed two or three mortar bombs on to the roof of the Monastery.

As already described the German propaganda machine had sought the plaudits of the civilised world for the measures taken by their soldiers to save priceless works of art from destruction. Later, categorical claims were announced that there were no armed German soldiers within three hundred yards of the walls, although it was stated that the Abbey still housed a few monks and a handful of refugees. How then could the British and Americans even contemplate the destruction of the ancient building, with its great religious significance, especially when, the Germans claimed, it was not manned for defence and had no tactical value whatever?

Even if overdone and coloured by the propaganda experts the outraged cries of protestation from the Germans struck an uneasy chord in many hearts. In the early days of February a lot of time was spent in Headquarters Fifth Army trying to decide whether or not to believe the Germans' claim that none of their soldiers were inside the walls of the Abbey. Nothing conclusive was produced to prove or disprove the Germans' story nor is it thought that any evidence will ever come to light to answer this question. Possibly the real truth will never be known and even if it were, then it could not help to resolve the dilemma that faced the Allied Generals in

1944 or change the decision they took after days of hesitation and agonising thought.

The simple brutal truth was that the Abbey stood on the summit of the key point at the heart of the Cassino defences. The German High Command had selected the best possible position from which to off-set the advantages the Allies possessed with their air superiority which gave complete aerial observation over the battlefield. Only from the highest vantage points on these mountains could the Germans direct artillery and mortar fire on to any part of the battle that threatened danger. As N. C. Phillips wrote: "Once the enemy had decided to include Monte Cassino in his defensive system the building on its summit inevitably became a legitimate target; for though the mountain might have been defended it could not have been captured without attention to its summit—it is the nature of war not to be played to the whistle between white lines".

On the Allied side the Generals could not agree among themselves as to whether the Abbey should be destroyed or not—for example, General Mark Clark was opposed to it. He, and others, were more concerned with sifting evidence which would prove or disprove the claim that German soldiers were inside the Abbey walls. Mark Clark's immediate subordinates, Generals Keyes and Ryder, supported him in saying that the bombing of the Monastery was unnecessary—although, as said before, the American officers and men in the precincts of the Monastery had bitter feelings about the views of their superior generals.

Up to February 12th no definite plans had been made nor had any decision been taken. The matter was brought to a head by General Tuker after he had learnt that his Division had been nominated for the task of assaulting Monastery Hill. His paper to the New Zealand Corps Commander started with the words: 'After considerable trouble and investigating many bookstalls in Naples I have at last found a book dated 1879 which gives certain details of the construction of the Monte Cassino Monastery'. He then went on to describe its formidable dimensions; one, and only one, entrance through a huge gate, 15 feet high walls of solid masonry which were at least 10 feet thick at the base, and as the Abbey had been constructed as a fortress in the 19th Century, loopholes had been made in the walls. Tuker stated that only 'block-buster bombs' from the air could be effective against such a building and, in a bitter tone, concluded by saying that when a formation is called upon to attack and reduce such a place then detailed information should have been readily available, "without having to go to the bookstalls of Naples to find out what should have been fully considered many weeks ago".

General Freyberg's immediate reaction was to ring up Clark's Chief of Staff and say, "I want the Convent attacked". This started a series of conversations by radio and telephone between Clark, often at Anzio, Alexander at 15 Army Group Headquarters and Freyberg in his advanced headquarters near the battlefield of Cassino. Freyberg was once more asked to confirm that he considered the bombing to be a necessity. After his reassurance had been repeated, Mark Clark reluctantly endorsed the proposals which finally went to his superior commander in Italy, General Alexander. The commanders of the soldiers, who in a day or two would be asked to risk their lives in an attempt to capture Monte Cassino, Freyberg and Tuker had felt that an all out attack on the Monastery by all available means and weapons was a military necessity. This was sufficient reason for Alexander who felt that his duty to the attacking troops was paramount over all other considerations. Quietly but firmly he supported the request. The Monastery would be bombed.

It is very much to General Alexander's credit that he has always maintained that there was no other decision open to him as the overall commander in time of war. Eighteen years later he wrote in his Memoirs, "When soldiers are fighting for a just cause and are prepared to suffer death and mutilation in the process, bricks and mortar, no matter how venerable, cannot be allowed to wear against human lives. Every good commander must consider the morale and feelings of his fighting men and what is equally important, fighting men must know that their whole existence is in the hands of a man in whom they have complete confidence. How could a structure which dominated the field of battle be allowed to stand? The Monastery had to be destroyed". Likewise, at a much lower level, a junior American Lieutenant, H. L. Bond, wrote: "When a choice is to be made between a museum-piece and the lives of young men then there is no need for long debate, although the Abbey stood for a belief in human dignity and individual worth". He went on to say that the tired American infantrymen who saw the bombing were to cry for joy as bomb after bomb crumbled it into dust.

Let this be the end of the debate. War, any war, is brutalising and the significance or otherwise of an ancient building is soon lost in the desire of men to survive and thence to win. Due respect can be paid to the scruples of General Mark Clark because he never liked the decision and said so at the time. Nevertheless he was not in direct touch with the fighting men of Cassino and did not appreciate their bitterness and frustration at being ordered to observe the sanctity of the Monastery. Of his many preoccupations Anzio was the one that gave him the most concern at this time, so that he was not able to gauge the feelings of the troops near Cassino.

The decision having been taken, events moved at an extraordinary speed as far as arrangements for the bombing programme work were concerned. The Chief of Staff, Fifth Army, General Gruenther, asked the Air Forces to bomb the Abbey on the following morning, that is, 13th February but bad weather intervened and caused a postponement. On the afternoon of 14th February leaflets in propaganda shells were fired by the artillery which fell close to the Abbey. These read as follows: 'Italian friends BEWARE. We have until now been especially careful to avoid shelling the Monte Cassino Monastery. The Germans have known how to benefit from this but now the fighting had swept closer and closer to the sacred precincts. The time had come when we must train our guns on the Monastery itself. We give you warning so that you may save yourselves. We warn you urgently leave the Monastery, leave it at once. Respect this warning. (Signed) THE FIFTH ARMY'.

Not unnaturally such a message caused the monks and the refugees to panic. Many dashed out at once to seek cover in nearby caves; some crept into deeper shelters while others put their faith in the Almighty by staying in the Basilica praying that God would not allow the tomb of St. Benedict to be destroyed.

Messages were sent by the old Abbot to the Germans who agreed that the remaining monks and refugees should be evacuated during the night of 15/16 February. Events, however, moved faster than the German plan because the weather cleared up on the 14th February and the Allies decided to begin the bombing of the Monastery at 0930 hours on the following morning, the 15th February.

HQ Fifth Army's main reason for the sudden decision to carry out the bombing as quickly as possible was the critical situation at Anzio where General Von Mackenson's offensive had begun to threaten the beach-head itself. It was intended that the Air Forces would complete their Cassino mission quickly so that they would be free to concentrate their full support over the threatened Anzio battlefield. However, it is sadly apparent that Fifth Army did not worry whether Freyberg had time or not to coordinate the bombing programme at Cassino with the ground attacks of the Second battle about to be delivered by his New Zealand Corps. Freyberg himself appeared to treat the bombing as a bonus, a gamble that might win the day, but no evidence has been found to show that any serious efforts were made to delay the bombing even if, as happened, the soldiers on the ground were not ready to attack at the same time as the air strike was made against Monte Cassino.

In the meantime, Fourth Indian Division, now without General Tuker, had taken over the sector on the mountains from the Americans by the early hours of February 14th. What they found was grim and forbidding. Dead bodies were strewn everywhere. Some of the living Americans were so exhausted that over fifty of them had to be carried down the mountainside on stretchers. Even more alarming was the fact that units of 7 Infantry Brigade took over their sector only to find that Point 593 was firmly held by the Germans although maps back at the headquarters of 34 Division had shown this rocky peak to be occupied 'by our boys'.

In the cold grey light of 14th February, Fourth Division, and 7 Brigade in particular, faced the realities of the situation in a none too optimistic mood. The CO of 1 Royal Sussex, Lt. Col. J. Glennie wrote in his diary: "We were therefore in full view of the enemy from all sides—we had no reserve rations and barely one blanket per man . . . everybody behind worked hard to get us supplies but the shortage of mules, the length of the daily march—seven miles each way after dark—and the heavy shelling and mortaring of mule tracks, all combined to keep the admin situation bad".

Patrols were sent out locally to familiarise themselves with landmarks but they could only move a few yards before drawing German fire. German outposts around Point 593 were less than seventy yards away. There was no elbow room for deployment, no cover behind which men could be concentrated before an attack and no time in which to change local dispositions. Major General Howard Kippenberger commented in his book: "Poor Dimoline (the acting Divisional Commander of 4 Division) was having a dreadful time getting his men into position. I never really appreciated the difficulties until I went over the ground after the war. He got me to make an appointment for us both to see General Freyberg as he thought that his task was impossible and his difficulties not realised. The General refused to see us together. He told me that he was not going to have any soviet of Divisional Commanders".

No Corps commander ever wants to be faced by subordinate Generals 'ganging up on him', nevertheless Freyberg's refusal to see Kippenberger and Dimoline proved to be a mistake because he was unable to appreciate the problems Fourth Indian Division faced in trying to get ready for the attack. Therefore, it is not surprising that the Army Commander, Mark Clark, wrote in his diary that Fourth Indian was slow in deploying and when its infantry units attacked, they did so in penny packets when the occasion urgently demanded a strong and well coordinated assault—but, alas, he and Freyberg had failed to give them time and the opportunity to do otherwise.

The morning of 15th February dawned with the sky clear and with the omens favourable from the air force point of view. The Germans and the terrified occupants of the Abbey sensed an air strike was due. So it was—at 0930 hours the first wave of the armada of bombers made its appearance over the Monastery of Cassino. Just fifteen minutes before, a frantic message had reached Brigadier Lovett in 7 Brigade headquarters to say that the bombers were on their way. It is no wonder that the commanding officer of the Royal Sussex was to comment in bitterness and frustration: "They told the monks and they told the enemy, but they didn't tell us".

All the controversy before and after the bombing was to be of little significance compared with the inescapable fact that the important decision to bomb the Monastery was nullified by a complete lack of coordination between the ground and airforces. A wonderful opportunity to crack open the kernel of the German defences was to be lost. The timing of the bombing had been decided by the vagaries of the weather and not by the readiness or otherwise of Fourth Indian Division to follow up with a ground attack.

As a direct result of this tragic error, it was going to be the fighting soldiers, the men in the shadow of the Monastery, who would pay for the folly of their superiors.

9

The Second Battle Begins

The bombing was an impressive and awe-inspiring spectacle carried out with a degree of precision against the Monastery with but token resistance being offered by a few anti-aircraft guns. The Allied Air Forces paid the Benedictine Abbey full honours with some 255 bombers arriving in wave after wave over the target from 0930 hours until a little after 1.30 p.m. The angry Brigadier Lovett in his headquarters wrote: "At that moment I was called to the blower and told that the bombers would be over in 15 minutes. I started to blow up myself but even as I spoke the roar drowned my voice as the first shower of eggs came down".

Near to Point 593 the diarist of an Indian battalion, the 4/16 Punjab Regiment, described the bombing: "We went to the door of the command post, a derelict farmhouse, and gazed up into the pale blue sky. There we saw the white trails of many high level bombers. Our first thought was that they were the enemy then someone said 'Flying Fortresses', then followed the whistle, swish and blast as the first flights struck against the Monastery. Almost before the ground ceased to shake the telephones were ringing. One of our Companies was within 300 yards of the target and another 800 yards. All had received a plastering and were asking questions with some asperity. We could not offer any explanation but just 'grin and bear it'." Luckily most of the casualties in these two shaken Punjab Companies were bodies bruised by pieces of the Monastery which were hurled great distances through the air in all directions.

General Mark Clark declined to watch the bombing and sat in his command headquarters trying to concentrate on reports from Anzio. His deliberations were interrupted by sixteen bombs, released by mistake from the American planes and a few landed near the command post, fortunately without causing any casualties. Meanwhile the majority of the planes continued to pulverise the appointed targets, dropping their bombs from heights between

18,000 ft. (Fortresses) and 10,000 ft., the Mediums which were much more accurate. The roof of the Monastery was blown away and the interior of the building reduced to a shell—although the mighty walls were not split from top to bottom as had been anticipated by the experts.

Inside their shelter the Abbot, his faithful band of monks and the remaining civilians, understandably thought that death was imminent. In terror they knelt in prayer when not only the building but the whole mountain shook as if in the throes of a giant earthquake. A large number of refugees were buried under the ruins, the exact figure will never be known but estimates varied between one and three hundred.

At approximately 1.45 p.m. there was silence and the inferno seemed to be over. The Abbot and the surviving monks climbed out into the open to be confronted by a terrible spectacle of utter destruction. The once beautiful Basilica was no more; only the stumps of shattered pillars remained as evidence that the huge building and its precious treasures had ever existed, with rubble and debris piled high over many of the once familiar landmarks. It was indeed a picture that proclaimed more eloquently than any words the futility of war. But the ordeal of these helpless people was not yet over for it was the whine and crump of Allied artillery that began a further onslaught against the ruins, and caused the survivors to hide yet again.

Churchill was to write: "On 15th February after the monks had been given full warning, over 450 tons of bombs were dropped and heavy damage was done. The greater walls and gateway still stood". (In fact, this giant entrance remained undamaged to the very end of the last battle.) Churchill concluded by saying: "The result was not very good". However, the result was as expected: the building had been turned into ruins ideal for defence. This might not have been a matter of great consequence if New Zealand Corps had been ready to follow up the bombardment with ground attacks. Instead nothing happened during the daylight hours of 15th February and as each hour ticked by, it was the Germans who reacted to the situation with speed and efficiency.

Without further delay, they arranged for the evacuation of Gregario Diamare (the Abbot of Cassino), and his followers and this was carried out on the following day, 16th February. Holding aloft a long Crucifix the eighty-year-old man of God led those who remained alive out of the ruins and down the hillside to a hastily arranged reception by the Germans. Dr Goebbels' propaganda machine made the most of such an opportunity and broadcast a statement signed by the Abbot immediately after the bombing had ended. This proclaimed: "I certify to be the truth that inside the enclosure of the Sacred Monastery of Cassino there were never any German soldiers; that there were for a certain period only three military police for the sole purpose of enforcing respect for the neutral zone which was established around the Monastery but they were withdrawn twenty days ago".

The next thing the Germans did was to send soldiers from their Parachute Division into the rubble of the Monastery. General Senger commented: "Now we could occupy the Abbey without scruple especially as ruins are better for defence—we had a commanding strongpoint which paid for itself in all the subsequent fighting". Without wishing to reopen the controversy about the destruction of the Monastery, it seems all too evident that the alert German propaganda machine, and the quick efficient occupation of the Monastery after the bombing, were both results of a firm conviction by the German High Command that the Allies would be forced to attack the Monastery if they were determined to open the Liri valley by capturing Monte Cassino.

While the Corps artillery continued to pound away at the ruined Monastery throughout the afternoon of 15th February frenzied attempts were made to organise an attack which would exploit some advantage from the bombing. General Freyberg wanted an assault to be mounted after darkness fell but he was unaware that Point 593 was still in German hands and he had no conception of the deployment problems facing Fourth Division in the front line positions. The acting Fourth Divisional Commander, Brigadier Dimoline, found that Brigadier Lovett at 7 Brigade Headquarters would not agree to an attack on the Monastery until the whole of Point 593 was in his Brigade's possession. Dimoline had no alternative but to agree. A handful of Germans on Point 593, by their machine guns and controlled mortar fire, could disrupt any attack on the Monastery itself. Time was precious to both sides but only the Germans were in a position to utilise fully the minutes as these went by during the late afternoon on 15th February. A decision was taken by Dimoline to postpone the main 7 Brigade attack for a further twenty-four hours so that the Royal Sussex could capture Point 593 in the interim period.

The whole of the Corps was affected by this decision, an inevitable one as far as the Indians were concerned but a cruel one for the New Zealand Division who had watched the bombing of the Abbey with taut nerves, keyed up with the thought that their attack would begin soon after it was over. The anticlimax was not made any easier to accept when they realised that the delay was to the advantage of the German defenders who were ready to fight for every position they held.

The spotlight now switched onto the men of the Royal Sussex who had to eliminate Point 593 before anything else could start. Lieutenant Colonel Glennie, the CO, was forced to wait until dark before his men could make any attempt because movement by day was quite impossible. Scope for deploying large numbers of men was so limited by the ground that he decided to attack with C Company, a total of 3 officers and 63 men. These early tactics adopted by 7 Brigade caused Mark Clark to comment: "The attack was slow in getting under way and of a piecemeal character so that the enemy was able to chop up first thrust and turn back the advance piece by piece".

It was possible for a senior commander not completely acquainted with all the facts to make such a critical comment. Clark failed to understand how a sudden decision to bomb the Monastery, without waiting for the ground troops to get into positions from where they could follow it up, had forced Fourth Division, 7 Brigade, and the Royal Sussex, into making piecemeal attacks. The second battle of Cassino was a victim of Anzio but the cause of Anzio would have been served better if the Air Forces had been made to wait or were switched back from their missions over the Anzio beach-head to Cassino a few days later. Expediency at the top overruled tactical planning on the ground so that the senior Army Commanders cannot be absolved from the charge of having grasped at the Air Forces' promise to neutralise Monte Cassino, without carefully considering how this was to be achieved by joint ground and air action.

Although C Company Royal Sussex moved forward with the utmost care and caution, it was quite impossible to muffle all noises from the alert Germans, many of whom were less than a hundred yards from the Royal Sussex positions. The Germans held their fire—until the British had begun to think that they had gained complete surprise but, on a signal, the defenders opened up with sustained machine gun fire as well as hurling a deadly shower of stick grenades which descended on C Company as they tried to crawl and wriggle their way forward. All their efforts were unavailing: they were checked and matters were made worse when their stocks of grenades were exhausted—in contrast to the Germans who seemed to have an inexhaustible supply of stick grenades so ideal for close quarter fighting. The Germans had every advantage and when C Company, under Major Dalton, was recalled, they had suffered thirty four casualties.

The implications of this reverse were out of all proportion to the small number of troops involved or the casualties incurred, regrettably high though they were for one company. As far as ground attacks were concerned nothing could be attempted during the hours of light next day; and the lessons of the abortive night attack were clear, painful, and obvious. More than one company would be needed if Point 593 was to be taken and held against German counter-attacks. Surprise would be impossible because the German positions were within one hundred yards of the nearest British outpost. A generous supply of grenades was required if the men from Sussex were going to hold their own against the tough paratroop soldiers and, even if the British managed to secure the Calvary Mount, it could only be held thereafter if strong reserves were available nearby. After the night of 16th February had come and gone, these lessons led to a further conclusion that any attack by a single battalion was doomed to failure as it could never capture the hill, called Calvary Mount by the Germans and Point 593 by their opponents, and hold it against immediate counter attacks.

Once more the fighter bombers attacked the ruins of the Monastery during 16th February while the officers of the Royal Sussex, having received their orders at 1100 hours, spent the rest of the day making their plans and thereafter briefing the soldiers. Colonel Glennie was most unhappy at the prospect of an attack that very night: "We needed 48 hours for recce, planning, building up our ammunition supply, etc. Oblique air photos of the objective were a real necessity but were not available. However, we got on with it because: a. it was repeatedly emphasised that we must do something to take the pressure off the Anzio beach-head which was in imminent danger of collapse; b. we had so far always been successful. We had the superiority complex common to the rest of Fourth Indian Division and we were not given to belly-aching".

The Royal Sussex did not belly-ache but quite rightly Glennie insisted on the time of the attack being put back so that the mule train could arrive in their position, bringing up the precious grenades. In fact, the attack was twice postponed by half-an-hour because the mule train was late; when it did arrive it brought only half the number of grenades asked for, which were quickly handed out to the three companies before the assault finally began at midnight.

The Allied gunners were not able to fire on and neutralise Point 593 because of the short distance that divided friend from foe. Other strongpoints in the rear and on the flanks were selected as targets but even then the shells passed a few feet above the attacking battalion, and a large number failed to clear the crest and caused casualties in the Regiment as it formed up on the start line. This resulted in a degree of disorganisation before the attack began. Thereafter, the story of C Company's reception by the Germans was repeated when after about fifty yards the leading men ran into withering machine gun fire and dozens of grenades landed in their midst. The Germans from the cover of 'sangars', and from foxholes protected by rocky ledges, buffeted their British assailants with every weapon at their disposal.

D Company worked its way round the left of Point 593, supported by a platoon from A Company. A forty foot wide crevice checked their progress but many of the men got round and in small groups forced their way up on to the main crest of Point 593, where fierce hand to hand fighting ensued. The Germans immediately sent in reinforcements which met the British soldiers face to face. The situation became so confused that control was virtually impossible. To the problem of control was the added difficulty that ammunition supplies had begun to dwindle and once more the British companies found themselves short of grenades.

Glennie decided to commit his reserve, B Company, which he had held back for its original role, to consolidate on Point 593 and exploit forward from the feature after it had been captured. Just before dawn the company tried without success and with heavy losses to force a way between the other companies towards the objective. To add to the confusion of the battle, the Germans fired three green Verey lights which some men of the Battalion thought was the signal for a withdrawal and as these men filtered back, others followed their example. However, by this time, the outcome was inevitable because there was little ammunition to fire, the first signs of daylight were approaching, and there was no cover available to hide behind, with the German grenades and machine gun fire becoming more and more effective as the light improved. The attack was called off but the damage had been done and the morning battle casualty report was gloomy reading: Ten officers and 130 men out of a total of 12 and 250 who had taken part in the battalion attack were killed, wounded or taken prisoner—and if C Company casualties were added to the list, then CO Royal Sussex had lost 12 officers and 162 men in a little over 24 hours.

Lieutenant Colonel Glennie summed it up: "The battalion fought hard against a very determined enemy, fighting at night on his home ground in ideal defensive positions". But two failures by an outstanding battalion to seize a preliminary objective indicated, with unmistakable clarity, the magnitude of the task that confronted Fourth Division up in the hills. General Freyberg decided that no longer could the battle be fought by one unit in 7 Brigade and that the time had come for the Corps to begin his original plan of a pincer movement which would end with the capture of Monte Cassino.

If the British were dismayed, then the Germans were puzzled by the comparative inactivity in the battle after the bombing on 15th February, until the Corps plan was set into operation three days later. General von Senger commented: "The lull in the battle seemed to drag on so that as a tactical prelude the destruction of the Abbey appeared to have no significance". The major reasons for the delay have already been discussed: the complete failure to harness the ground offensive to the bombing programme or, more accurately, to delay the bombing until the soldiers were ready to begin coordinated attacks; the failure of Freyberg and his scratch Corps Headquarters to appreciate the deployment and logistical problems facing Fourth Division; and something not to be underestimated, the absence of General Tuker at this all too critical period. No disrespect is intended towards Brigadier Dimoline, who found himself promoted from Commander Royal Artillery to be Divisional Commander overnight, but it was inevitable that as a temporary, stop-gap Commander, his voice could not carry the same weight in discussions with General Freyberg or indeed when dealing with his fellow brigadiers in Fourth Indian Division.

The New Zealand and Indian Divisions began their main attacks during the night of 17th February in conditions that did not allow either Division to deploy its full strength. The extreme difficulties experienced by the Indian Division in carrying out the relief in the line of the Americans, in supplying their forward troops and in trying to obtain a satisfactory start line for local attacks, have been mentioned. In the valley the New Zealanders, under the newly promoted Major General Howard Kippenberger, also faced problems. The deliberate flooding of the Rapido Valley by the Germans prevented them from attacking on a wide front so that the only approach from the west was along and astride the railway causeway. The causeway itself was known to be heavily mined and breached in several places so that no tanks or supporting arms could move forward until the engineers had opened and cleared a suitable track. Although Kippenberger had designated his 5 Brigade to attack across the river, the advance had to be spearheaded by two companies only—because there was not room for a bigger force until the railway station had been captured.

It posed a lot of difficulties for Howard Kippenberger who wrote: "I felt a little unlucky having to deal with so awkward a problem in my first battle as a Divisional Commander". He could but give directions to 5 Brigade and then ensure that all possible means of support were readily available to help them achieve their mission. Self-propelled guns, 17 pounders, machine guns and mortars were brought forward as close as possible to Cassino in order to keep the German Garrison (211 Regiment, 90 Panzer Grenadier Regiment) under fire and also to give the illusion of an attack on a broad front. The hope was that the leading unit of 5 Brigade, 28 Maori Battalion, would seize the railway station quickly so that there were sufficient hours of darkness to allow the engineers to clear the mines and breach the gap before daylight came on 18th February. Only if tanks were up with 28 Maori Battalion before dawn broke did the operation stand a reasonable chance of succeeding—if they were not, then it was doubtful if the Maori infantry could survive on their own throughout the day against German tanks and heavy support weapons. The local prospects were no more than fifty/fifty and even then any long-term value of the New Zealand advance still depended on who held Monastery Hill above them.

The night of 17th February was a cold, bleak one as the two companies of the Maori Battalion began their advance at 2130 hours. In the darkness they moved forward under intense mortar and machine gun fire through barbed wire and minefields towards the strongly defended railway station. After a stirring advance, followed by a fierce assault at about midnight, the station was taken, but a block of houses to the north of it, and a small knoll to the south, still remained in German hands. So far, so good but the capture of the station would only be of benefit if the engineers behind the Maoris could open up a route for tanks to follow them before daylight came.

Although the engineers worked heroically throughout the night, regardless of heavy casualties to officers and men, their efforts were to be in vain. Only by the narrowest of margins did they fail to bridge one gap and aided by spotters in the mountains, the German mortar fire drove the engineers into seeking cover. Looking at the slopes of the mountains looming above the Cassino railway station, General Kippenberger had to decide whether or not to use smoke in an attempt to conceal the sappers who had been trying to work in full view of the German observers above them. He knew that smoke would be a double-edged weapon as it could allow his opponents the opportunity to put in a counter-attack under cover of the smoke screen, shrouded from any observation by the Allied artillery. Kippenberger did not hesitate for long—smoke had to be used if his sappers were to carry on their urgent work.

Just after 7.00 a.m., the sun rose and was to set at half-past five in the late afternoon, and for nearly eleven hours, the two companies of Maoris faced heavy odds with nothing but the weapons they carried, friendly artillery fire that came quickly on call but could not always be accurately controlled, and a heavy pall of smoke which was at the whim of the wind. The Maoris were heavily mortared after dispersing the first German counter-attack during the morning. Thereafter a continuous hail of machine gun and mortar fire, mostly from Monastery Hill, rained on them while the gallant engineers worked hard to complete their task under conditions of great danger and intense discomfort.

Reinforcements were unable to reach the station and the supply of smoke shells was being exhausted as the forward companies kept sending back urgent pleas for the smoke to be thickened. Nevertheless the fact that they were still holding firm until after midday caused hopes to rise in the New Zealand Headquarters but thereafter as the long day dragged by, fresh reports were received that the Germans were preparing to deliver a strong counter-attack on the isolated group of Maori soldiers.

Shortly after 1400 hours, the Germans moved forward with two tanks making their way towards the station while infantry of 211 Regiment advanced along the railway line under a heavy curtain of fire. It was not long before the German tanks were in the station yard and one platoon of Maoris was overrun. They had no heavy weapons to fire at the tanks and the remaining men of the two companies had to withdraw back to their original start position. The venture was over. Between 1600 and 1900 hours survivors from the original force of some two hundred all ranks arrived back across the Rapido. This foray resulted in about one hundred and thirty casualties plus thirty from the engineers who had laboured for so long to no avail.

A disturbing thought is that even if the Maoris had succeeded it is very doubtful whether a breakthrough into the Liri valley could have resulted as the Germans still held Monastery Hill and thus they completely overlooked the railway station, nearly 2,000 feet below them. As soon as 7 Brigade's attacks ended in failure on the mountains, then there was little point in the Maoris' gallant attempt in Cassino town. The Maoris' conduct in this attack added to their reputation. It was, however, a gesture which gained one small bridge head over the Rapido but had no real significance in the overall battle for Monte Cassino.

10

The Second Battle Ends

On the 17th February, the same night as the Maoris mounted their attack, three battalions from Fourth Indian Division were ready to begin their part in the capture of Monte Cassino. Room for deployment was so limited that the plan adopted was but an elaboration of what had been tried before by the Americans. It was the direct approach but there seemed to be no alternative to the Brigade Commander at the time—nor did there appear to be any alternative to the author when he visited the peaceful scene a quarter of a century later. As his superior commander had ordered him to mount a direct assault on the Monastery, Brig Lovett had little choice in selecting a plan.

The 4/6 Rajputana Rifles of 11 Indian Brigade was to pass through the sector held by Royal Sussex and storm Point 593, exploiting if possible to the end of the Snakeshead Ridge. Then at 0215 hours, with the help of the rising moon, two Gurkha Battalions, the 1/2 and 1/9 Gurkha Rifles, were to make a direct assault on to Monastery Hill, cutting straight across the boulder strewn elbow of Snakeshead Ridge and passing to the left of the now infamous Point 593. If their efforts were crowned with success, then two battalions from 5 Brigade would move into the north of Cassino town and link up with the Maori Battalion. Only the opening moves of this plan were even attempted.

The key to the battle lay in the hands of the two Gurkha Battalions, both of which had magnificent records in past battles fought during the African campaign. In an attempt to avoid the experiences of the Royal Sussex, whose ammunition supplies had run out at a critical period in their two battles, soldiers from the third Gurkha Battalion in the Fourth Indian Division, the 2/7 Gurkha Rifles, acted as porters in support of the assault made by their fellow countrymen. The Gurkhas, attackers and porters alike, waited for the moon to rise while the first moves were made at midnight by the Rajputana Rifles against Point 593.

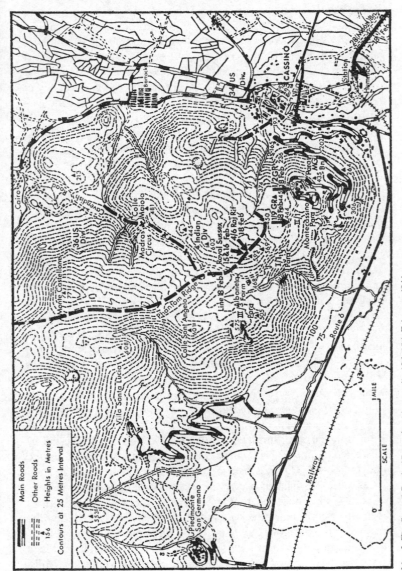

Map 5: The Second Battle (Operation 'Avenger'), 15th-18th February 1944.

Heroes of many past encounters, the Indian soldiers began to make their way along the ridge towards Point 593, but once again the Germans raked the slopes with fire and after about an hour the Rajputana Rifles found themselves pinned down less than one hundred yards from the objective. Nevertheless, isolated groups of gallant men did reach the crest only to perish inside a ruined fort while they tried to repel fierce German counter attacks. In a final attempt to win the position, the CO sent in his reserve company at 0430 hours but the Germans stood firm. The Rajputana Rifle casualties amounted to one hundred and ninety-six all ranks and only two British officers escaped unscathed from the night's fighting. The Battalion, which had contained many veterans, was never the same again and it was a sad and costly defeat after a string of victories in past battles.

Prior to crossing an undemarcated start line in a night filled with the noise of the Rajputana Rifles' battle, the 1/9 Gurkhas had to cover an approach march of four miles up the crowded track that served as the supply life-line to the troops fighting for Point 593. It was not an auspicious beginning to their attack which started at 0215 hours with Point 444 as the first objective, some three hundred yards to the left of the Indian Battalion. The movement of the Gurkhas was detected instantly because many of the defenders of Point 593 were not directly concerned with beating off the frontal assault made by the Indians and were experienced enough not to neglect their flanks. The two leading companies, C and D, were buffeted by heavy fire of all descriptions and pinned down within a small area of hillside, while behind them, the other two companies were unable to even leave their 'jump off' positions. The small and shallow penetration was the only thing achieved by these piece-meal operations because the third unit, the 1/2 Gurkhas, was to fare no better than the unfortunate Rajputana Rifles, and, in the end, the small patch of ground won by the 9th Gurkhas had to be abandoned before dawn. Their losses were the lightest of the three assault battalions but still totalled 94 all ranks; the tough German paratroopers had thrown back the second unit attack mounted by Brigadier Lovett, and the omens for the third one being successful were most unfavourable.

After the Second Battle was over, a story was published which described how a few Gurkha soldiers reached the Monastery walls, only to perish there, after hand-to-hand fighting. No evidence has ever been forthcoming to prove such a story but if any Gurkha soldiers did reach the Monastery then they might have been from a platoon of C Company 1/9 Gurkhas who disappeared into the darkness under a young British officer, Captain Bond. Later a wounded signaller crawled back to say that his officer and a handful of men had reached the Monastery. However, no bodies of Gurkha soldiers were ever found there, so it is more than likely that Bond's gallant little party perished on the eastern slopes of Point 593, well short of the Monastery walls.

In the small hours of 18th February, the third unit to attack, within the small battle area of no more than one thousand yards, was the 1/2 Gurkha Rifles. The supreme prize of the battle, the capture of Monastery Hill, had been entrusted to this experienced Battalion with its many victories over the Germans during the Desert and Tunisian Campaigns. Now, each of the four rifle companies was given a clear-cut task which it was hoped would end with the capture of Monastery Hill.

After midnight, when the Battalion was forming up the heavy Allied guns and the retaliatory German fire added to a night of noise, confusion and thunder. On the right, the 'burp burp' of the German sub-machine guns indicated that the Rajputana Rifles and 9th Gurkhas were at close grips with the defenders of Point 593. The men of the Second Gurkhas had to wait until early morning when it was their turn to top the crest of the ridge of Point 450 and advance down the slope towards the looming pile of the Monastery, nearly eight hundred yards away.

At once pandemonium broke loose. German 'spandau' groups and machine guns shot at the Gurkhas from the right flank and from posts dug in under the walls of the Monastery. Ahead of them lay scrub which had to be crossed but which might give them a measure of protection. Dashing into cover the leading companies found themselves in a death trap because the scrub proved to be thorn thicket, sewn with mines and booby traps, ingeniously threaded together with trip wires. Men were blown up, killed and maimed as they floundered around in the thicket so that within fifteen minutes most of B and C Companies had been struck down. A few men broke through but had to fall back and dig in on the near side of the scrub belt.

Meanwhile the CO, Lieutenant Colonel Showers, led the other two companies over the crest only for their assault to be greeted with a blaze of fire. Showers fell, wounded in the stomach, while around him the casualties quickly mounted. Those coming behind tried to press the attack and one or two enemy posts were captured, but the accurate machine gun fire from points along the northern slopes of Monastery Hill had halted the Gurkhas. As dawn broke the broken remnants of the companies were forced to consolidate close to the start position which they had used less than two hours before, two hours in which twelve officers (British and Gurkha) and 138 other ranks were casualties with not a yard gained from the Germans.

In these battles fought by the Rajputana Rifles, by the Ninth Gurkhas and finally by the Second Gurkhas, stories of indomitable heroism and individual acts of courage were too numerous to mention in such a narrative as this. In spite of the terrible shock as men were cut down in the opening minutes of these assaults, there were always those who shouted "On, on" and who took the fight towards the Germans, reasonably confident in their defences behind rocks and concrete reinforced shelters—and with their weapons aligned on the approach routes used by the Indian Division.

General Alexander wisely decided that it was profitless for the Fourth Indian and New Zealand Divisions to continue the assault as the original plan was already sadly awry. Like its predecessor, the Second battle had touched success and the outcome was in doubt at times, but in the end there were no gains: In the mountains Points 445 and 593 had been attacked but could not be held. In the valley the Maoris had won a temporary bridgehead which the tanks had been unable to reach and without their support, the early gains could not be held. One major lesson was that the seizure of ground near Cassino meant little, and would continue to mean little, just as long as Point 593 and Monastery Hill remained in German hands.

The Allied generals had other problems to ponder over. In the hills north east of the Abbey more than one brigade of infantry was required to overrun the mutually supporting German outposts but the supply problems, stemming from the maintenance of even one brigade, would be accentuated if more fighting soldiers were sent into the bare and rocky forward areas. And the lesson that 7 Brigade learnt at such a terrible cost, was that, ideally, the German outposts had to be attacked at the same time or as second best, overrun with the minimum of delay between each phase of the attack. Another headache was the inhospitable weather which continued to hamper the Air Forces, artillery, supporting arms and tanks, all of whose aid was essential if the Germans' hold around Cassino was to be prised open.

These unresolved problems confronting the Allies had contributed to the victory gained by the Germans in the Second battle but there were two reasons of even greater importance. The first was the tragic failure to harness the bombing of Monte Cassino to the New Zealand Corps plan for the ground attack, an omission that made the decision to destroy the Monastery completely meaningless. And the second was the combination of an almost impregnable defensive position with the magnificent fighting qualities of the German paratroopers. The soldiers of New Zealand Corps were hurried and harried into a battle for which they could not plan properly against opponents who had prepared themselves to withstand a series of onslaughts and, by training and past experience, were used to fighting in small, isolated groups. The courage displayed by both sides under terrible conditions was most remarkable but the odds were always on a victory being gained by the defenders.

Back at New Zealand H.Q. Kippenberger wrote: "It was no use repining. Two editors from New Zealand were at my mess and we had a particularly gay evening joined half way through by the General (Freyberg) and his mess. Soldiers should not worry. You do your best but you do not cry over spilt milk".

New Zealand Corps had done its best under difficult conditions. All ranks grieved the heavy casualty list which made them even more determined to win the next encounter. They expected and deserved a sound plan and to be given enough time for their preparations for battle to be completed. They hoped that their commander, General Freyberg would adopt a plan that would make the Third battle of Cassino the decisive one and win the victory which would lead to the capture of that elusive city of Rome.

11

The Third Battle—Freyberg Plans Again

The reverse suffered by the New Zealand Corps during the Second battle was a grievous blow, particularly as the situation at Anzio was still fraught with danger and the outcome of the struggle there remained very much in the balance. Adolf Hitler had been quick to appreciate that if the German Army eliminated the small Allied beach-head then the victory would have far-reaching repercussions throughout the world. To the German people struggling against heavy odds on land, sea and air, the tonic of success would restore, to some extent, Hitler's waning prestige. Equally important, if the Allies were thrown into the sea then it might compel them to revise, and delay, their plan for the invasion of France. Any changes which involved a bigger striking force might have precluded a landing in 1944 and valuable time would have been gained for the development of Hitler's 'secret weapons'. Without doubt, therefore, the fate of the Anzio beach-head was of vital importance to both sides. Churchill wrote: "The ease with which they (the Germans) moved their pieces about the board and the rapidity with which they adjusted the perilous gaps they had to make on their southern front was most impressive. It all seemed to give us very adverse data for Overlord".

At the height of the Second battle the Germans renewed their efforts to smash a way through to the sea at Anzio. By the 17th February they had reached the positions which the Americans had seized on the first day of the landing so that VI Corps' situation was critical in the extreme. Mark Clark commented: 'We were back to a line which had nothing much behind it except the beaches and the sea. We were obviously going to take it on the chin with everything Mackenson could throw at us on the following morning'. But on the other side of the hill, Field Marshal Kesselring had decided to stop the attack; unbeknown to Mark Clark, the German casualties had been very severe and the Allied superiority in artillery and air power had convinced the Field Marshal that the last few miles to the sea could not be won without terrible losses. Hitler ordered that the offensive be resumed before the end of February—heavy rain caused the actual date to be put back from the 25th to the 28th February—but by this time Allied plans had been made at Cassino to launch the Third battle and, once again, its military purpose was to ease and divert German pressure away from Anzio.

The alternatives to another direct head-on assault against Cassino and Monastery Hill were carefully considered by Generals Alexander, Clark and Freyberg. The heavy, almost incessant rain, had turned the Liri valley into a quagmire so that any chance of a breakthrough there was ruled out. Once again Juin pleaded for his French Corps to be reinforced in order that the route north of Monte Caira into the Atina basin might be opened. But the weather at the end of February was so bad that the long difficult way over the mountains would have taxed available logistic resources to the extreme limit, although a personal opinion is that an earlier attempt at the end of January might have succeeded, before the winter of 1944 turned from neutrality into direct opposition to the men and mules living on the harsh rocky mountains.

Another attempt along Snakeshead Ridge, a repetition of Fourth Indian Division's suicidal attack, was ruled out by General Freyberg. That left but one alternative if an attack had to be launched before the spring weather came, and for the sake of Anzio, such an attack was deemed to be necessary. For political reasons, Churchill was keen that his American and Russian Allies should see that the Italian Campaign had not deteriorated into an ineffective battle of attrition; in his eyes, Rome was still the prize to be won at as early a date as possible. An attack had to be launched, therefore, and Freyberg decided that the plan that stood the best chance of success was one that involved a heavy saturation bombardment from the air on to Cassino town itself. His outline proposal was presented to General Alexander who wrote: "Accordingly on the 20th February, after discussing the plan with Generals Clark and Freyberg, I decided that we would next attempt to capture the town of Cassino after heavy bombardment with the New Zealand Division which would then push past the southern face of Monte Cassino along Route 6, then making contact with the Indians north west of the Monastery and thus encircle the enemy positions. This would give us a big bridge-head over the Rapido and an entry into the Liri valley".

It is evident from the statement above that the final decision to attack the pile of masonry on Monastery Hill, and the battered town below, was made by Alexander and not at Fifth Army or New Zealand Corps level. In retrospect, it may seem strange that Alexander had fallen victim to the magnetic attraction of Monte Cassino, like his subordinates Clark, Keyes and Freyberg before him. Until the end of February 1944 the key to this puzzle can be found in the lack of time and in the terrible anxiety about Anzio, feelings shared by Winston Churchill who continued to prod Alexander with a series of strongly-worded telegrams. Time was indeed a commodity in short supply, for although the Second battle only petered out on the 18th, the plans for the next offensive were ready by the 20th, with the attack scheduled to begin on the 24th February. Under the circumstances and remembering the many pressures on the generals concerned, it is not surprising to find that the suggested plan was one which could be put into effect quickly and, equally important, a plan that again relied on the still untested effect of a pounding by the Strategic Air Forces against a small target area. Hopes were high that such a bombardment might win the day without heavy casualties to the New Zealand Corps—and as stated before, General Freyberg was well aware that public opinion in New Zealand would be outspoken if losses were severe and he knew that a disaster would be strongly felt by that small nation. Freyberg sought victory, but not at any price; Clark demanded immediate help to save the soldiers at Anzio; and Alexander decided that one more attempt to seize the strongest bastion in the whole of the Italian Campaign was justified.

A detailed plan was produced. Kippenberger's opinion was: "It was not a bad plan, a subsequent (Fifth) Army report stated that it was the best that could have been produced in the circumstances". Once again, it should be noted that there was no firm conviction among the leaders that victory would result; there was the same strange fatalistic attitude which pervaded the Allied Headquarters from the Rapido fiasco and continued until the early days of May came, almost as if events were too much for the Allied commanders and no one general was master of his own destiny. The German commanders, however, were under no misapprehension about their role in the battles, realising that there was to be no retreat whatever or quarter asked or given, and every post and position had to be defended for as long as the Fuehrer ordered. This is not to imply that the lot of the German soldier was in any way an easy one; in many respects the Parachute Regiments and Panzer Grenadiers had to endure far greater tribulation from the heavy air and artillery bombardments than their opponents were required to undergo. Their lot as soldiers was hard but their commanders did not lack confidence and continued to be optimistic that they could hold on as long as the Italian winter continued to prevent the full weight of the Allied thrusts against other parts of the front.

Before we study the plan prepared in haste by New Zealand Corps the German situation must be looked at in a little detail. 90 Panzer Grenadier Division, which had suffered severely and lost many casualties during the February fighting, was in urgent need of rest. Field Marshal Kesselring chose 1 Parachute Division to relieve it, a choice that soon proved to be a wise one, as the soldiers of New Zealand Corps were quick to discover to their cost. On the 20th February General Baade's 90 Division was finally relieved and three Parachute Regiments took over Cassino town, Monastery Hill and Point 593, the Calvary Mount. The commander of the Parachute Division, Lieutenant General Heidrich, assumed command of the eight mile wide sector held by his Division on the 26th February.

15 Panzer Grenadier Division remained in occupation of the Rapido sector although General von Senger's original intention had been to relieve its units by battalions from 71 Infantry Division. In the event only one regiment was ever withdrawn because 71 Division was used piecemeal to bolster up and reinforce threatened weak spots elsewhere. Up on the mountains 44 Hoch Und Deutschmeister Infantry Division and further north still, 5 Mountain Division, continued to hold their own against Juin's French Corps but, by now, the winter with its snow, sleet and fierce winds had reduced the activities of both sides to minor clashes.

The Parachute Division had to hold the eight mile front with depleted numbers; most of its battalions could muster two hundred men each, and their companies rarely more than forty soldiers apiece. General Heidrich had an extremely difficult task in resupplying his Division as movement by day was quite impossible with the Allied artillery punishing anyone who dared to emerge from cover. By night, however, the same sort of activity occurred behind the Parachute Division lines as took place on the Allied side of the battlefield; lorries with darkened side lights delivered stores which mules then carried up the mountain tracks to a point from where fatigue parties could manhandle the precious loads of ammunition, food and water to the OPs on crests, and the machine gun teams in foxholes, often less than one hundred yards away from the Fourth Indian Division. Life for the German soldiers was never less hard and exhausting than it was for the Indians, Gurkhas, British and New Zealanders who opposed them.

General Heidrich sensed that another attack was imminent and that General Freyberg only awaited an improvement in the weather before it began. His paratroopers were feverishly employed in constructing new defence posts and improving those already in use. The rain and snow, which made conditions difficult for the working parties, at the same time gave the Germans longer time to complete their preparations without too much interference. Within the battered town new strong points were selected and the old ones were reinforced with any available materials, so that the occupants might stand more chance of survival should another holocaust break above their heads. In short, the Germans were content to endure the inclement weather and use it to their advantage while their opponents fretted and cursed at the delay.

Delay there had to be because the crux of General Freyberg's plan was the carefully planned air bombardment on Cassino town when the Air Forces would drop about 1,000 tons of bombs into a target area of no more than one square mile. Thereafter, the artillery would lob somewhere in the region of 200,000 shells into approximately the same congested area. If anyone survived bomb and shell then it was expected that they would be too shocked to fight the Kiwi soldiers who would follow up and enter the town as quickly as possible, although the vexed question of a safety limit caused concern. A distance of a thousand yards was decided on which meant that there would be an appreciable delay after the bombing had stopped before the attacking troops could even enter the ruined town with its debris and rubble. . . . Only after much deliberation was this possible flaw accepted as being inevitable, because no senior Allied General was prepared to risk his troops being hit by the American or British aeroplanes.

The role of Fourth Indian Division was to storm a way up the mountainside after the New Zealanders had cleared the town from the north, and seized Castle Hill at the foot of Monte Cassino. From Castle Hill 5 Indian Brigade would climb up the steep slopes and capture the Monastery: the way to Rome would be open with 78 Division and an American Task Force, Combat Command B of 1 US Armoured Division, ready in reserve, poised to exploit the breakthrough into the Liri valley.

The major drawback was that although the two divisions were attacking side by side from the north, the operational front was very narrow indeed. The town could only be entered along a single road, because the ground on both sides was flooded and mined, and this meant that battalions could only be fed into the battle through this funnel instead of hitting the men from the German Parachute Division at various points, with a series of heavy blows. Moreover, 5 Indian Brigade had to enter and follow the same route before they reached the slopes of Monastery Hill: it was not the ideal way to deliver such an attack and, once again, there was a strong possibility that the initial blows would have to be delivered in a piecemeal manner against one sector of the town. Misgivings there were but the hope was that the Air Forces would remove the defences of Cassino, and demoralise its defenders, as had been promised before the Second battle.

The Parachute Division and the two divisions of the New Zealand Corps faced each other with the strong suspicion that the next battle would be as bitter and costly as the ones that had gone before. The Germans sensed that another gigantic air strike was inevitable even if they could not foretell where and when such a bombardment would take place. The timing depended on essential, reasonable climatic conditions and the weather changed for the worse before the date planned for the operation, 24th February.

Winter struck with all the violence of a fresh enemy, rain froze into sleet, sleet into snow, which strong winds turned into blizzards. Now there could be no chance of aircraft even flying, let alone carrying out pinpoint bombing against Cassino town. The bombers were grounded while tanks and vehicles churned help lessly and ineffectively in a sea of mud. Nothing could be don ther to improve positions or to launch any fresh attacks a and foe, German and Indian, clung to exposed positio mountains as the worst storm of many an Italian wi mountain crests in its icy grasp.

The Fourth Indian Division historian described this new turn of events as follows: "On the crests and along the hillside the infantry clung to their meagre shelter under the continuing buffeting of the elements. When darkness fell the men emerged from a freezing cramp to prepare for the next inevitable day. The Germans likewise came to life searching the paths and assembly areas with mortar and artillery fire in the hope of intercepting the supply columns. These interminable flights of shells which passed overhead with the rasp of tearing cotton brought unrelenting labour to the rear echelons couped in the upper Rapido Valley. Porters and mule trains assembled nightly at the dumps, signallers moved out to repair or lay new wires, field companies shelved their tools and squelched off through the mud, ambulance convoys crept forward to pick up the day's wounded. Along slippery ice-covered ridges, these groups with endless delays made their way forward. . . ."

Long drawn out days when movement was impossible followed by nights of activity meant that the morale and physique of the men of the forward positions was severely tested. 7 Brigade under the shadow of Point 593 and the ruined Monastery suffered sixty casualties a day, many of whom were victims of severe exposure or sheer exhaustion. The recollections of the author in his diary are similar to those in the quotation above. "Time seems to have stopped; it is as if we have been condemned to live forever in a cold, damp hell on earth, each of us obtaining but meagre shelter behind rocks or in holes in the ground. Each night we pray that the following morning will bring a change in the weather, a respite from the rain and snow and the endless vigil that is never a quiet one as the whine and crump of the gun and mortar continue by day and night. As day succeeds day the anxiety about the next attack has changed into a desperate longing to do anything rather than sit for ever undergoing an ordeal that tests minds and bodies alike".

Although the weather continued in all its fury until the second week in March, the next German offensive at Anzio, due to begin on 28th February, did not last long. On that day too, rain poured ??? and Kesselring was quite prepared to ask Hitler for a further ??? ment, although at the request of his troops in LXIII ??? rps, he refrained from doing so and the attack was ??? t day. Fortunately the Allies were favoured with an ??? in the weather over the beach-head and their naval guns and aircraft were able to harass the attackers and operate without restrictions. No ground was given and the German attack came to a standstill. On 1 March Kesselring decided to break off the offensive which had been a failure even though the beaches still lay within the range of the German heavy artillery and the Allied soldiers could never enjoy any period of rest or quiet. The crisis was over and the urgent, dire necessity of a further attack by New Zealand Corps at Cassino was to disappear when the fighting at Anzio died down and ceased to be critical.

The question must be asked as to whether there was any military justification for continuing with the plans for the third attempt to capture Monte Cassino, so soon after the failure of the Second battle, and before larger forces were available and the weather was more favourable. A delay of some six weeks would have seen winter turn to spring, when alternative routes through the Aurunci Mountains would have been open to a strong force of men, armour and vehicles. In retrospect, the decision to launch the First battle is sound, the inevitability of the Second one is accepted, but the third offensive in March, planned for the specific purpose of relieving Anzio, makes little sense if military reasons alone are sought. General von Senger und Etterlin decided that: "This battle will go down in history as one of the most perplexing operations of war". The Germans were puzzled and the soldiers who fought in the New Zealand Corps have asked the same sort of questions: Why was the Third battle fought? What was the object of launching it in March and who really expected it to succeed?

Perhaps the last query is the easiest one to answer. The Air Forces were supremely confident that an aerial bombardment, delivered on such a grand scale, would so reduce Cassino to rubble and its defenders to shocked apathy, that exploitation by the Allied soldiers would achieve the long sought breakthrough to Rome. Some of the generals had doubts but without any examples of such an airstrike being made, with so much power on to a small target area, they were not prepared to rule out the possibility of success. Victory had only just eluded them in the past battles even to the extent of General von Senger requesting that Cassino should be abandoned at the end of January. The generals could argue that there was as much chance in this battle of winning the prize of Monte Cassino even if the military reasons for launching it in the middle of March were unconvincing and obscure. Since 1944, the question that has exercised many military historians is why it was not delayed until spring. Was it, as General Fuller maintained, just a case of "bombing conquers, all else follows up?" He infers that a blind faith in the effects of aerial and artillery bombardment influenced General Alexander into having one more attempt at snatching a victory, a victory that would have been a real tonic to the British and American Governments, after the severe winter fighting in Italy which had cost them dearly and brought so few rewards. The Russians had been reproaching their Allies for months past, implying that their soldiers on the Eastern front had been carrying the whole brunt of the war against Hitler. Stalin was suspicious about the procrastination shown by his Allies in starting their invasion of France. A complete deadlock in Italy would have been interpreted by him as showing how inefficiently the Western Powers were waging their one small land campaign against the common enemy. To offset such a criticism, the Anglo-American armies had to keep attacking; they did not have time to regroup even if climatic conditions had allowed such a large-scale deployment of men and guns to have been carried out, speedily and efficiently. It all added up to the truism that in modern warfare commanders-in-chief are rarely, if ever, able to take decisions in a vacuum, without political factors influencing and often overruling military considerations.

During the early planning stages of the Third Battle, Alexander's Chief of Staff, General John Harding, prepared the military appreciation from which the decision to regroup the Fifth and Eighth Armies was to stem and it was to be the back cloth to the spring offensive by the Allied Armies in Italy. He advocated that a three to one ratio of infantry superiority had to be obtained at vital points on the front and his plan envisaged encircling movements away from the hard centre of German resistance around Monte Cassino. Harding's brilliant appreciation became the basis for the final plan for the Operation called Diadem. The irony of it was he was writing proposals for these plans at the same time as the New Zealand Corps was ordered to take on the Germans in another venture—the success of which could be prayed for but its outcome could by no means be guaranteed. Recalling General Senger's remarks, it was perplexing to be planning a future offensive at the same time as a single Corps of two divisions began to carry out a frontal attack on Monte Cassino: it indicated that General Alexander had doubts about the result of the New Zealand Corps' next attempt.

Meanwhile, the soldiers of the Indian and New Zealand Divisions waited from day to day for the weather to clear. As the rain and snow fell, a daily, codeword signal was flashed to all units with monotonous regularity: "Bradman won't bat today". Cricketers could not perform, it was not fighting weather, and the bombers which were to be the star performers could not even take off the ground. Such a winter could not go on forever, even at Cassino, and on the 13th March the skies began to clear and prospects looked brighter.

Appropriately enough the date selected to begin the third offensive coincided with the Ides of March—15th March. The long awaited codeword 'Bradman' was circulated through the Corps on the 14th; after the war the New Zealand Official History commented: "Those who affected sporting language speculated on the state of the wicket and the historically minded noted that the morrow was the Ides of March". Freyberg, like Julius Caesar, could but trust to fate in the knowledge that his two elite divisions were ready even if both had lost their original commanders. The sick General Tuker, who had been replaced first by Brigadier Dimoline and then by Major General Galloway, was not destined to return to his Division while the New Zealand Division suffered an equally grievous blow when Major General Howard Kippenberger lost both feet when blown up by a mine on Mount Trocchio. At a critical time, Major General Parkinson, his relief, took over as an untried Divisional Commander and the wealth of experience that Tuker and Kippenberger possessed was to be sadly missed by Freyberg in his daily councils of war. It is, however, profitless to surmise what their advice would have been or, more important, whether Freyberg would or could have been influenced by it. It was a pity that the plans, so carefully nurtured for the long delayed third assault, were to allow little deviation once the battle started, and the slender pipeline through Cassino along which the second wave of assault troops, to maintain the momentum of the attack had to pass, proved to be too narrow when speed was essential during the early, crucial stages of the battle.

12

The Third Battle is Launched

On the 12th March, the Allies used the giant sledgehammer of air power with its terrible destruction, pounding Cassino town at 0830 hours in the morning. Official sources disagree about the exact number of aircraft that took part but some five hundred bombers, of which nearly three hundred were 'heavies', dropped over a thousand tons of bombs on the town in three and a half hours. To a War correspondent like Christopher Buckley, the bombing was gigantically one-sided—"a horrid vision of the potentialities of mechanised war." To a young British officer, cowering down in his foxhole below Point 593, it was a terrifying exhibition of sound and fury. He wrote in his diary: "After a few minutes, I felt like shouting that's enough; but it went on and on until our ear drums were bursting and our senses were befuddled. Several bombs fell on my company and I found myself shouting curses at the planes. The chance of being killed or maimed by one's own side is somehow more terrifying even if the end result is the same; 'Dear God, take pity on those poor devils in the town':"

As soon as the bombing started, "Cassino was shrouded in swirling billows of smoke and dust and that soon hid it from observers", amongst whom were General Alexander and a group of senior officers, standing on the hill near Cervaro. They watched the terrifying spectacle, so one report alleges, in a light hearted atmosphere. The bombers followed, wave upon wave, and it was later estimated that about half the bomb load fell within the confines of the town. There were unscheduled targets which included Allied gun areas, Fourth Indian Division's B Echelon where some fifty men and one hundred mules were casualties, a Moroccan Military Hospital, and over one hundred Italian civilians at Venafro, a town ten miles south of Cassino that suffered because it had been built at the foot of a hill, similar in shape to Monte Cassino. Within the correct target area, the devastation was terrible and: "already battered from weeks of siege, Cassino was now utterly laid waste—not a single building stood intact and streets lost their identity in a wilderness of rubble". The desolation of war was complete.

Bohmler in his book on the Monte Cassino battles declared that the German garrisons were astonished and relieved when the Monastery was not included in the target area. He wrote: "This was a bad blunder since the roofs and cloisters would hardly have stood up to another heavy bombardment. The defence would have been largely neutralised and the Indians would have been able to capture the hill without much difficulty." It is not possible to prove or disprove this statement except to point out that it was not the last ditch defences around the Abbey that were to halt and defeat the New Zealand and Indian Divisions' efforts during the days that followed the bombing.

In this hell the German paratroopers lived and died in an inferno that seemed endless. Walls collapsed, bombs tore craters in gardens and fields, trees flew through the air and the noise was quite indescribable. Lt. Schuster commanding 7 Company: "We could no longer see each other; all we could do was to touch and feel the next man. The blackness of night enveloped us and on our tongues was the taste of burnt earth. I had to grope my way forward and through a dense fog then down came the bombs again. Direct hits here, here, and here—when I got back the men read in my face what I had seen. The same unspoken thoughts were in all our minds—when would it be our turn?"

Lt. Jamrowski, a Prussian commander of Sixth and Eighth Companies recorded similar experiences: "There was nothing we could do but crouch, tense and expectant, where we were. Bombs were now falling like rain and in our underground shelter the thought struck me that we were just like submarine crews whose U-Boat was being pursued by depth charges". Later, when the entrance to the cellar was completely blocked he and his men set to work clawing at the rubble and the earth. All sense of time was lost and after hours of labour a small cleft was made and they saw light. Eventually they escaped but scores of their comrades died under the debris in other parts of the town.

In spite of the terrible ordeal undergone by the garrison in the town, the German High Command decided to stand firm and go on holding Cassino. Although casualties were heavy, they had been less than expected in proportion to the material damage caused by the pulverising aerial bombardment. At noon, the bombing was followed by the shells from six hundred guns which continued to fire on the ruins as the leading soldiers of 25 New Zealand Battalion began to move from their start point, about a mile away from the town. The long awaited battle was about to begin.

The battlefield of the next few days lay before the New Zealanders as the two leading companies of 25 Battalion moved down Caruso Road towards Cassino. The town with the mountains above it formed the bottleneck which had to be cleared before the entrance to the Liri Valley could be reached, barely a mile from Cassino Railway Station. The town itself covered half a mile square, still containing many fortified strong points and concrete reinforced cellars, several of which had survived the bombing. On Monte Cassino there were four key points which would soon feature in communiques for many days to come. A steep rocky knoll, some three hundred feet high, stood at the foot of the mountain. It took its name, Rocca Jamula (Castle Hill) from the old Roman fort on its top, a fort that had originally been built as an outpost to defend the Abbey in days gone by. The importance of Castle Hill lay in the fact that it was linked by a saddle of rock with Monastery Hill, which made it an ideal spring board for the battalions of 5 Indian Brigade in their assault on the next two objectives—the early capture of Castle Hill by the New Zealand 25 Battalion was a vital part of the overall plan.

Above the Castle the switchback road, which wound its way up the mountain to the Monastery, formed a couple of hair pin bends which were identified by friend and foe as Points 165 and 236 (map contours). These bends on the shoulder of the mountain formed natural defensive positions and overlooked the slopes below.

Finally, the fourth intermediate objective that was soon to become world famous, Point 435, was formed by a jutting platform of rock about two hundred and fifty yards below the walls of the Monastery. On the rock platform which would give a measure of protection to assaulting infantry, toiling up the steep slopes from below, stood a broken pylon which had originally carried an aerial ropeway from the town below to the Monastery above. From the valley below it resembled a gibbet so that it was to be called 'Hangman's Hill', a name that the Ninth Gurkha soldiers, and

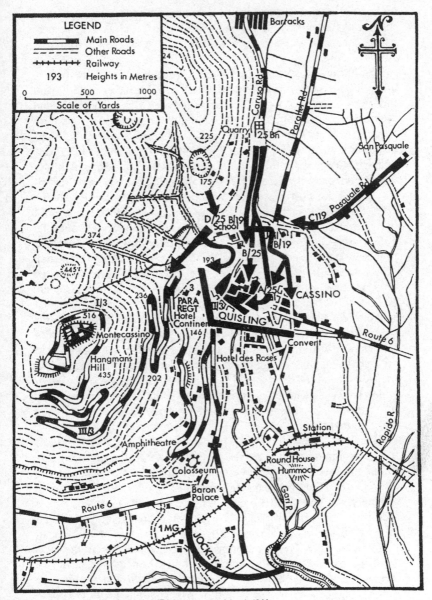

Map 6: The Third Battle (Operation 'Dickens'), 15th March 1944.

their British and Indian companions, who inadvertently swelled their ranks during an epic stand, will never forget as long as past battles are recounted by old soldiers in Nepal, India or Great Britain.

The battlefield selected by General Freyberg was a narrow strip into and through the rubble of Cassino, on to Castle Hill, and thence to the Abbey itself. The restricted area was both a help and a hindrance to the attacking units. No great number of troops were required which from the point of view of keeping down the number of casualties was a distinct blessing. Both the divisions in New Zealand Corps had taken a heavy knock in the Second battle which added to Bernard Freyberg's cares, because he was, as always, conscious of his direct and personal responsibility to the New Zealand Government, watching the casualty figures to ensure that the price paid in lives was not an excessively high one. To nullify any virtue in channelling the attack through a restricted funnel in the ruined town, was the fact that if any of the strong points were still manned by German soldiers, who were untouched or unaffected by the bombardment, then it would be extremely difficult to isolate and by-pass them. Could the surviving German soldiers still fight after such bombardment? If the answer to this was in the negative, then the battle plan would lead to victory at a relatively low cost of lives. On the other hand if they could man their machine guns to fight and defend the town, then once again the New Zealand Corps would face a hard struggle, the outcome of which would depend on several factors, including the readiness by the attackers to accept heavy losses if it developed into a long slogging match.

The New Zealanders quickly discovered two things as their leading companies, supported by tanks, reached the northern sector of the town: firstly, heavy German machine gun and rifle fire greeted their arrival causing them to move cautiously; and secondly, the Allied Air Forces had presented the Germans with a first class anti-tank obstacle. The bombing had failed to kill and destroy all life in Cassino and this was an unpleasant set-back in the detailed plan. However, of greater consequence were the messages flashed back over the radio that the tanks of New Zealand 19 Armoured Brigade could not penetrate the town and support the infantry. Huge piles of rubble and debris, combined with deep craters, had brought the tanks to a complete halt. The most strenuous efforts were made by bulldozers to clear a way for the tanks but thirty-six hours were to elapse before even a narrow corridor reached the centre of the town. This gap enabled tanks to move but not to manoeuvre, to be near the infantry but not to give them that close and intimate support so necessary when attacking strong points in a restricted area.

The German paratroopers, the survivors, had crept out of their holes and cellars and although few in numbers, grimly defended their positions against the understandably cautious 25 New Zealand Battalion. "They had beaten us to the draw," said Mark Clark and ruefully added, "aerial bombardment alone never had done and never will drive a determined enemy from his position". The Kiwis were to learn the truth of these words just as the Americans did in Vietnam a quarter of a century later. The leading companies had to split themselves into small groups in attempts to get into and around rubble that was often quite impassable or to by-pass a group of Germans who stood firm and fought to the death with sub-machine guns and rifles and grenades. The much planned and practised infantry-tank cooperation was the first big casualty in the Third battle: fighting under a heavy pall of smoke it was an infantry battle in which the crack New Zealand soldiers took on the equally elite Paratroopers with hand grenades and small arms fire. With no recognisable streets or landmarks under the choking smoke which hung like a dirty sheet above the town, the task of controlling and coordinating attacks was difficult in the extreme and, at times, completely impossible.

Many survivors of this grim battle, Germans, New Zealanders, and men from the Fifth Indian Brigade, who followed in the wake of 15 New Zealand Battalion ready for the next phase, have suggested that, had two brigades struck at Cassino on different axes, the town might have been captured on the first day instead of the meagre gains won, inadequate ones that enabled the paratroopers to reoccupy 'last stand positions' in and around the Continental Hotel, a pre-selected strong point that stood some five hundred yards south of Castle Hill. In support of this theory, many German authorities have maintained that the New Zealand attack, delivered as it was on a narrow front, was too confined, too slow, and not strong enough in numbers, all of which meant that the defenders were able to delay the hesitant probes forward for long enough and thus enable reinforcements to infiltrate back into the town.

In retrospect, there is little doubt that the bombardment had raised hopes of the commanders and their staffs to an unrealistically optimistic level so that uncommitted troops were held back in reserve during the crucial opening stages, for the sole purpose of exploiting a break-through by the armour that never came. One more brigade from these forces might well have cracked the nut but it would be realistic to point out that the coordination of a double-pronged attack by two brigades, on different axes, would not have been an easy operation in the rubble heap that once bore the name of Cassino town. Extremely difficult but not necessarily impossible, providing that the plan had not relied on streets to act as boundaries or on recognisable landmarks for phases of the attack, because no longer were there streets nor did little stand which could help soldiers recognise their positions during any battles in the rubble. If more troops had been used in the opening stages then one tactical ploy that might have been successful would have been a series of blows on two parallel axes, with the spear head units in the van, being relieved and changed over at quick, regular intervals. However, such tactics would not have led to a quick break through and heavy casualties would have been inevitable—it would have been an unsubtle 'direct approach', abhorred by Liddell Hart.

Both the opposing Divisional commanders, Heidrich and Parkinson, had many worries, not the least of which was the lack of accurate information about what was happening in the town. General Heidrich by chance was visiting the battle headquarters of 3 Paratroop Regiment when the bombing had started and there he had to stay. From mid-morning all wireless and telephone communications had stopped and he could no longer contact his superior headquarters at XIV Corps. Reinforcements could not be called forward or sent into the town by daylight but Heidrich succeeded in directing heavy artillery fire against concentrations of New Zealand troops on the outskirts of the Northern sector of the town. This undoubtedly delayed the impetus of the attack and the German High Command acknowledged the fact by a communique that specifically mentioned the 71 Mortar Regiment. The Germans' faith in their mortars was not misplaced in the struggle for Cassino —these weapons had many advantages over the heavier guns which supported the Allied soldiers, being especially suitable for searching out deep ravines or striking at targets on reverse slopes or at men crouching behind walls or buildings. By the time heavy rain had begun to fall, Heidrich had a clear idea of the battle so that he was able to make the decision to infiltrate reserves into the town. About two-thirds of the town had been lost but the way, the vital way to the Via Cassilina, Route 6, was still blocked in the centre.

By 16.00 hours, General Parkinson had realised his error in expecting that one lone New Zealand battalion could cope with the double task of clearing the town and capturing Castle Hill. Reinforcements were required: initially, 24 New Zealand Battalion was asked to send one of its companies ('B' Company) and then an hour and a half later 26 Battalion was also asked to advance into the town. At the same time the one piece of cheering news was that 'D' Company 25 Battalion captured Castle Hill after a most skilfully conducted operation. Its 16 Platoon climbed up an almost vertical rock face unopposed—a climbing feat in itself with or without a live enemy waiting at the other end—and then spearheaded the rush onto the fort itself. By 16.45 hours the feature was theirs at a loss of six killed and fifteen wounded in the whole of 'B' Company. Although in the long and seemingly endless struggle at Cassino this action was but a small one, it was a classical example of good basic infantry tactics by first class soldiers. Unfortunately, HQ 25 New Zealand Battalion did not receive any information about the success for some time and this led to a delay in the relief of the New Zealand troops on Castle Hill by 5 Infantry Brigade.

The Ides of March, and Fate, produced another unforeseen event for Freyberg and his men when rain fell in torrents as dusk descended. If General Heidrich had had the power and ability to call for rain at any stage in the Third battle then it is doubtful if he would have changed the date and time that Fate selected on his behalf. The heavy rain lashed down turning craters into ponds, ponds into small lakes, and making the engineers' task of clearing one narrow approach route through the rubble doubly difficult. No glimmer of moonlight appeared so that confusion, always likely in any night operation, was increased. Behind the leading sections and groups the men of 5 Brigade and the Kiwi Supply Echelons scrambled about and jostled each other as a way was sought through the ruined town. Major D. A. Beckett O C 'C' Company 1/4 Essex later commented: "To understand this I think we have to realise that the damage caused by the bombing and the close quarter fighting going on at the foot of Castle Hill made control very difficult. We were trying to move up in single file along a tape and then when it ended, up a path to the Castle. Any other method in the darkness and over rocks and rubble was impossible. From time to time we met parties of Germans and close quarter fighting developed. In one such instance my batman Heather was shot in the leg by a burst from a sub-machine gun and a signaller was also hit. By the time we had cleared them and arranged for evacuation more time had passed".

Delays were inevitable under these appalling conditions and the Allied soldiers in the town were paying for the unduly optimistic outline plan which despatched them through one narrow pipeline to the funnel mouth at the base of Castle Hill. Each and every time the leading troops were stopped, platoons and companies, all in single file, came to a halt or edged an uncertain way forward for a few more steps. Minutes slipped by, hours passed, time the attackers could not afford to lose as it gave the defenders a chance to recover their balance and take steps to harass, hinder and disrupt the next phase in the attack as it was being mounted.

In order to view the unkind and inopportune bad weather in perspective, it can be said that it was an important factor in the loss of valuable time but on its own not a vital one. Nevertheless, an example of how it hindered forward movement, 26 New Zealand Battalion, whose objective had been beyond the Railway Station, found the going so difficult, because of deep mud and numerous craters, that the CO decided to consolidate in the vicinity of Route 6 rather than attempt any further attacks until dawn next day.

Meanwhile, the relief of 'D' Company 25 Battalion on Castle Hill had been timed for 1930 hours but the weather, the debris and the German paratroopers all combined to make this impossible. Only at midnight were the leading elements of 'C' Company 1/4 Essex established in the Castle itself, with the other three Companies strung out in the rear around Point 175 across the ravine and on the approach to the Castle from the outskirts of the town. It could be said that the base for 5 Indian Brigade's assault up Monastery Hill was in friendly hands but it could not be claimed that it was securely held. In this area the Germans, too, had suffered a setback which men from the Essex Regiment exploited by taking Point 165 so that the whole sector of 2 Company 3 Para Regiment was now in New Zealand Corps' hands. Only one survivor of 2 Company succeeded in escaping to the Monastery to give the men there the news of the disaster, while 5 Brigade prepared to advance on the next two objectives as previously planned; first to pass through the door held open by the Essex Regiment was to be 1/6 Rajputana Rifles which was directed on to the two lower hair pin bends of the mountain road. From there the 1/9 Gurkha Rifles would move up to Hangman's Hill, to form the last base from where the coup de grace on the Abbey could be delivered by the Essex Regiment, supported by as many of the Ninth Gurkhas as could be spared.

So much for the hopes and plans of Brigadier Bateman (5 Brigade)—now to see what happened to his two battalions as they clambered up the steep slopes to their objectives. The adjective 'steep' is used advisedly as the Brigade axis of advance up to the Monastery entailed a climb of 500 metres for every 1,000 metres covered horizontally, and climbing it in peacetime by daylight is no easy matter. First to struggle up was the Indian battalion, the 1/6 Rajputana Rifles, who had already met with disaster when prior to arriving at the Castle, a vicious and accurate German artillery concentration had smashed down on the two rear Companies, 'C' and 'D', as they were inching their way forward along the congested tracks. Ahead of them, the leading companies, 'A' and 'B', waited for their comrades near the Castle until 0245 hours on the 16th March. Time was pressing so 'A' Company was ordered to begin the next phase—to move across the hillside and capture Point 236 which stood above the second hair pin on the road to the Abbey. By 0430 hours the Indian soldiers were within two hundred yards of their objective but the alarm was given by a German sentry and accurate small arms fire pinned the Indians down. Any idea of advancing proved quite impossible and they had no alternative but to seek refuge in the Castle below before dawn broke on the 16th March.

Lieutenant Colonel G. S. Nangle, commanding the 1/9 Gurkha Rifles, was faced with a difficult situation when his men reached the northern outskirts of Cassino by 0100 hours. An officer has described the move through the town in these words: "There were numerous 'stops and starts' which were exasperating when enemy snipers and grenadiers were active around us. Slowly and surely we found our way in the darkness past heavy German tanks blown completely upside down amongst the piles of rubble from collapsed buildings. We trod on the bodies of many German dead wedged in the rubble without fully realising it". CO 1/9 Gurkha Rifles had been given instructions to support the Rajputana Rifles during their attack on the two hair pin bends and thereafter, to continue the next phase of the Brigade plan, the attack on Hangman's Hill itself. The news that greeted Nangle indicated that only two companies of Rajputana Rifles had reached the Castle and, what was more important, that no-one had as yet secured the intermediate objectives between Castle Hill and Point 435 (Hangman's Hill). No orders were forthcoming from Brigade Headquarters and Colonel Nangle had to decide between holding back his whole Battalion or sending it forward over an uncharted, and possibly an enemy held hillside. In an agonising dilemma for any Commanding Officer to resolve, Nangle decided to carry on with the original plan by sending up 'C' and 'D' Companies to attack Hangman's Hill, with the rest of the Battalion following in single file after the leading companies had strung out and moved off. With the main track up through Castle Hill under constant German fire, 'C' and 'D' Companies were sent by an alternative route which then split into two tracks, both of which appeared to lead in the right direction. 'D' Company went one way only to walk into spandau groups and snipers, and fifteen men fell victims to German fire, so that it was dawn before the company could be brought under control, and made ready for any further advance.

'C' Company skirted the fringes of the town and disappeared into the night. No one saw or heard them until as dawn was breaking the German defenders in the Abbey caught sight of the small, tough Gurkhas clambering their way up the rugged slopes by Hangman's Hill. Within seconds machine-guns, fired from behind loop holes and sandbags, had driven the intruders back behind shelter of the outcrop of rocks by Point 435. The Germans had learnt about the extraordinary arrival of 'C' Company 1/9 Gurkha Rifles on their own doorstep before Nangle who still waited anxiously during the morning of 16th March, for some sort of message from the company that had melted away into the darkness of the night.

The exploits of 'C' Company 1/9 Gurkha Rifles were not to be known for several hours to come, but are mentioned here in the

Top: Panoramic view of Cassino. *Imperial War Museum*

Above: A pre-war view of the Monastery at Cassino (1927?). *Imperial War Museum*

The Monastery at Cassino before it was bombed in March 1944.

This picture was taken on 15th March 1944, as 2,500 tons of bombs rained down on Cassino. When the barrage lifted, the fight for the ruins began.
Imperial War Museum

Fifth Army, Cassino Area, 'Hangman's Hill' and Monastery from edge of
Cassino in North end of town. *Imperial War Museum*

A medical orderly moves forward, under protection of a flag at Cassino.
24th March 1944. *Imperial War Museum*

German troops captured by the New Zealanders being held beside a Sherman tank. *Imperial War Museum*

Men of the (2nd Bn Somerset) Light Infantry climbing the narrow mule-track of a ravine in the hills behind Sujo, on the North bank of the Garigliano River. 20th March 1944. *Imperial War Museum*

Every house not completely demolished could contain enemy snipers, and these infantry-men search one partly-demolished building in Cassino. 24th March 1944. *Imperial War Museum*

Contact with the troops in the town is kept by radio. Pte John Totman (nearest camera) and L/Cp Arthur Ould operate the wireless set in the Cassino area. 26th March 1944. *Imperial War Museum*

German Army in Italy. Paratroopers fighting among the ruins of the Monastery at Monte Cassino in April 1944. *Imperial War Museum*

75mm gun on a Sherman tank fires to silence sniper posts. *Imperial War Museum*

From their positions among the ruins, (Guards) Bren gunners cheer the fall of the town. *Imperial War Museum*

(214) Field Coy RE Staffordshire Territorial Coy of 78 Div. working on a Bailey bridge and a track for tanks. This bridge has been built in two days, under continuous fire, and is about 1,000 yards from the River Gari bridges. *Imperial War Museum*

A view of the Abbey on Monastery Hill, Cassino, after its capture by Allied troops in May 1944.
Imperial War Museum

correct chronological order. Under their young commander, twenty year old Captain Michael Drinkall, the Company walked up the track in the darkness of a wet night and moved in single file diagonally across the hillside to a point where they dumped their packs. This was below Hangman's Hill and in silence they crept up on the objective and surprised a German outpost in a small cave, killing two of the men they found there. Those who escaped raised the alarm which was followed by heavy mortar fire on to the Gurkhas as they sat tensely in positions as dawn broke.

During this 'stonk' both the Company Commander and his Gurkha Officer Second in Command were wounded. Undoubtedly more casualties would have resulted had not a Gurkha NCO stalked the German mortar post and put it out of action. The wounded Drinkall, who continued to command his men from a stretcher, had no communications with his colonel as the Company radio set failed to transmit. Two runners were sent off down the hillside towards Castle Hill, but were seen and nearly intercepted before returning from an abortive attempt. 'C' Company's position was not a happy one and Drinkall was on the point of arranging a withdrawal as soon as it was dark when, suddenly and dramatically, the Company wireless, after much tinkering, began to work and communications were established with Battalion headquarters on the edge of the town. In this way New Zealand Corps learnt that Hangman's Hill was held by the company that had disappeared into the darkness of the night before.

Meanwhile the morning sitrep of 16 March as read by General Freyberg was indeed a confusing one with 5 Indian Brigade in much disarray after a hard night's fighting. To an experienced general like Freyberg such a situation was not a new and unexpected one and there was consolation in the thought that his opponents had problems of equal magnitude to resolve. Although New Zealand Corps' outline programme and 5 Brigade's detailed plan had not gone as scheduled, the Germans were no better placed and were sending for the few reserves which were readily available. For them the disquieting information was that 1/4 Essex and companies of 1/6 Rajputana Rifles had a firm grip on Castle Hill, the entrance to the Abbey above. South of Castle Hill a mixed force of 1/9 Gurkhas and Rajputana Rifles awaited an opportunity to move forward and take advantage of the unplanned incursion made by the 'missing' C Company of the 1/9 Gurkhas, less than three hundred yards from the Monastery walls. Both Generals Freyberg and Heidrich were in a somewhat similar situation, hampered by incomplete reports of the night's fighting, and a mixture of welcome and unwelcome news to add to the confusion. The balance of the battle could be tipped either way depending on which side reacted with speed, tenacity and a strong faith in the final outcome. Perhaps the latter quality was one that Heidrich had in greater measure than Bernard Freyberg because every available man in the Parachute Division would be used, if necessary, whereas Freyberg was not prepared to seek a victory at any cost. For the sake of the men he led such an attitude was admirable; the horrors of the First World War fought in their youth remained a strong influence on Freyberg and many of his contemporaries in the British Army. However, his reluctance to commit reserves at moments of crisis did lead to several attacks of a piecemeal nature and thus a prolongation of the agony at Cassino. It is tempting to consider what the result of the Third battle might have been if Heidrich and Freyberg had exchanged roles. Perhaps, a direct confrontation at Cassino might never have taken place for the Germans—admittedly with the advantage of hindsight—claim that their generals would have avoided Monte Cassino in the way that Juin and Tuker had advocated, by attacking across the hills towards Terelle.

As soon as he was able to re-establish efficient communications from the morning of 16th March onwards, the personality of Lieutenant General Richard Heidrich played an important part in the fighting. His previous reputation as a trainer and ruthless leader of men had been well earned and his leadership was to pay dividends at Cassino. Heidrich drove himself hard, made heavy demands of his troops and he expected his officers and men to keep up the same high standards, eschewing all ideas of personal comfort when necessary. He was an aggressive leader and his paratroopers were stamped with the same mark: they were individualists, self reliant and skilled in all the arts of soldiering. When two or three men were cut off from their parent section or sub-unit they fought as if such a situation was a normal one. The comradeship, esprit de corps and efficiency of the German Paratroopers was to earn the praise and recognition of all who fought against them and by the end of the Third battle, was to save, yet again, Adolf Hitler's cause at Cassino. Paratrooper prisoners taken directly after the terrible bombing complained of little except "a few split eardrums, a thorough dusting and a bad scare". General Alexander tells a story of how he visited Caserta Base Hospital and entered a ward full of German prisoners. On the command of the Feldwebel (Sergeant Major) all of them lay at attention while the Warrant Officer reported them as being present and correct to Alexander. Such soldiers, fighting or wounded, were not invincible or superior but they made the task of the New Zealand Corps one that Freyberg assessed to have no more than a fifty-fifty chance of success.

During the daylight hours of the 16th March the New Zealanders renewed their efforts to clear the rest of Cassino town. At 0615 hours the infantry attempted to eject the Germans westwards from a sector north of Route 6. 'A' Company of 25 New Zealand Battalion had little success and were pinned down by small arms and mortar fire throughout the day. Without tank support the infantry soldiers found that each move from the cover of a mound or a pile of rubble was to offer themselves as a target to German snipers: to attempt a concerted rush on an enemy post immediately attracted the coordinated fire from machine guns in other positions. 'B' Company of 24 New Zealand Battalion did make a little progress when two of its platoons seized a house but they were soon isolated and surrounded. During their stay the Kiwis beat off and defied German raiders who shouted at them in English to surrender—but after midnight these men had to be withdrawn from their abortive foray.

26 New Zealand Battalion had a fruitless morning although the arrival of three tanks at the eastern sector of the town in the late afternoon raised morale and promised an encouraging success in the immediate future. To get these tanks forward as far as the Convent in the town had taken a prodigious engineer effort which included the construction of a Bailey bridge over the Rapido and the spanning of two huge craters nearby. All this had taken long hours of work by American (48 US Engineer Battalion) and New Zealand (17 Field Company) sappers to enable three tanks, the forerunners of the much cherished plan of attack by the mixed infantry and tank force, to arrive twenty hours after the bombing had ended. The Allied armour did not and could not play a decisive role in the Italian campaign, a fact that Winston Churchill failed to appreciate as can be seen from his message of frustrated anguish to General Alexander: "What are you doing sitting doing

nothing? Why don't you use your armour in a great scythe-like movement through the mountain?" As always, Alexander's reply was courteous and patient. He understood how the restless mind of Winston Churchill continually worked for and sought a solution to the deadlock in Italy, which persisted throughout the long winter of 1943/44.

The slow progress made in the town during the 16th March caused Freyberg to postpone yet again his original idea of a Kiwi attack on Cassino Railway Station, synchronised with an attack by 5 Indian Brigade on the Monastery. As a supplement to the dual attack, a tank thrust from the village of Caira up to the south west of Snakeshead Ridge was due to be mounted. At 1830 hours on the 16th all available reports of the day's fighting were studied at a conference, held at (New Zealand) 6 Brigade Headquarters. The generals listened to the latest briefing which indicated that two-thirds of the old built-up area of Cassino was in New Zealand hands, and nine supporting tanks had entered the town. Unfortunately, it later transpired that six of these could not move until a lot more work had been carried out by the sappers. By now, the German resistance had been pin pointed as being based on the rising ground in the area around the Continental Hotel. No one was in any doubt about the next objective which was the Railway Station and the area of the Colosseum where Route 6 turns into the Liri Valley. However, there was a lot of argument about the desirability of strengthening the infantry in the town. Clark was sure that more battalions were required, Freyberg felt that he had enough in the confined area, and the temporary Commander of Fourth Indian Division, Major General Galloway, said he was "completely convinced that the best way to clear Cassino is to put infantry in and go on doing so until it is cleared". Freyberg's views prevailed at the time but later opinions expressed by the Germans tend to favour Generals Clark and Galloway. Bohmler summed it up: 'Just one more minor push and the trap would have been closed. Victory was beckoning to Freyberg but he failed to seize the unique opportunity given to him'. Instead the New Zealand troops in the town were to continue to attack north, using infantry already there, and these thrusts would be renewed after daylight on 17th March. It was to be a quiet night for them and the events of the night 16/17th March belong to 5 Indian Brigade.

The mystery of the missing 'C' Company of 1/9 Gurkhas had

been finally resolved when their radio sent out a faint message early in the afternoon: every radio set in the Battalion had been opened up in a frantic effort to gain contact. Prior to that, small figures had been seen on Hangman's Hill by the New Zealand gunners, and the whole of the New Zealand Corps now learnt the unexpected news that a small body of Gurkhas, by some extraordinary piece of fortune, had captured 5 Indian Brigade's second main objective, while the Germans still held the lower ones around the hair-pin bends on the road to the Abbey. 'C' Company had to stay where it was and the rest of the 1/9 Gurkhas would move to its aid as soon as darkness allowed them to climb across and then up the mountainside. It would be an exaggeration to suggest that the toehold near the Abbey was a great gain but equally it was an opportunity to try to force open a way to the Abbey, and this might be achieved by sending the rest of the battalion to Hangman's Hill—as originally planned. On hearing this Major Evans of the Ninth wrote: 'We thought what a bloody relief it was to get out of the town where we were losing men and achieving nothing'.

Men of the 1/9 Gurkhas began their move up to reinforce 'C' Company at 2100 hours. The night was clear and the moon picked out the silhouettes of Castle Hill and the Monastery. Once again, it proved quite impossible to advance in any other way than single file, which meant that it was a slow and frustrating business. When the leading soldiers left the out-skirts of the town they found that the track leading up to Castle Hill was being fired on by German snipers so that an alternative way into the Castle had to be found. The original curtain walls ran from the fort down the side of the hill and were obstacles until a hole was found through which, one by one, the Gurkhas passed and thence made their way up to the Castle itself. It was nearly 0400 hours on the 17th March before the whole force had reached the Castle and ready to cover the last part of the journey up to join 'C' Company on Hangman's Hill.

During the same night 1/6 Rajputana Rifles had launched an attack with two Companies ('A' and 'B') on to Point 236, the higher of the two hair-pin bends on the road to the Abbey. A knoll was seized and held until dawn against a series of heavy counter attacks but shortage of ammunition eventually forced the Indians to fall back onto a none too securely held Point 165. The other two companies from the same Battalion were successful in taking their objective, Point 202, which they stubbornly defended throughout the daylight hours of 17th March. Without doubt these dogged, tough battles allowed the Gurkhas to wend their way below the Indians, and above the Continental Hotel to Point 435, without any disaster or major clashes with the Germans occurring. On the steep hillside the three Gurkha companies managed to fan out into some sort of open formation where they were inter-mittently shelled by an Allied tank crew who, in the fog of war and in ignorance, must have assumed that the slopes above Castle Hill were completely in German hands.

As dawn was breaking the first sub-unit to reach 'C' Company's position was 'D' Company and it arrived at an opportune moment because the Germans had launched a sharp attack which threat-ened to overrun the whole Company position. The wounded Drinkall with a revolver in his hand, had inspired his men to hold on until the rest of their Battalion arrived. The Germans were beaten off and they retired to the Monastery taking with them the knowledge that a substantial force of Gurkha soldiers was now within a matter of yards from the outer walls of the building. As soon as possible, Colonel Nangle deployed his Battalion into a tight little perimeter, ready for the next phase in the Brigade plan which he expected would begin shortly afterwards. His Gurkhas had taken their objective moving up the mountain with little beside their weapons and light scales of ammunition: no-one expected this to be more than a temporary pause before the next move, without any suggestion of these lightly clad men having to endure a long sojourn on the rocky slopes of Monte Cassino. Major Evans commented: "Now began our nine days' wonder!"

13

The Third Battle—The Climax

If a situation map was studied, showing the dispositions of the contestants as they existed on the morning of the 17th March, it would give a false picture to the reader of this book. Such a map would be too tidy and neat—and the struggle for Monte Cassino, throughout the Third battle in particular, was never a tidy one. It was a rare occasion when a unit commander had all his sub-units directly under his control in one area of responsibility. Groups of men sometimes found themselves being commanded by nearby sub-units from another battalion and, on other occasions, they had to fend for themselves in isolation until some semblance of control was established. The map might show the Rajputana Rifles holding Point 202 but in fact, there were men from that battalion helping the Essex defend Castle Hill—and later there were to be others sharing the lonely vigil of the Ninth Gurkhas on Hangman's Hill. If a student at a Staff College was able to produce an exercise on the lines of this, the Third battle, it is doubtful whether his chances of promotion would be enhanced—even if it had taxed his powers of imagination to the limit. The Third battle was an untidy muddle, a bloody encounter between two sides with soldiers often confused and frightened, and invariably deafened by the noise of battle as it rolled along the mountains around Monte Cassino.

Many of the local victories reported in sitreps were won by groups of men rather than by a unit or even sub-unit and the normal chain of command was often ineffective and sometimes impossible. Junior commanders invariably exerted far more influence than brigadiers, or their equivalent, frantically seeking accurate information from the scattered groups under their command. And further up the command structure, Generals Freyberg and Heidrich were victims as well as commanders in this struggle between infantrymen from Germany, New Zealand, India and Nepal. Heidrich had committed all his major reserves so that he could but pray that his paratroopers would stick it out. Freyberg had reserves but he hesitated until it was too late and until the price of victory went beyond the limit he was prepared to pay.

Daybreak on the morning of 17th March found the three features, Hangman's Hill, Points 202 and 165, in the hands of the 1/9 Gurkhas and 1/6 Rajputana Rifles. On the other hand Point 165 was under heavy German pressure so that possession of the southern slopes of Monte Cassino was still under dispute. The advantages of having the Gurkhas near the Abbey were offset by the fact that their links back down the hill and through the Castle were tenuous ones. The importance of Castle Hill had never been underestimated by the Allies and likewise, its great significance as an artery to the 9th Gurkhas was soon to be appreciated by General Heidrich. If the continued occupation of Castle Hill by 1/4 Essex was disputed by the Germans then any further offensive moves by New Zealand Corps would be disrupted; if Castle Hill were ever to be retaken by the German paratroopers then any attack on Monastery Hill by the 9th Gurkhas, or any other troops from Cassino town, would be doomed to failure.

The tasks for the Germans on 17th March were clearcut ones. They had to stop the New Zealanders clearing the town and they had to ensure that no reliable route from Castle Hill upwards was available to 5 Indian Brigade or used with impunity by any of its units. Naturally, the Allies sought the opposite aims. Freyberg urged his subordinate, Major General Parkinson, "to put great energy into clearing it up on a broad front; it is essential that we should push through to the Gurkhas tonight, anything you can push into the town do so".

General Freyberg's instructions were given at 0800 hours but by that time 25 New Zealand Battalion, together with a troop of 19 New Zealand Armoured Regiment, had begun to thrust westwards in an attempt to clear the Germans from north of Route 6 and to destroy pockets of resistance in the area of the Continental Hotel, as vital to the Germans as Castle Hill was to the Allies. The power of the tanks began to tell and, although under heavy shelling, the Kiwis fought their way forward slowly to their final objective. By 0900 hours they were right up against the Continental Hotel but the outlook for the drive on to the second objective was still far from promising. Nevertheless, even this limited progress caused Freyberg to exhort his men: "Push on, you must go hard. Task Force B must go through as soon as possible. The limit is the roof

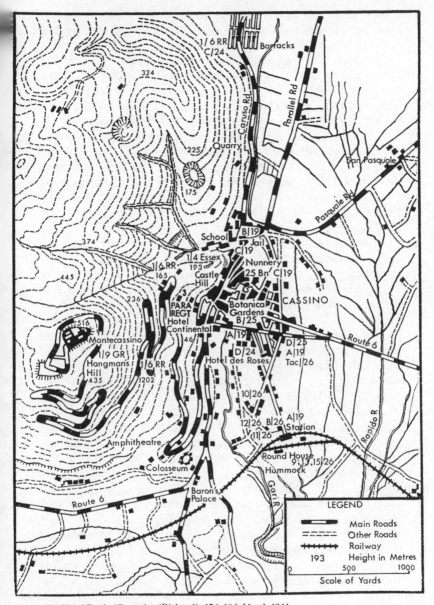

Map 7: The Third Battle (Operation 'Dickens'), 17th-18th March 1944.

—push hard". To Clark who continued to urge him to send in more infantry into Cassino town, Freyberg stated that he had hopes of "a certain amount of movement".

At about this time the German Headquarters at 14 Panzer Corps and Tenth Army had also received and digested reports on the recent fighting. In the normal confusion of war the Allied gains had been reported as being more extensive than they were and Tenth Army confessed to Kesselring that "things are not too splendid here". The heavy fighting in the town had caused losses that were critically heavy, with the units of 1 Parachute Regiment being in a bad way as far as fighting strengths were concerned. General Heidrich had his worries but he took reassurance from the fact that the western parts of the town and the ruined Abbey on Monte Cassino were still held by his paratroopers. The Fuehrer sent Heidrich a personal message of congratulations at the same time as two battalions of 155 Panzer Regiment were put under divisional command as reserves. Heidrich acknowledged the message and gladly accepted the reinforcements which he used to relieve paratroopers in the less exacting sectors. It is typical of Heidrich and his men, that they declined to share the honours of Cassino with any one, and this included recently arrived units.

Thrusting towards the second objective 26 New Zealand Battalion's attack was, as N. C. Phillips put it: "a rough and rugged affair". Nothing went as planned because of serious communication problems and this resulted in an artillery concentration being fired at 1100 hours, which heralded an advance by tanks of A Squadron without the infantry being aware that the attack had begun. The tanks set off for the Railway Station but in spite of an earlier reconnaissance, were unable to rediscover the crossroads which marked the way to the Station because the maze of rubble was so deep. Another way round was sought and found; the troop of tanks advanced southwards under a hail of machine gun bullets until two of their number were set on fire by German anti-tank guns. Eventually two tanks did reach the Station at mid-day where they had to await the arrival of 26 Battalion to support and guard them, if further progress was to be made.

'C' Company of 26 Battalion was ordered to follow up the tanks while runners sought the other companies in the centre of the town to give them a similar message. Their forming up was carried out in frantic haste as groups of soldiers arrived from different places at a rendezvous near the tactical headquarters in the Convent, prior to beginning the advance of about a thousand yards towards the Station.

'C' Company did manage to join up with the two lone tanks and exploited forward for some two hundred yards. By this time the company had a strength of only forty men, while the rest of the battalion continued to arrive in dribs and drabs, tired, depleted and bewildered. The confusion and loss of control were reduced, to some extent, by the initiative and determination of junior leaders bravely supported by the small groups of men who followed them. By dusk the battalion had about a hundred men in the Railway Station but a later count showed that the cost was a casualty list which contained over seventy names, half of whom had been killed during these actions.

The capture of the Station was a success—even if it had been achieved at a cost and the time taken had been far longer than had been hoped or anticipated. Unfortunately the other New Zealand battalions had made little progress as they battered away at the German defence posts in the western part of the town. The resistance around the Continental Hotel and the Hotel des Roses continued to be as unremitting and determined as ever while the vital stretch of Route 6, where the road turns right at the base of Monte Cassino, still led through a fiercely contested battlefield.

Freyberg's hopes which had been high on the morning of the 17th, with the confident aim of thrusting a way through to the Gurkhas on Hangman's Hill, had suffered setbacks as the hours ticked by. His troops had not lacked support with the Air Forces flying over four hundred sorties, with the artillery firing a prodigious amount of shells, and with tanks in the town supporting the three battalions of infantry. On Hangman's Hill, the 1/9 Gurkhas still sat in isolation, suffering a lot of discomfort from an almost continuous smoke shoot by the Allied artillery. The object of this was to form a screen behind which the Kiwi sappers could labour on the Rapido crossing. The artillery observation officer on Hangman's Hill was as irritated as the Gurkhas; "Our shelling continued throughout the afternoon with such accuracy that the Gurkha commander's sangar received three direct hits from shells. Attempts by the battery commander urged on by the Gurkha CO to shift the target proved fruitless. Relations in all directions seemed to be in an atmosphere of strain". Another officer added:

"No matter how much we cursed and swore about this we could not stop it! To cap it all, several HE shells of the 'drop short' variety made an unwelcome landing on our positions, causing more casualties". Perhaps the most annoying aspect of the whole business was that no one had seen fit to warn Lieutenant Colonel Nangle or his Gurkhas that the smoke screen was going to be fired. The sudden and almost continuous arrival of shells was the first indication that something was afoot. As the day went by, the watchers on Hangman's Hill had increasing doubts about the usefulness of the smoke screen, particularly as the most important German observation post in a twin-pronged piece of masonry in the Monastery, continued to direct German guns and mortars on to the New Zealand tanks, rendered immobile by the rubble and craters on the road or waiting at the edge of the town.

Freyberg received divided counsel as to how he should conduct the battle. His New Zealand subordinates, Major General Parkinson and Brigadier Bonifant (commander of the 6th Brigade) agreed with him that no further reinforcements were required in the town itself. Generals Clark and Galloway continued to press for more infantry to be sent into Cassino, even if it meant taking a brigade away from 78 Division, which was standing by as 'the follow up force', ready for the pursuit into the Liri valley. Freyberg, like Keyes before him, was loth to weaken the potential of a dramatic breakthrough; the second phase of the plan appeared to influence the two Corps commanders more than the necessity of winning the first one. Mark Clark strongly urged Freyberg to launch an attack on the Abbey from Hangman's Hill in conjunction with a tank thrust from the hills to the north east. Freyberg had natural and well founded doubts about committing his force to these moves before the supply route to the Ninth Gurkhas was secure, while General Galloway maintained that such a route could never be secure until the New Zealanders had completely cleared Cassino town. One thing the generals on the spot did agree on was the vital necessity to resupply the Gurkhas on Hangman's Hill and to make their life-line through Castle Hill a secure one.

The first prerogative, that of resupplying the Gurkhas, proved possible to achieve but the second was to be the rock on which victory in the whole battle depended—and eventually foundered. Shortly after dark a porter column escorted by two companies of 4/6 Rajputana Rifles arrived on Castle Hill. Here they were delayed while men from Essex repelled a German raid on the lower hairpin bend of the mountain road. The noise of fighting plus heavy shelling, which had caused nineteen casualties to the porters, so upset the men from the Indian Pioneer Corps that they refused to go up the hillside to Point 435. Such an attitude was not surprising as the men had no weapons and had been asked to undertake something far removed from their normal specialist duties. Nevertheless ammunition, and to a lesser degree supplies, had to reach the 1/9 Gurkha Rifles on Hangman's Hill for they had not taken any reserves with them in their initial advance. Some records state that two of the 4/6 Rajputana Rifles were ordered to take on the porters' loads: the author prefers to rely on his memory, corroborated by friends who were in the Castle, who recollect that the companies, under Captain French of the Rajputana Rifles, volunteered to make their way through to Hangman's Hill, fighting for their precious loads if necessary. They set off and three hours later a message was received reporting that the Indians had run the gauntlet with the loss of eight men, one company arriving at dawn after nearly walking into the Monastery! By that time the first rays of light on the 18th March were breaking so that these soldiers of the Rajputana Rifles took up a position on the right flank of the Gurkha perimeter, prepared to play their part in any fight that might ensue. Military necessity had dictated that the loads they had carried contained ammunition rather than food which was now in very short supply on Hangman's Hill. Water, too, was a problem: "the Kiwis who were down below us on the lower slopes (Point 202) kindly let us use their water well after we had found a mule in ours at low level!"

During the night the New Zealand Division made plans which would, if successful, clear the Germans out of their two Hotel strong points, using Point 202 as a base from which the attacks would be launched. A gallant assault by 'C' Company 24 New Zealand Battalion reached Hotel des Roses and was defeated only when the leading platoon commander was killed literally outside the Hotel door. No more progress proved possible so that, with six killed and five wounded, the company had to withdraw and its platoons were forced to consolidate above the town around Point 202.

The Germans made the first move after dawn of the 18th when some sixty men of the Parachute Machine Gun Battalion (Motor

Cycle Company) made an attack on the Railway Station. The attack was pressed home with great determination and only after stiff fighting were their efforts repulsed. This act of aggression was significant as it showed that the Germans had recovered their poise and confidence: after the bombing, and prior to this, it had been a question of delaying tactics and of holding on where they could. Reinforcements had continued to enter the town, some of them walking through underground tunnels from the area of the amphitheatre. Now they had given notice that counter-attacks and aggressive moves could be expected against the three points of the triangle held by New Zealand Corps—Point 193 (Castle Hill) garrisoned by the Essex Regiment; Point 435 (Hangman's Hill) occupied by the Gurkhas; and the Railway Station defended by the Kiwis. Of the three points, Castle Hill was the most important. As long as it was retained by the Allies an attack on the Abbey through Hangman's Hill was a possibility, but if the position were lost then any force on Hangman's Hill would be doomed. Likewise the New Zealand hold on the station area would be even more precarious should the German paratroopers retake Castle Hill from where they could overlook and dominate the town. The struggle for the Monastery depended on the outcome of the battle for Castle Hill and the importance of this position was fully realised by General Heidrich.

Also on the 18th March the German Air Force paid a lightning visit to Cassino with 'planes making sneak raids on the Railway Station area in support of the German ground pressure, which continued throughout the day in a struggle in which neither side achieved any important gains. 26 New Zealand Battalion had to endure continuous mortaring, sniping and shelling as well as being bombed by 'hit and run' raiders from the Luftwaffe. Nearby, 25 New Zealand Battalion had been ordered to clear German snipers and machine gun posts from houses at the base of Castle Hill—the snipers were exerting more than a nuisance effect on the British hold on Castle Hill and were firing at the main track. It was to take 'C' Company all day to clear one strongly defended house but the Germans still clung to others nearby—and continued to snipe at men on the main track to the Castle; one of their targets was the author of this book who had to crouch behind rocks before darting to the next piece of cover—an experience he has never forgotten. Meanwhile the third New Zealand unit, 24 Battalion, held their

142

ground "at a respectful distance from the Hotel Continental and
its neighbouring bastion, the Hotel des Roses", two hundred yards
to the south. Plans to mount another thrust towards the southward
stretches of Route 6 were disrupted when a house collapsed, in
which many of the company were sheltering, and this disaster was
followed by another dive-bombing raid. By the time the troops had
sorted themselves out it was too late to carry on with previous
plans for the attack.

By the evening the Germans appeared to have stabilised the
whole of the battle with the situation on Castle Hill becoming
more and more difficult because German snipers continued to fire
on the tracks that led up to the old Fort from the base of the hill.

The stalemate in Cassino was to the advantage of the defenders
and a growing sense of confidence was reflected in one of their reports: "the enemy's fierce assaults continued all day but paratroopers held firm and kept command of their position . . . the artillery again played a great part in the success of the defenders
bringing acceptable relief to the hard-pressed infantry with destructive concentrations on the enemy's forming up places. Fresh
reserves were brought up to strengthen the very weak garrison of
the town". Now the day of crisis had been overcome, General
Heidrich was full of optimism for the future.

What the Germans had feared was a sudden and sharp influx of
infantry from the New Zealand Corps, before the holes in their
defence had been plugged up, but it was only after a lot of argument and not until the late afternoon before Freyberg decided to
commit a further battalion. 28 (Maori) Battalion was to move in
the early hours of the 19th against the German posts at the base
of Castle Hill. Freyberg's hesitation was influenced by the attitude
of his subordinate, Parkinson, who continued to maintain that
there were enough troops in the town. Unfortunately the indeci-
sion and vacillation shown by General Freyberg made the task of
his adversary, Heidrich, that much easier.

Time was running out and opportunities to win the battle were
slipping by: New Zealand Corps decided that the following day,
19 March, was to be the one on which the Monastery would be
captured. The Maoris, it was hoped, would have overcome the
Germans in and around the Continental Hotel and cleared the
area below Castle Hill before dawn. The remnants of the 1/6 and
4/6 Rajputana Rifles, now merged into a composite unit, were

to relieve 1/4 Essex in the Castle so that the British battalion could move up and join the Gurkhas on Hangman's Hill. Then the final dash up and into the Abbey was to be undertaken by the Essex and 9th Gurkhas together. The plan was bold but it was also a desperate one as if the New Zealand Corps realised that there could only be one more chance to win the battle. Even if the Germans had waited passively for each phase of the plan to unfold itself, it is doubtful whether the tired and depleted striking force of the Essex and 9th Gurkhas would have been strong enough to have captured and retained the large ruined Abbey. Such problems had been considered by Freyberg but he put considerable faith in the surprise thrust by a small armoured force of 7 Brigade Recce Squadron, reinforced by some tanks from the New Zealand Regiment, along Cavendish Road from the north towards the Monastery. Provided the timing of such a diversionary action was coordinated with the attack through Hangman's Hill on the Abbey, then New Zealand Corps Headquarters had grounds for guarded optimism.

Such a plan meant, of course, that the 9th Gurkhas on Hangman's Hill had to be given more supplies if they were to take an active part in the final assault as well as continuing to hold their isolated position in the face of German pressure. It was decided to resupply them by dropping containers from about fifty aircraft and this was done during the afternoon of the 18th March. Many containers bounced down the hillside into the hands of the Germans but when it is remembered how small the target area was, the efforts made by the air crews were remarkably efficient—and remembered with gratitude by Colonel Nangle and survivors from Hangman's Hill. The choice of rations for the battalion, the majority of whom were high caste members of the Chhettri clan, was not imaginative but hunger and necessity overcame religious scruples. Some casks of rum were received, with gratitude not only by the able bodied Gurkha soldiers but by the many wounded, laid out in an open culvert below Battalion Headquarters.

The hopes of victory for 'Operation Revenge', the code word for the 19th, withered before dawn had broken. Unbeknown to each other, both sides had resolved to force a decision before the day was out. New Zealand Corps made the first move when the composite Rajputana Rifle force took over the defences of the Castle. At first, the relief went smoothly and the two leading Essex companies started across the slopes of Monte Cassino to join the 9th Gurkhas. In the Castle itself, the other two companies had almost finished handing over to the Indians when a fierce hail of machine gun fire swept the walls. A sharp bout of gunfire and some vicious mortaring heralded an attack made by some two to three hundred men from the 1st Battalion 4 Parachute Regiment, who rushed down from the Abbey and overran the shaken and surprised Rajputana defenders on Point 165 and in positions near the lower hairpin bend, on the mountain road. The leading assault elements not only reached the Castle walls but threatened to overrun the defenders who were firing, through loop holes and from behind broken masonry, at the reckless German soldiers.

The Germans' decision to throttle the life-line from the Castle up to Hangman's Hill meant that it was a major attack and it was pressed home with much tenacity. The garrison consisting of two companies of Essex, two platoons of men from the Rajputana Rifles, some sappers and a few gunners, manned the walls and 'something approaching a mediaeval siege took place'. Grenades showered over the walls into the courtyard and on the other side some of the paratroopers died but a few yards from their objective. The Germans suffered heavy casualties from the Essex Vickers machine guns which fired at their flank, from the crest of the adjacent Point 175, and after about twenty minutes a signal flare recalled the men from the 1st Battalion.

The lull that followed proved to be a short one and soon another attack was mounted. The defenders under Major Beckett were not taken by surprise: "Defensive fire was therefore laid on very close in and as soon as the attack started a full blunderbuss of artillery, mortars, a medium machine gun and small arms fire was brought to bear". During the attack a part of the west wall of the old Castle fell in, burying about a dozen of the small British force. At the time it was thought that a tank shell had caused the damage; it has since transpired that the Pioneer Battalion of 1 Para Division succeeded in blowing the breach in the outer wall although they were unable to penetrate into the Castle itself and their attack was repulsed. Major Beckett, twice wounded, set a magnificent example to the men in the Castle and his leadership was a big factor throughout the 19th March when the situation around Castle Hill remained tense and serious.

If Castle Hill had been lost during these attacks then it is more than probable that the small garrison on Hangman's Hill would have been eliminated. To this extent the Germans had failed but their aggressive action spelt the end of any attack on to the Monastery by the mixed Essex and 9th Gurkha force. Although the Germans did not possess the hill side above Castle Hill, their snipers aided by accurately controlled mortars and artillery continued to harass and strike against the Gurkhas. A New Zealand NCO in the valley below described one of several bombardments on Hangman's Hill: "In the darkness shells and mortars crashed among the rocks, burst in spraying red circles of flame on the flinty surfaces and their echoes rolling down the hillside. Our own guns from behind and before Trocchio replied with a hurricane of shells that rushed over our heads and plastered the face to the south west of Hangman's Hill. I thought I could see the occasional flash of grenades. As the storm subsided through the comparative silence came the rip of an occasional spandau—and by contrast the slow rattle of a Bren in reply. The Indians (Gurkhas) were still there".

The confused and conflicting reports about fighting on the lower slopes of Monte Cassino led to many strange orders being given. The author once wrote the following, based on his diary: "Down in the quarry we awaited instructions about our new tasks which, when they came, rocked us back on our heels. We were to go up to a feature called Castle Hill, a hill below the main Monastery Hill and thence using the Essex Company there as a firm base, launch an attack towards the Monastery itself. An entry in my diary contained the remark, 'God help us all' ".

'God did help us—using His influence through a certain Major Denis Beckett of the 1/4 Essex who was commanding a company of Essex on Castle Hill. They were under severe pressure from the German Paratroopers who were slowly and skilfully trying to cut off Castle Hill from the town below. Within the Castle, battered for weeks past, was congregated a mixed force of survivors—British, Gurkhas (1/9 GR), Sikhs, Indians. Others had tried to battle their way up the mountain towards the Monastery only to trickle back in groups to the relative safety of the old Castle. Denis Beckett was determined not to add A Coy 2/7 GR to the list of defeated men, particularly as he wanted us to help him hold the hill. He refused to let us commit suicide and told Brigade Headquarters accordingly.'

By 1015 hours Nangle's forces had received reinforcements in the shape of B and D Companies of the 1/4 Essex who had left Castle Hill before the German paratroopers had begun their attack. The companies had wanted to turn and engage the unsuspecting paratroopers from the flank but Brigadier Bateman of 5 Brigade had ordered them to continue on to join the 1/9 Gurkha Rifles. Such an assignment proved to be a dangerous one and only after heavy fighting did some seventy men reach Hangman's Hill, many of whom had been wounded in encounters with Germans during the hazardous journey.

General Freyberg had decided to postpone the assault on the Abbey until 1400 hours and it was for this reason that the two Essex companies had been ordered to carry on up to Hangman's Hill. He still hoped that the New Zealanders could clear the town, and of more importance, that the situation around Castle Hill would be eased before midday. However, even if the fortunes of New Zealand Corps had changed for the better in the town and at Castle Hill, it is doubtful if Lieutenant Colonel Nangle's force would have been strong enough to crack the kernel of the German defences, without the support of an equivalent attack being made simultaneously against Point 593 by the rest of Fourth Indian Division.

The Third battle is the most interesting, certainly the most perplexing, and undoubtedly the most tragic of the four battles at Cassino. It is full of inexplicable decisions which the study of records fails to resolve without doubts and numerous arguments. Records show that the assault on the Monastery was postponed until 1400 hours on the 19th March but what is shrouded in conjecture and mystery is the apparent decision to allow the armoured attack from Cavendish Road to be launched early in the morning, without any regard being taken about the main assault from Point 435. Fourth Indian Division records indicate that it was felt to have been a justified risk to let the tanks make their diversionary thrust on the assumption that the postponed 9th Gurkha attack would definitely take place at 1400 hours. Be that as it may, the armoured sortie was made and it came as a complete surprise to the German paratroopers.

Unfortunately the tanks moved forward without any infantry support as the depleted 7 Brigade was fully committed in holding the whole sector up on the hills to the north west of the Monastery. The tanks found the going difficult although their sudden appear-

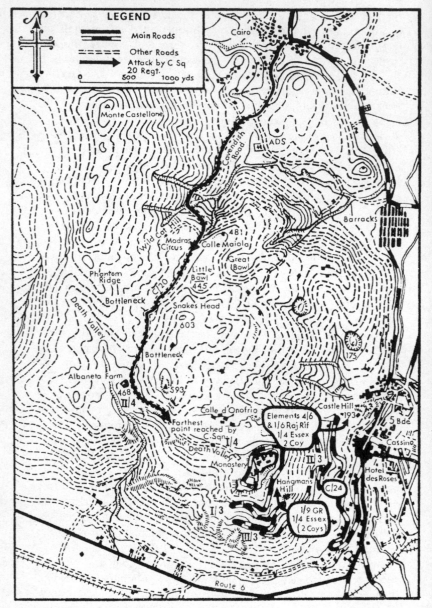

Map 8: The Third Battle, 19th March 1944.

ance in such rugged country came as a distinct shock to the 2nd Battalion of 4 Parachute Regiment. Frantic messages were sent back to an equally amazed headquarters as Shermans of C Squadron 20 Armoured Brigade thrust their way up between Albanette Farm and the southern shoulder of Point 593. The leading tanks reported that a way to the Abbey lay ahead over a rough cobbled road but unfortunately there were no infantrymen to go with them. One by one the tanks were knocked out or disabled, with so little ground to cover to their final goal, and by late afternoon, the inevitable decision to recall the last of the tanks had to be taken.

In retrospect there is little doubt that this small operation, which owed so much to the magnificent preparations carried out by the engineers in secret beforehand, and the skill and courage of the tank crews during the action, had given the Germans a severe shock. The tragedy was that carried out in isolation such a gallant diversion had no chance of winning the overall battle—it was a gesture, full of dash but with little tactical significance.

During the 19th March the third major setback that befell New Zealand Corps was the repulse of 28 (Maori) Regiment in its attempt to eliminate the German positions around the Continental Hotel. The tanks of 19 Armoured Regiment were not able to move with the infantry they were supporting because of obstructions caused by rubble and deep craters. The Maoris fought well, took a batch of prisoners, but their efforts could not reduce the main centre of resistance. More and more did it become obvious that German reinforcements were slipping into the town so that the capture of one or two houses by the Kiwis had little meaning as long as the Germans were able to infiltrate snipers into parts of the town that had been already 'cleared'.

General Freyberg's two-pronged attack which sought the capture of the ruined Abbey had resulted in the abortive armoured thrust and a larger but still isolated force awaiting developments on Hangman's Hill. Under these circumstances, the Corps Commander had no option but to postpone any idea of a further assault on to the Abbey until Castle Hill was securely held and Cassino town effectively cleared. He found that General Galloway continued to be a strong advocate for more infantry to be sent into Cassino; Galloway maintained that without such support his Fourth Division would be powerless to attain a victory on the hills.

In effect, there were two options open to Freyberg. The first one was to recommend to Generals Alexander and Clark that the battle should be called off before a complete stalemate developed. To have done so, however, immediately after the great efforts made on that day, 19th March, would have had a disastrous effect on morale, particularly when a major success had been nearly achieved. The second course was to revoke an earlier decision and use part of 78 Division in an attempt to garrison the town against interlopers and to sweep it clean, once and for all. By late afternoon, General Freyberg had made up his mind and given orders to this effect. 78 Division was to take over some of New Zealand Divisions' responsibility in Cassino, with one of its battalions, 6 Royal West Kents, relieving the Castle Hill garrison, before launching an attack to recapture Point 165. 5 New Zealand Brigade's task would be then to clear the rest of the town and open up Route 6 to the south so that the small garrisons on Hangman's Hill and Point 202 would no longer be isolated.

14 Panzer Corps faced the events of the day with composure but not with complacency. Any major threat from Hangman's Hill was now discounted as a result of their counter-attack against Point 193 (Castle Hill). What caused most concern was the increasing effectiveness of Allied tanks in the town which, although confined to certain tracks in the maze of rubble, nevertheless caused a lot of casualties to the defending paratroopers. Within the town area fighting was severe and the grim bitter nature of the struggle was reflected in the small number of prisoners taken—as at 19 March, the Allies had taken only fifty-one Germans and the number captured by their opponents was much the same. Every yard was contested, no quarter given and yet, in the desperate struggle for supremacy, the decencies of war were observed to an astonishing degree.

Examples of feelings akin to comradeship can be found in many stories, told by soldiers who fought at Cassino. Major Beckett recounts one experience: "One of our few prisoners saved my life by grabbing hold of me and pushing me down when one of their snipers shot at us and he later gave me his black gauntlet before he was taken back". Likewise at Castle Hill when the wall collapsed and buried several British soldiers, nearby German paratroopers helped the defenders dig out a number of men from the rubble while both sides evacuated wounded during the short truce. And a third story concerns the Regimental Medical Officer of the 1/9

Gurkha Rifles who on three occasions went up and down Hangman's Hill to attend to and bring back casualties. Each time he
was stopped by German paratroopers and searched. On the second
occasion he was handed a written note which declared that no
more evacuations would be permitted. This did not deter the gallant Captain Sonnie from making his third sortie and, although he
was intercepted, the Germans still allowed the doctor and the
wounded in his care to pass unmolested. In his turn, Captain Sonnie strictly obeyed the Geneva Rules and refused to disclose, to an
irate British brigadier, information about the Germans he had seen
on his journeys up and down the hillside. Such phrases as 'fanatical Nazi paratroops' had little meaning to the men of New
Zealand Corps who remembered their opponents as magnificent
soldiers and in the heat of battle, the contestants had a mutual respect and understanding of each other's problems. Many
wounded men survived because, like those under Captain Sonnie's
care, the stretcher bearers were allowed to carry out missions of
mercy in the forward areas.

With units from 78 Division at last being used, the new dispositions gave the New Zealand Corps Commander one faint chance
of victory which he realised had to come within forty-eight hours
because the Gurkhas on Hangman's Hill and the New Zealanders
on Point 202 could not remain in isolation for much longer.
Freyberg greeted 20th March with an ironical entry in his diary:
"Another lovely day—climatically". Winston Churchill telegraphed
Alexander on the same day: "I wish you would explain to me why
this passage by Cassino Monastery Hill, all on a front of two or
three miles, is the only place you keep butting at. About 5 or 6 Divisions have been worn out going into these jaws—it is very hard to
understand why this most strongly defended point is the only passage forward and why . . .".

General Alexander's reply explained that the winter weather
had not allowed other venues of attack, stressed the unexpected
delays caused by the complete destruction in the town, and paid a
whole-hearted tribute to the German Paratroopers: "Considering
they were subjected to the whole of the Mediterranean Air Force
plus the best part of 800 guns in the greatest concentration of fire
power which has been put down and lasting six hours, I doubt if
there are any other troops in the world who could have stood up
to it and then go on fighting with the ferocity as shown". Never-

theless it was also clear from Alexander's message that he sensed the battle had been lost and already he had decided to transfer the Eighth Army to the Cassino sector "and to deliver the decisive blow in the next battle".

General Freyberg was not the only senior general who was loth to call off the Third battle at Cassino. His immediate superior, General Mark Clark, had been able to devote much more of his time to affairs of the main Fifth Army front, because the situation at Anzio had changed from a critical one to an uneasy acceptance of a temporary stalemate by both sides. Victory at Cassino before the British Eighth Army moved across to take over the sector was a prize dear to General Clark's heart. His Fifth Army had been repulsed twice and was on the verge of another defeat. That the troops who had failed twice since mid-February were from New Zealand, Great Britain and India, and not America, mattered little because the battles had been directed by General Clark and his Headquarters. As Army commander, Mark Clark dearly wanted victory but like Alexander, he had his doubts after the events of 19th March. To Freyberg he said: "I think you and the Boche are both groggy". Nevertheless, Freyberg was given a further thirty-six hours although it was made clear that Alexander would not allow any attacks to continue unless there were definite signs of a quick success. He had already decided that it would be better to concede a temporary victory to General Heidrich and his men rather than prejudice a greater victory in the spring: a victory that could lead to a collapse of German resistance south of Rome.

In the same context, General Juin had given identical advice to General Clark: "It seemed inadvisable to commit oneself too deeply to a local operation which had already proved to be costly and which would become more costly every day—and all for the sake of a meagre success. I mentioned again my own ideas regarding large scale comprehensive operations as the only means by which a breakthrough in depth could be achieved and such formidable obstacles as Cassino overcome by means of an enveloping movement . . . I can only hope that the affair will come to a swift and victorious conclusion for, from the broader aspects, I cannot but ask myself in what sort of condition will the British troops emerge from the battle".

New Zealand Corps began its attempt to close the battlefield against German reinforcements on the night of 20/21 March. If these moves proved effective one more effort would be made to clear the town for the final breakthrough. One company from the 2/7 Gurkha Rifles in 7 Brigade was ordered to seize Point 445 so that the Germans could no longer infiltrate reinforcements down the ravine between Castle Hill and Point 175. The Gurkha company kept up their attack for two hours but were unable to cover the last few yards to their objective; a continued blaze of defensive fire caused some twenty casualties and the attempt had to be abandoned.

Above the Castle, another 'leak', through which the paratroops were moving down to the south of Castle Hill, was Point 165. As a consequence a company from 6 Royal West Kent was ordered to leave the Castle and attack the lower hairpin on the road to the Monastery. The advance had only just begun when the leading men walked into a newly planted minefield and amidst the explosions, casualties were suffered. Of even more importance any chance of surprising the Germans was lost and their accurate shooting down the hillside caused the Royal West Kents to abandon the attack.

Once more, inside the town, the New Zealand battalions tried to drive up the slopes of Monastery Hill and join forces with their detachments on Points 146 and 202. By daybreak they had achieved little and the stoutly defended Continental Hotel still remained the rock of resistance which defeated and foiled their efforts. The problem of street fighting in a mass of rubble was never solved by the Kiwis, gallantly though they tried throughout the Third battle: one lesson they did learn was that the defender, and his snipers, were favoured by the destruction of the town.

The reports sifted at the end of 21st March did not contain any news that gave rise to optimism in the Allied camp. Progress continued to be measured by a building or two captured after costly and grim fighting. After personally checking prospects with, amongst others, the commanding officer of 21 New Zealand Battalion, Freyberg decided to seek Alexander's permission to persevere with the attack for yet another day while Churchill, in London, had also been wondering if a decision to call off the whole battle might not be delayed: "Surely the enemy is very hard pressed too", ended his signal to Alexander. Both men, soldier and statesman, friends for many years, sensed that the margin between defeat and victory was still a matter of yards, of a few buildings, expertly prepared for defence, and capably and efficiently protected by soldiers who refused to give in, and were hard pressed but not, as yet, to the verge of defeat.

Plans made to renew the attack on the 22nd were forestalled by the 1st Parachute Regiment who sent a company supported by a detachment of engineers against the Royal West Kents in the Castle. The defenders in the shape of the British battalion won the encounter and not only inflicted many casualties, but captured some thirty prisoners—but the action temporarily postponed any ideas of aggression from the Castle Hill base.

Elsewhere the defenders were also successful locally, but they were the Germans and not the British or New Zealanders. In spite of spirited support by tanks of 19 Armoured Regiment, and lavish help from the artillery, the tired New Zealand battalions in the town were unable to clear the eastern base of Castle Hill. As on the previous day one or two houses were captured, but the German resistance never slackened and by late afternoon any further probing forward was considered to be a waste of lives. It had been a frustrating day with no successes to bring any cheer to Freyberg and his commanders.

A final conference reviewed the situation on the morning of 23rd March. The problems and realities of Cassino were thoroughly examined with different views being expressed by those present. One fact that could not be hidden was the state of the New Zealand Corps; both Divisions were exhausted and at the end of their tether. Over six weeks had been spent exposed to the rigours of the weather, the dust, the mud and rain, and the noise of battle that never ceased. Officers and men were tired and could no longer believe that a victory would be won by buffeting away at Monte Cassino or spending hour after hour trying to dislodge fanatical defenders from a single strong point. Six battalions had suffered excessive casualties, with the Corps as a whole losing over 2,000 men killed, wounded or missing. Before the conference ended, Freyberg was convinced that the battle could not be kept going any longer. Alexander agreed with this assessment, something that he appears to have been convinced about two days before, although he did not try to assert himself at that time; one more of the several puzzling features that historians find perplexing when they consider the battles of Cassino.

Thereafter decisions were made quickly and put into effect at once. New Zealand Corps would wind up the battle without taking any steps which would make their intentions too obvious; the isolated posts on Hangman's Hill and Point 202 were to be given up, but other hard-won gains were to be retained, even if the positions of the troops in the town and the south were known to be tactically unsound. To offset these disadvantages, posts were to be wired and mined for defence as soon as possible. New Zealand Corps, after being relieved by 13 Corps from the British Eighth Army, would be dissolved after its short history of some six weeks containing two gallant but costly failures.

The disengagement of the troops on the hillside above the town caused concern because since 19 March they had been supplied exclusively from the air. By now the Germans had ceased to send any ground attacks against the 1/9th Gurkhas on Hangman's Hill, although there had been a lot of sniping, with mortaring and shelling taking a daily toll of victims. Several casualties had managed to make their way down the hillside under a Red Cross Flag, but for the more seriously wounded evacuation had not proved possible. Two young medical orderlies from the Essex Regiment remained on Hangman's Hill until the final evacuation in order to tend the wounded, carrying out operations and even amputations when emergencies so demanded.

The story of how the orders for withdrawal were transmitted has been told in many accounts on Cassino. For security reasons it was decided to ask for officer volunteers to slip through the German outposts and give the orders by word of mouth. On the night of 24/25 March three volunteers set out, each carrying a carrier pigeon, Major Mallinson (1/4 Essex) and Captain Normand (1/9 GR) both reached Hangman's Hill but the third officer, Lt Jennings (4/6 Rajputana Rifles) was intercepted and forced to return to the Castle. The two pigeons which arrived, carried in the battle dress blouses of Mallinson and Normand, refused to fly back to their base after being released in the early hours of the morning. Only after the light had improved, and by dint of a considerable spot of shooing them away, did these important winged messengers return to 5 Brigade Headquarters. Meanwhile the New Zealand detachment on Point 202 was also warned about their imminent withdrawal by messengers.

Withdrawal from Hangman's Hill began after dark on the 25th of March, with the tired force moving down the route used by the messengers, after booby-trapping everything they could. Various distractions were made such as a raid from the Castle by the Royal West Kents; artillery concentrations were fired on certain German outposts; in the town, New Zealand tanks displayed aggression in as noisy a manner as possible. The way down the hillside was nerve-wracking and a considerable strain for men who had endured so much for so many days, but it passed without any major incident. Bohmler's version of the evacuation from Hangman's Hill is not borne out by accounts from other sources, Allied or German. His story of how the Gurkhas moved in groups under a Red Cross Flag undoubtedly refers to the wounded who had done this on three or four occasions under the gallant Captain Sonnie. In fact, the Germans appeared to have had scanty information about the two isolated Allied outposts, chiefly because they had decided to let them wither away rather than attempt to remove them by force in a direct confrontation. It appears that the withdrawal from Hangman's Hill was actually reported to 14 Panzer Corps Headquarters on the 26th March, that is, twentyfour hours after it had been completed.

Down from Hangman's Hill, Nangle led a party of eight officers and 177 Gurkhas of the 1/9 Gurkhas, two officers and 50 soldiers from the Essex Regiment, and 40 Indian soldiers from the Rajputana Rifles. In spite of their ordeal the Gurkhas had expressed deep disappointment when told that they were abandoning Hangman's Hill without relief. Bohmler states that the German patrols eventually counted 185 dead Gurkhas in and around Hangman's Hill, the price the battalion paid for the nine days spent under the shadow of the Abbey. From Nangle came warm-hearted praise for the support given by the gunners, in particular 1 Field Regiment; "we loved them after Hangman's Hill", the signallers and porters, and finally, for the incredible courage, patience and fortitude shown by the wounded as they lay in the open, awaiting evacuation, or in many cases, death. For Nangle and his Ninth Gurkha Rifles came messages of congratulation from many quarters; General Freyberg's words were: "What I particularly liked was at no time was there any belly-aching from 9 GR".

The New Zealand detachment of C Company 24 Battalion also made its way unhindered from Point 202. The spotlight had tended to light on the Gurkhas in their more exposed position near the Abbey, but it must not be forgotten that the men of C Company had undergone an ordeal on Point 202 which was tough and exacting. Their very presence had kept the insecure life-line open from Castle Hill to Hangman's Hill—as well as providing water from their well for the Gurkhas, higher up the mountain. They were tired, hungry and cramped from lack of exercise, but like 9 GR, they would have continued the struggle if any value could have been achieved or if there had been any chance of a victory.

Relief, too, came for 7 and 11 Indian Brigades on the hills near Point 593 who had patiently waited for a chance to exploit the elusive breakthrough. Life had been cruel and a constant strain during the six weeks they had confronted the Germans on the higher ridges. Continuous harassing fire had taken a daily toll of casualties while the weather had claimed victims from frostbite, from the heavy rain, and from constant and wearing exposure to the elements. A complete state of exhaustion was revealed when tired groups of men made their way back across the Rapido valley after handing over the forward areas to units of 78 Division. A junior officer wrote: "The distance was probably less than five miles but for most of the battalion, the men had hardly walked at all for six weeks. Men were cramped, unfit, mentally exhausted, without any willpower. Even though the ordeal was nearly over, the fact did not seem to be understood. . . . Never will I forget that nightmare of a march. Officers, British and Gurkha, shouted at, scolded, cajoled and assisted men as they collapsed. At times we had no alternative but to strike soldiers who just gave up interest in anything including a desire to live. By dint of all the measures we could think of, most of them reached their transport before daylight appeared; to survive and fight another day".

By 26th March the Germans had appreciated that the battle was indeed over. General von Senger wrote: "This battle of Cassino has ended in our favour, but the enemy will probably launch another major attack in the Corps Sector very soon, he will hardly lie down under defeats as they represent a loss of prestige for him . . . there is no indication yet just where the enemy plans to strike next".

General von Senger's cautious claim to a victory was a true assessment because the defenders had undoubtedly won the battle; but it was a victory dearly bought because the initial bombardment on the 15th, followed by continuous and exceptionally heavy artillery fire, had caused severe losses. XIV Corps War Diary for 23rd

March mentioned that the battalions in the forward areas had fighting strengths varying from 40 to 120 men, units in name trying to carry out tasks requiring a full complement of men.

Meanwhile, General Tuker, still in hospital, had heard that he was to return to India to take up another appointment and consequently would not see his beloved Fourth Division again. He wrote that he would never forget "the courage, daring, utter devotion, utter endurance unto death of the Division", but his subsequent assessment of the Third battle revealed his sorrow at the result: "Fourth Division lost more than a battle, they had lost some of its very substance in the shape of the men who had moulded it".

Such words applied in equal measure to the New Zealand Division. Courage and selfless devotion to duty had not been able to defeat the resolute men of the 1st Parachute Division. Outnumbered, outgunned, with few tanks near them and meagre air support at irregular intervals, the Germans were the victors of the Third Cassino battle.

14

The Third Battle in Retrospect

No battle ever started with such a prelude of noise and destruction as the one that New Zealand Corps launched on 15th March. Why then did the sledge-hammer fail to crack the kernel of the Cassino defences? Historians, and soldiers, especially those who fought at Cassino, will continue to argue and ponder over such matters for years to come. The author can but give a personal assessment of the facts as already described.

The seeds of failure were sown not on or just before 15th March, but six or seven weeks before that date. In the past, commentators on the Cassino battles have been prepared to show that the Fifth Army Commander, General Mark Clark, or the Corps Commander in two of the battles, General Sir Bernard Freyberg, failed to coordinate certain matters or to act decisively at a particular crisis. At the same time there has been a definite reluctance to implicate General Alexander with any of the major decisions made, with two important exceptions; the bombing of the Monastery in February and the humane and wise decisions to call off both the Second and Third battles as soon as stalemate had been reached. In fact, it was Alexander who decided when all the battles were to begin, who agreed to the overall tactical concept and who remained in close touch with developments throughout. He did not, it is true, plan or fight the day to day operations, but he was always in a position to have said: "A direct assault against Monte Cassino will not succeed, we must try again elsewhere, using different tactics".

The strongest defences in Europe were attacked by a single Corps, consisting of two divisions, on a narrow front in the heart of winter without any attempt at diversionary operations on the main Fifth Army sector. And the final decision was made by General Alexander. How then could an experienced and able commander continue to seek victory at Cassino after a similar attempt to rush the Monastery by the Americans had failed? Part of the answer to this query lies in the overall strategy of the British Government which, under Churchill, sought ways, and by all possible means, to keep the Germans at full stretch before the Second Front was opened.

Churchill's claim that the Campaign in Italy was 'the Third Front' could mean little if stalemate reigned from the Adriatic to the Tyrrhenian Sea. Allies who doubted the value of the Campaign and its long-term benefits had to be reassured by deeds which meant that continuous pressure had to be exerted; only then could the claim of containing elite German Divisions be justified. Such an effort had to be made before the spring weather made a further large scale offensive possible. Pressure against Cassino was exerted for motives that were not influenced by military tactics alone; although an unbounded faith was put in the heavy bombardment from the air which, it was anticipated, would win the day without too high a price in lives having to be paid by the New Zealand Corps. However, the air strikes, terrifying though they were, did not crack and destroy the will to fight of the German defenders, nor did the bombs pave a way through to the Liri valley. On the contrary, the terrible and complete devastation helped the defenders by enabling them to fight the infantry on even terms. Such a situation was becoming evident to the Allied generals within twenty-four hours after the first bomb had fallen, but when nothing like the scale of the bombardment had ever been tried before as a tactical weapon they had no experiences on which to assess their chances. Alexander and his subordinate generals gambled on a quick painless victory; their reward was a slow costly stalemate and a resounding failure with no material gains to offset the cost in lives suffered.

Once again, events had showed that direct assaults against Monte Cassino were doomed to failure unless made in conjunction with thrusts elsewhere, which could threaten the German flanks and force Kesselring to spread his limited reserves across the front at crucial points.

During the first three battles, the struggle at Cassino was one in which the defenders had the advantage of terrain and the attackers had overwhelming superiority in materials. However, it is wise to qualify the last statement by saying that the material disparity lay in tanks, aeroplanes and guns, but not in infantry. The attacker requires a superiority in infantry of about 3 to 1 if he is to capture hill features or carry out street fighting successfully: New Zealand Corps could have deployed up to twenty-four battalions at a critical period in the battle and these units could have been opposed by a maximum of fourteen battalions under command of the German 1 Parachute Division. Such a modest superiority in infantry was not enough to win the day especially when the climate and terrain did not permit the scores of tanks, the dozens of aircraft, or the tremendous expenditure of shells to be used to the maximum advantage—more infantry was required not more guns.

It is clear, therefore, that the decision to keep on attacking Monte Cassino was accepted by Alexander, even if he was 'jockeyed' into an unenviable position by strategic and political considerations. General Alexander's great ability in being able to weld together and lead a team of many nationalities was helped by his charm, equable temperament and accessibility. Nevertheless there were seeds of weakness in the virtues and there were occasions when he displayed a reluctance to override his subordinates or to interfere in their handling of day to day affairs. Such an occasion occurred on the 22nd March when Alexander was convinced that the Third battle was bound to end in failure and had already given out preparatory orders for regrouping before his big Spring offensive. In spite of this, his subordinate generals were able to obtain his agreement to one more throw of the dice before the Third battle was finally brought to an end.

If the strongest point in the German Gustav Line defences had to be attacked by a frontal assault—for reasons other than military —then could success have been achieved by a plan different from the one adopted by New Zealand Corps? It must be conceded that no one could possibly have forecast the effects of the bombing without previous experiences to provide lessons for study. For this reason the operation's dependence on the bombing can be accepted by posterity. What must be queried was the original decision to keep such a large force out of battle and in reserve for the final exploitation into the Liri valley. These units were not employed in any active role at the time when German survivors in Cassino were improvising defences and shaken by the bombing, and when the outlook for General Heidrich and his troops was grim and difficult. Freyberg was to take a lot of persuading before he decided to deploy extra soldiers from 78 Division into Cassino and, by then, it was too late as the Parachute Division had recovered its poise and the Allied thrusts had been blunted and stabilised.

Undoubtedly the crucial hours were those that followed the bombing on the 15th March up to the 17th, when only two New Zealand battalions were actually at grips with the Germans in the town. The optimism of the pre-bombing period seems to have remained with Freyberg and his New Zealand subordinates throughout the 16th of March. In the early stages casualties were not heavy so that any idea of a long tough battle had not yet entered the minds of the commanders in the New Zealand Division. It seems probable, therefore, that more infantry in the town before the 17th March might have won the day; after that date, a much harder struggle became inevitable, in which the cost of victory would have been heavy, even if extra infantry battalions had been deployed in the rubble and debris called Cassino town.

Having argued that more infantry might have pressed home early gains, a factor which supports the opinions of Freyberg and Parkinson has to be mentioned in this last 'look' at the Third battle. The scene of the conflict was a small, tight area and accounts of the struggle at Cassino tend to exaggerate it all in terms of space. 1/9 Gurkha Rifles were, it is true, isolated on Point 435 (Hangman's Hill) but nearly all the major incidents, described in the previous chapter, took place within a distance of one mile from their position—and the Gurkhas were at the far end of the circle. With progress measured in yards, in the possession of one or two houses, it was not quite as simple as it sounded to say: "Send another brigade or battalion into Cassino". It was especially difficult to decide and define where and how they would operate alongside troops already scattered into groups among the ruins. Suffice to say that it was never tried so that no one can really say how events would have transpired.

Attackers and defenders alike faced problems of great magnitude in this, the Third battle, but in spite of their initial setbacks, the Germans can claim to have solved many of theirs so that victory was their reward. The high quality of the Parachute Division has been mentioned and due accord has been given to General Heidrich for the way he commanded his men, with his intelligent use of artillery and mortars, and the way he organised and launched quick local counter-attacks against points where danger threatened. New Zealand Corps' part can best be summed up by quoting N. C. Phillips: "where so much is obscure, it is clear that there was no easy solution for the attacker, the critic of the solutions that were in fact adopted must first arm himself with better ones".

Were there better ones if such an attack had to be delivered into the jaws of Cassino? We can but ponder over the words of General Tuker, written in his book 'Approach to Battle': "An extraordinary obsession in British commanders' minds that they must challenge the enemy strength rather than play on his weakness . . . may do for games; war is neither a game or sport unless staking men's lives can be regarded as sport . . . that thought may yet make some pause before undertaking the responsibilities of command on the battlefield . . . the waste of hammering at the enemy's strongest point is seen at its most extreme form later on in Italy, at the battle of Cassino in the spring of 1944, where men were hurled time and again against a mountain position which had for centuries defied attack from the south and which in 1944 was not only the strongest position in Italy, but was held by the pick of the German troops in that theatre of war. These battles in fact were military sins no less".

15

The Fourth Battle: Operation Diadem

After the 23rd of March the name Cassino rarely appeared in the main Allied communiques during the following six weeks. On the other hand German propaganda continued to extol the exploits of the gallant defenders and, indeed, began taunting the British and Americans with promises that any further attacks on Cassino would end in failure. Such statements caused Kesselring some anxiety because he not only hoped that Alexander would try another direct thrust, but he also realised that the Spring weather would open up many other possibilities on land, from the sea and by air. Although Doctor Goebbels might proclaim that the German Army was invincible, Kesselring knew that his men would have to face a combined onslaught before the summer was out; moreover his problem was to obtain up-to-date intelligence on Allied intentions, a task that was made extremely difficult by the ineffectiveness of the Luftwaffe. Kesselring was unable to find out when or where Alexander would strike. Such a situation allowed Alexander and his staff ample opportunities to prepare their plans in detail, while at the same time deliberately allowing certain aspects of their preparations to be noted by German agents. Deception was to be a big factor in influencing the German dispositions before the main battle began.

Kesselring had several problems to face after the Third battle was over. All his divisions, whether in the Cassino sector or holding the beach-head around Anzio, were tired and under-strength. A period of rest would have been welcomed but such a respite depended on the Allied plans. Of even more significance was the strain put on the German organisation by the all out efforts of the Allied Air Forces against targets behind the battle zone. Railway lines, bridges, main roads and depots were struck by day and night in an effort to strangle supplies and disrupt administration. In North Italy the Alpine passes were bombed and attacked with monotonous regularity. A severe strain was put on the lines of communication—that it did not break down was chiefly due to fore-thought in arranging to stockpile supplies of ammunition in central Italy plus a large measure of resupply by sea done at night. In addition, maintenance teams located at various 'danger spots' nullified, to a certain extent, any major disruption to the railways and roads by their energetic and untiring efforts to repair damage caused by the Allied bombers.

The German Armed Forces under Field Marshal Kesselring's command included a pitifully weak Luftwaffe and few naval craft of any significance. There was little they could do to stop another sea-borne landing, nor did the German Air Force have the capability of finding out where such an invasion might take place. Kesselring was convinced that the costly rebuffs at Cassino meant that the Allies would use their unchallenged superiority at sea and in the air in another effort to end the Italian Campaign: from this fear stemmed his decision to keep the mobile Army Group reserves well behind the main front so that they could keep a wary eye on the most likely of beaches for a landing. If a further invasion had taken place then such dispositions would have taken a terrible toll of the landing forces. On the other hand, if the Allies decided to launch an offensive on the main front, with or without assistance from the troops at Anzio, then the locations selected by the German Commander-in-Chief suited their purpose in every way.

The crux of the Allied deception plan was to encourage the Germans into accepting that another landing was inevitable and imminent. Kesselring felt that the La Spezia-Leghorn area would be selected by the Allies for a major landing: 'Such an operation would have brought about the collapse of the front in Middle Italy and dealt a fatal blow to the Army Group.' Unbeknown to Kesselring, however, was the hard fact that the Allied combined Chiefs of Staff had already confirmed a previous decision which placed 'Anvil' (landing in the south of France), as top priority in the Mediterranean area. A landing anywhere on the Italian coastline had been firmly ruled out by those set in authority above Alexander, thus forcing him to fashion and design a victory by an offensive on land. Such a venture only stood a chance if the Germans were caught off balance in the initial stages. Not only was it essential that Kesselring should dispose his divisions with a view to countering another landing, but equally was it vital that the Allied regrouping for the offensive should be shrouded in secrecy. In both respects Alexander and his Chief-of-Staff, General John Harding, were to succeed beyond measure, with the staff work brilliantly executed, so that the seeds of victory were sown for Operation Diadem. However, an examination of the German dispositions must be completed before Allied plans are discussed in a little detail.

Although Field Marshal Kesselring had come to the conclusion that the landing would be in the La Spezia-Leghorn area, he sensed that the main offensive might first take the form of an advance through the Aurunci mountains to Cassino before a direct thrust into the Liri valley was attempted. In addition, he could not and did not discount the possibility of a subsidiary attack being made by an airborne force after landing, somewhere in the north of the Liri valley. Being an able and imaginative commander, the Field Marshal was able to consider all the possible courses open to his antagonists; but what concerned him most was the paucity and scarcity of information to give him significant pointers on which to base plans for the defence of the Gustav Line—and Rome.

For example, the French Corps disappeared from the area north of Cassino but its movement thereafter remained secret. In Kesselring's words: "The whereabouts of the French Corps was a constant source of anxiety to me; Tenth Army, and its subordinate commanders were directed to regard as a matter of urgent importance any information on the subject and to report it forthwith to Army Group, whose ultimate decisions might well depend upon it".

An attempt was made to build up a reserve behind the main front, a task of considerable difficulty because the divisions were already overstretched. The front was divided between LI Mountain Corps under General Valentin Feuerstein and General von Senger's XIV Panzer Corps. General von Senger was bitterly disappointed to find that the Cassino sector, still defended by Heidrich's Parachute Division, passed to the control of LI Corps. His feelings can be appreciated after some four months of responsibility for the overall defence of Monte Cassino, but Kesselring believed that the next crucial battles would not necessarily be the ones fought in the immediate area of the Monastery. The all important Army Group reserve divisions were to be held back until the offensive had been launched and the threat had been established so that the chance of them being used at the wrong place and time could be minimised. As a guard against a sea landing 92 Infantry Division and the Hermann Goering Division were in the Civitavecchi-Leghorn area. Further south the 26 and 29 Panzer Divisions were located near the Anzio beach-head to act as a reserve as well as being ready to counter any fresh landings near Anzio. The possible Allied airborne threat had influenced the German Commander-in-Chief into positioning 90 Panzer Grenadier near Frosinone. Under the circumstances, and with the scanty information available to help him, it is difficult to see how Kesselring could have located his reserves in any other way, assuming as he did that another seaborne landing was a certainty.

The major regrouping of the German forces was planned to be completed by the middle of May: at a lower level unit and subunits within divisions were relieved for short periods to allow rest and recuperation after the hard winter's fighting. Such a scheme entailed a degree of disorganisation as far as the command structure was concerned, and formations had to be split so that holes could be plugged. The middle of May would have seen the defenders correctly organised and with their commanders and key personnel back from leave. As an example, Field Marshal Kesselring had allowed General von Senger to go back to Germany; the latter had left behind an order of the day warning his formation that the Allied attack could be expected at any time after May 24th, a date that would have seen the General back in command of his Corps.

'Diadem', launched on 11th May, completely deceived the Germans as to the time, place and power of the main thrust. More than half the victory was assured before the first shells landed just before midnight on the 11th May.

The Germans had to plan in the dark in their attempts to anticipate the various courses open to General Alexander; what they could not know was that the seeds of a successful 'Diadem' had already been sown, firstly by Alexander's aim which laid down that such an offensive would destroy the right wing of the German Tenth Army and to drive what remained of the German Fourteenth Army to the north of Rome; and secondly, in a masterly appreciation by his Chief of Staff, General John Harding. This appreciation had been originally written at the end of February and thereafter formed the basis for the final plan, even though there was a delay of a month before official approval was given to 'Diadem' by the Combined Chiefs of Staff. The plan envisaged a striking force of some twelve Divisions producing the necessary local superiority of 3 to 1 in infantry at the critical point; favourable odds that had never been forthcoming throughout the winter of 1943-44.

In order to obtain such a superiority time was required to plan and carry out large scale regrouping, and to await the arrival of fresh divisions; six to seven weeks was the estimated period during which no major operations could be attempted by the two Allied armies in Italy. Such a proposal was viewed with doubt by General Sir Maitland Wilson, Commander in Chief Mediterranean Area, who continued to advocate unceasing pressure across the front rather than any curtailment of operations that would allow the Germans rest and respite or grant them the opportunity to withdraw troops from Italy to be used to meet the impending invasion of France. Fortunately General Alexander was able to persuade his superior that preparations for the Spring offensive could not be hurried or the size of his forces truncated without accepting the grave risk of yet another rebuff. Their differences amicably resolved, the two British generals then had the problem of finding seven or eight extra divisions from somewhere within the Mediterranean command. Divisions there were, but they had already been earmarked for the projected 'Anvil' landing in the south of France. Would the Chiefs of Staff let these troops be used in 'Diadem' first thus accepting a postponement of 'Anvil'? Once more American suspicions about the British Mediterranean policy were aroused but eventually on 24 March approval was given—'Anvil' would await the capture of Rome; detailed planning could go ahead.

General Alexander had appreciated that the complexity of the staff work, and the logistical problems that had to be resolved before the regrouping could be effected, meant that the planning could not await the formal approval of his superiors. He revealed the true stature of a great commander by refusing to be diverted from his long term strategy by the day to day frustrations and delays—or indeed by the setback at Cassino during the Third battle. Coordinating conferences were held on 28 February and on 2 April, at which the senior commanders in Italy were told how the embryo 'Operation Diadem' would develop into the offensive to clear the Germans out of south and central Italy. A detailed description of the planning for 'Operation Diadem' could not be covered in the story of the four battles for Cassino, although it would be equally wrong to describe the last battle without mentioning the background of the Spring offensive. The hoped for fall of Cassino and the capture of the Monastery were prizes sought by all Allied soldiers in Italy. But Cassino was but a phase, albeit a crucial one, in the concerted plan made by General Alexander and brought to fruition by his Army Commanders, their staffs, and the men under their command.

Alexander's plan was to concentrate the bulk of the Fifth and Eighth Armies into a twenty mile front between Cassino and the Tyrrhenian Sea and then smash a way through the German Tenth Army. By achieving a vast superiority in infantry, guns, armour, and with the fair weather allowing the Air Forces to operate by day and night, the expectation was that the Tenth Army would be driven from the Gustav Line defences in complete disorder. The Allies knew that the Germans had prepared other areas for defence; the Hitler line around Piedimonte, about eight miles behind Cassino, and the Caesar line, north of the beach-head in the Alban Hills, had been reported by many Intelligence sources. It was essential, therefore, that the strength of the initial thrust did not allow the enemy to occupy either or both of these subsidiary lines; indeed the hope was that the Tenth Army would be routed and vigorously pursued north west to a point where General Truscott's VI Corps from Anzio might drive across their path and attack the retreating Germans in the Alban Hills.

Such extensive regrouping posed many problems for the staff, the biggest headache of all being the move of so many divisions without the Germans realising what was afoot. Absolute secrecy about the switch of the Eighth Army to the Cassino front from the Adriatic sector had to be maintained. The detailed measures adopted such as movement by night, wireless silence, elaborate camouflage, and many others, were remarkably successful and an outstanding example of organisation by the staffs concerned.

Hand in hand with the strict and absolute security went the imaginative deception plan which played on Kesselring's fears of another Anzio type landing in the Civitavecchia area. Reconnaissance planes flew many sorties over the beaches. Back in the Naples/Salerno area operation 'Nunton' saw the Canadian Corps and 36 (U.S.) Division carry out combined operation training with all the trimmings of an assembly area, ready to mount a big landing from the sea. These measures but served to confirm Kesselring's original appreciation that the Allies had decided to abandon direct assaults against the Gustav Line in favour of a third major landing on the west coast of Italy.

The result was that the precious mobile reserve divisions were given areas situated far from the main front, thus fulfilling Alexander's hopes in this respect. In the battle of wits before 'Diadem' was launched no one can doubt that General Alexander outsmarted his able adversary, Field Marshal Kesselring. It is to the latter's credit, however, that although the Allies possessed overwhelming superiority in numbers, on sea, land and air, in materials and weapons of war, and obtained complete surprise in timing and at the actual point of assault, they were still not able to crush the Germans into final defeat or cause them to abandon Italy.

A truly international army awaited D Day which was to be May 11th, a date that allowed the fresh divisions time to arrive in Italy and prepare themselves for battle, that promised moonlight to help the attackers, and for political reasons anticipated the early capture of Rome to divert the attention of the world from the last minute overtures and possible delays to 'Overlord'. The soldiers of Great Britain and the United States found themselves outnumbered by their allies, each of whom had contingents commanded by a general who had a direct political link to his own government. Never can a Commander in Chief have had such a mixed and varied team to command. Fortunately for the Allied cause in Italy, General Alexander's great gift of suggesting courses rather than ordering them, combined with his striking sincerity and complete honesty of purpose, achieved a wonderful sense of unity in both the Fifth and Eighth Armies.

General Mark Clark's leadership had already been tested from Salerno to Anzio; his qualities were known and his image as a commander projected with assiduous regularity by a high powered public relations team. His Fifth Army still controlled VI Corps at Anzio under its new commander, General Truscott. At first the overall plan for 'Diadem' had envisaged the assault from the beach-head preceding the one due to be launched along the main front, but Alexander finally decided to reverse the order so that VI Corps was warned and expected to begin the breakout from Anzio on about D + 4. The decision as to the timing of the breakout was to be made by Alexander himself; VI Corps' task would be to attack the German Fourteenth Army with the object of cutting Highway No. 6 in the vicinity of Valmontone, thus isolating the Tenth Army to the south. Meanwhile the task of the main Fifth Army was to first capture the Ausonia defile; then side by side its two Corps would advance on Army orders. On the left the men of U.S. II Corps moving along the coast had comparatively easy terrain ahead of them, but the French Expeditionary Corps on the right was challenged by mountainous country around the Ausenti Valley. Juin, however, was confident that his Moroccans, experienced and dashing fighters in mountain warfare, would open up the valley and burst into the Liri Valley from the south. Indeed Juin's fear, which he expressed before 'Diadem' began, was that the Eighth Army would not keep pace with his Corps; he predicted that the British and Poles would be involved in heavy fighting on his right flank and their progress would be slow. His forecast and anxiety were justified by events. Fortunately, too, General Mark Clark's final plan owed its inspiration to Juin's conviction that the weakest link in the German defensive chain was the Petrelle massif. Juin's faith in his troops was more than rewarded, so that it is pertinent to suggest that his opinions ought to have carried more weight in the Allied conferences. At the end of January the French General's plea that Cassino should have been by-passed to the north by a reinforced and strengthened French Corps had been disregarded. When the French set about the task of marching towards Rome through the Aurunci mountains the country was far more hazardous and difficult than that which had faced them around Monte Cassino in January and February that year. Precipitous mountains and determined Germans were unable to stop the Moroccans and Goums on May 11th and the days that followed.

Eighth Army's move from the east coast across to the Cassino sector had not passed unnoticed by the Germans. They, too, had thinned out troops holding the area near the Adriatic coast so that both sides openly disregarded the possibility of any attack on that flank. The build up of troops south of the Liri Valley could not be hidden from intelligence agents or the occasional reconnaissance plane that evaded detection in a high level sortie. What was denied to the Germans was accurate information as to where and when these troops would be used. In contrast, the new commander of the Eighth Army, General Sir Oliver Leese, had the advantage of detailed and up-to-date information on German dispositions, including pinpoint locations of most of their artillery and 'nebelwerfers'. Nevertheless, the task that faced General Leese was not an easy one: for one thing, he was in the unenviable position of being Field Marshal Montgomery's successor. Although his great predecessor had always treated Leese as heir-apparent, nevertheless the contrast between the two men could not have been greater. Field Marshal Montgomery's qualities and his methods of command have often been described and analysed. Leese was a robust competent General who, like the majority of commanders in modern times, exercised control through his staff; but he did not have the reputation or magnetism of his old commander to add to his solid and reliable qualities.

Eighth Army was given the biggest burden in the opening stages of the offensive. Not only did its divisions have to cross the Rapido into the Liri Valley, but the Cassino massif had to be conquered and captured, whatever the cost. With the spring weather came optimism and few now doubted that the Gustav Line could be turned and forced open by enveloping thrusts. Nevertheless, it was still an inescapable fact that the quickest road to Rome lay through the Liri Valley, guarded by Monte Cassino and its Monastery. General Leese had the same task that had confronted his predecessors, Generals Keyes and Freyberg, while the German paratroopers still held a third of Cassino town and the defences on the mountains were as strong as ever. But where the Americans and the New Zealanders had used two divisions, Eighth Army was in a position to deploy double that number and still have troops uncommitted, ready to force an opening or exploit a breakthrough.

From the River Gari to Cassino was General Kirkman's 13 Corps with its four divisions: 6 Armoured, 4 and 78 (British), and 8th Indian Divisions. General Kirkman's troops were to operate on the old ill-fated axis used by the American 36th Division in January, with the task of securing a bridge head over the River Rapido. By exploiting forward from the bridge head 13 Corps would meet determined resistance from the German infantry, aided by their well tried and organised artillery, but the weight of assault combined with a massive fire plan gave solid grounds for optimism. Moreover, if the situation required, ready to pass through or come into the line on the left flank, was 1 Canadian

Corps under General Burns. These Liri Valley defences were not only to be subjected to a massive coordinated attack by 13 Corps but simultaneously, Monte Cassino and its observation points, so invaluable to the Germans in the past, would be assaulted by the Polish Corps under General Anders.

Finally, on the right of the Allied line in the sector north east of Monte Caira, was X British Corps which included an under-strength New Zealand Division and 2 Parachute Brigade. X Corps' task was a subsidiary one during the impending operation, that of guarding the flank and simulating an attack on the German left wing in the direction of Atina. Alexander intended that the German defenders would be stretched from the very beginning of 'Diadem'; on this occasion it would not be possible for his opponents to plug holes by the use of local reserves as had happened in the Cassino battles. The German corps commanders had no reserves readily available and the Army Group mobile reserves were north of the Tiber, looking for an invasion fleet that never existed.

The Fourth battle of Cassino was about to start, not as an attempt to storm defences in isolation, but as part of a brilliantly conceived and carefully planned offensive. In this respect the Polish Corps was fortunate although the objectives sought by its men were still defended by General Heidrich's Paratroop Division. The ruined Monastery, the infamous Calvary Mount (Point 593), the strong points around the Continental Hotel; all these had to be stormed and taken before the Poles could claim that Cassino was theirs. Let us examine how they planned to conquer where others had failed.

Poland had decided to fight rather than accept subservience to German tyranny in 1939. In 1944 the country still lay subjugated under the iron heel of the Nazi invader. The spirit and will of her people had suffered a terrible blow when, in the autumn of 1939, Soviet Russia had cooperated with Germany in the joint occupation of their country. A few months later Adolf Hitler turned on Russia to begin the invasion which eventually bled the Third Reich to death and utter defeat. In spite of the fact that Russia became an uneasy ally of the Western Powers to fight the common foe, thousands of Polish prisoners of war remained for a considerable time in prisons and labour camps throughout Russia. An amnesty was eventually allowed so that the Poles could reconstitute an army under the leadership of a great patriot and commander, General Anders.

In spite of Russian promises and assurances, hundreds of Polish prisoners never tasted freedom nor were they given the chance to serve their country again. Many of those released were in poor physical condition as a result of the treatment they had suffered as 'guests' of the Soviet Union. But to all who were allowed to leave Russia a miracle had occurred; they were back in the Polish Army and would be given a chance to fight the Germans who had not only crushed their country by military power but had carried out numerous acts of barbarity against the civilian population under their occupation. No other incentives were necessary to make them train hard or to give everything they had got, nor was it necessary to instil hatred of the Germans into men who had seen their country damaged and broken by the war. Many of them had lost their families and had nothing left to fight for except Poland. If death came in battle then who would have grief for lonely men who had lost everything except love of their country and were left with nothing but a terrible hate of the Germans?

The tragedy was that the Poles under General Anders could but live for the present with little hope for the future. Already the Teheran conference decisions meant that many of the soldiers' homes would lie east of the Curzon Line in the Soviet sphere of influence. The majority of them, from General Anders down to the most junior recruit, had experienced Russian hospitality and were suspicious about Stalin's designs on Poland. They could but hope and pray that their American and British allies would not agree to the liberation of Poland from the Nazis only to hand over the country to the Communists. Bewildered, subjected to vicious Russian propaganda, which accused them of being British mercenaries, the Polish 2nd Corps put aside doubts and misgivings and prepared to fight and, if necessary, die in order to restore the honour of their country.

The 2nd Polish Corps, some fifty thousand strong, had come under the command of the Eighth Army in February 1944, but saw little action while the battles at Cassino were being contested between the German paratroopers and Freyberg's New Zealand Corps. General Anders had been warned that the result of the battle at Cassino would decide where and when his men would be used in Italy. A day or two before the 23rd March General Leese offered the Poles their task, that of capturing the Monte Cassino heights and then the town of Piedimonte. General Anders did not hesitate for long although under no illusion whatever about the complexity of the task and the heavy price in lives which his Corps might have to pay. Later, when the war was over, Anders stood by his decision by writing: "I agreed with General Alexander in thinking that the road to Rome could only be opened up by taking Monte Cassino." Once committed, the General and his staff lost no time in planning the next attack on objectives that had defied capture since the end of January.

Anders pays tribute to General Sir Bernard Freyberg who gave him a lot of useful advice, based on experiences culled during nearly two months' fighting at Cassino. To this and other recorded data, the General and his staff added the results of reconnaissances made by air or from vantage points that overlooked the battle field. Slowly and carefully an accurate picture of the main German dispositions was built up so that General Anders could consider how his Corps might overcome the Monte Cassino defences.

In effect, there were four possible ways of attacking Monastery Hill; all would exact a heavy toll of casualties, but which would bring victory? From the south, aimed at the simultaneous capture of Monastery Hill, Points 593 and 575, the attack would have entailed a full scale river crossing over the River Gari/Rapido before any assault up the steep mountainside could be launched. Such a hazard completely outweighed the obvious attraction of mounting attacks against the three key objectives at the same time. The New Zealand Corps had already tried attacking from the east during the Third battle; nothing had changed since then to make the chances of the Poles succeeding where the Kiwis and Indians had failed. The strong points around the Continental Hotel were still manned by determined troops and the steep climb up to the Monastery would always be a severe handicap to any attacker. Experiences in attacking from the north had been equally disastrous when Fourth Indian had made gallant but abortive attempts to seize Point 593 in the early days of February. One further possibility remained: that of attacking on a broad front from the north east. General Anders and his staff sensed that this might bring the victory they sought.

Anders appreciated that such a plan meant the Monastery itself would not come under direct attack during the initial phase. If his divisions first secured Snakeshead Ridge and Colle San Angelo then they would overlook Route 6 and so threaten to outflank Heidrich's garrison in Cassino town and around the Abbey on Monastery Hill. Such an attempt had been made by Fourth Indian Division, but under very different circumstances. Whereas the Indians had been able to deploy a single brigade against one of the objectives, the Poles could use two divisions simultaneously against both features, thus preventing the Germans from moving reserves from one spot to another, in order to stiffen resistance or to counter attack vital key points. To add to the German paratroopers' fear of being cut off, the British 13 Corps would be making its major assault across the Rapido to threaten the town from the west. The Poles could feel with justification that an attack from the north east was the only possible one that allowed them the chance to deploy their maximum effort at one time against the superlative defences created by the Germans. The decision having been made, detailed planning could go ahead and subordinate commanders were allotted tasks in the crucial battle that faced the men of the Polish Corps.

Unfortunately the Polish Corps only consisted of two infantry divisions, each of two brigades; 3 Carpathian and 5 Kresowa Divisions, supported by 2 Polish Armoured Brigade. One of the vital lessons from the past battles was that extra troops must be ready at hand to exploit openings or consolidate gains against the vigorous counter attacks which the Germans were past masters at organising so quickly. General Anders had to create such a reserve and was forced to place a battalion from each brigade under Divisional Headquarters' control: the shortage of infantry meant that casualties in either of the divisions might entail the whole formation being temporarily unfit for battle, but such a risk had to be accepted.

Preparation for the battle was made more difficult by the fact that ground reconnaissance patrols were ruled out; the overall plan made it important that the Germans had no chance of capturing prisoners and thus learning that the whole of II Polish Corps had been concentrated for an attack in the Monte Cassino sector. Nevertheless, this edict meant that the junior commanders did not have an opportunity to pinpoint German outposts or acquaint themselves with the best covered approaches to their objectives. Stringent security was the order of the day, and extensive measures were taken to conceal the preparations that went on by day and night and intensified as D Day, May 11th, approached. With dusk and darkness came scenes of hectic activity as supplies were brought forward and stockpiled, tracks were made or existing ones strengthened as guns, tanks and men eased their way forward into assembly areas. At daybreak all open activity ceased; vigilant German observers peered across at an area in which maximum and ingenious use of camouflage had been carried out. Equally intent radio intercept teams listened in to English conversations on allied wireless nets opposite the Cassino sector but heard no Polish language being spoken—British signallers had been attached to the Polish Corps for deception purposes.

Lots were drawn to decide which division should be responsible for the less glamorous right-hand role, the capture of Colle San Angelo, or which would attack towards the Monastery after seizing Points 593 and 569. To the 5th Kresowa Division befell the task of first seizing the mountain ridge around Colle San Angelo and then covering the 3 Carpathian Rifle Division as it battered a way through to the final goal, the Abbey. The overall plan envisaged both divisions attacking simultaneously, but the Kresowa

Division was to pause on an intermediate objective until their left flank was protected. This meant the early capture of the infamous Point 593 by the Carpathian Division; once more the bare rocky hill was to be the key position in the oncoming battle. The very nature of the ground allowed the Poles little scope in the choice of assembly areas, the direction of attack, the tactics they used. What could uphold their faith, however, was the weight of the blows about to be rained on the Germans along the whole front; in the words of Fred Majdalany: "an operation in C major with full orchestra."

On 11th May 1944 General Anders issued his order of the day: "Soldiers, the moment for battle has arrived. We have long awaited the moment for revenge and retribution on our hereditary enemy. Shoulder to shoulder with us will fight British, American, Canadian and New Zealand Divisions, together with French, Italian and Indian Troops. The task assigned to us will cover with glory the name of the Polish soldiers all over the world. At this moment the thoughts and the hearts of our whole nation will be with us, trusting in the Justice of Divine Providence we go forward with the sacred slogan in our hearts: God, Honour, Country."

The tragedy was that General Anders, a man who had been treated like a criminal by the Russians in the notorious Lubianka Prison in Moscow, had no alternative but put his trust in the Western Allies. Without such a trust the gallant commander could not have made the stirring cry for an all-out effort by his men. And equally clearly the Polish soldiers would not have advanced with such enthusiasm against the Germans if they had known that a large portion of their country had already been promised to Stalin by the Western Powers. In blissful ignorance of their bleak political future, the Polish Corps waited during the daylight hours of the 11th May with the utmost confidence. Detailed planning had been completed, the artillery had vast dumps of smoke and explosive shells ready to fire, and nothing had been left to chance that could have been foreseen. Slowly the hours ticked by until the appointed time—11.00 p.m. on the night of the 11th May.

17

The Fourth Battle: Victory Unfolds

Up on the mountain the Germans were in the process of relieving some of their men in the forward areas; their batteries were all but silenced so that the Allied guns would not be provoked into upsetting these reliefs. One of the quietest nights for a long time was suddenly filled with thunder when, at 11.00 p.m. the whole front burst into a crescendo of noise and fury. The artillery of the Fifth and Eighth Armies opened up with thousands of shells pouring on the defenders and, in particular, on to known German gun positions from the Tyrrhenian Sea across to the East. The guns kept up a furious barrage for some forty minutes before switching on to the first objectives due to be stormed by the infantry. The roar and crashes in the mountains became a continuous mixture of whining and explosions; during the ensuing twenty-four hours the guns of the Fifth Army, for example, fired over 170,000 rounds. Surprise had been achieved and support had been both generous and meticulously executed. It was now up to the infantry, the Americans on the coast, the French on the heights of Monte Faito, the British standing before the River Gari and the Poles attacking from Monte Castellone across the rocky battlefield that had already cost so many Allied lives. Each of the four Corps had an important part to play, but the most pressing was that undertaken by the British 13 Corps. If the two assaulting divisions, 4th British and 8th Indian, had not secured a bridgehead before daylight, a bridgehead that included tanks, then the Germans would be granted a whole day to recover and counter attack. The memory of 36 Division's attempt over the same river was still fresh in the minds of the Allied generals.

Beside the coast, General Geoffrey Keyes' II Corps made a slow start, partly because both the 85 and 88 Divisions had relatively little battle experience. The German 94 Division under General Steinmetz fought with great determination against the attack which benefitted from lavish support given by the guns of the Fleet and from swarms of fighter bombers. The Germans held up the American advance until the 14th May; thereafter progress quickened because 94 Infantry Division was forced to evacuate well prepared positions as a result of French pressure through the mountains towards the Liri Valley—Juin's Corps achieved startling results within the first forty-eight hours of the offensive.

The French Colonial troops hurled themselves against 71 Division on the upper Garigliano and seized Monte Faito (825 metres). German resistance stiffened, but could not stave off the Moroccan 4 Mountain Division after attacks on the key feature, Monte Maio. Juin had maintained that this pillar of the Cassino gateway could be taken by a bold aggressive thrust across the mountains; his prediction came to pass when it fell on 13 May and the French then advanced north west to reach the Liri Valley, south of Cassino by that evening. The decisive opening had been made for further thrusts into the Gustav Line, but as Juin had predicted, progress by the British 13 Corps had been a slow, tough process, and on the hills north of Cassino the Poles had met with costly rebuffs. A German opinion, as expressed by Bohmler, is that, once the French had made the rent in the Gustav Line, the Poles were laying down their lives in vain. Whether Polish efforts were a vital factor in the eventual capture of Cassino and the fall of Rome will be examined later.

In 13 Corps sector 4th British and 8th Indian Divisions each began crossing over the Gari/Rapido with two brigades leading. There was a thick mist in the valley which became a dense fog as the guns on both sides kept up a high rate of fire. The German guns had been badly knocked about by the ferocious bombardment before midnight and were unable to strike with such accuracy at the assaulting troops, as they had done in January, when the Texas Division had attempted a similar crossing. The defending infantry, however, were ready to fight it out and aided by extensive minefields, thick wire and well sited concrete emplacements, refused to be dislodged. When daylight came on the 12th May, although 4 Division had a narrow strip of bank in its possession, there was no bridge across the river, and one of its brigades, 28 Brigade, had been unable to consolidate its hold on the west side of the fast flowing river. The two battalions concerned, 2 Kings in the van followed by 2 Somersets, had been subjected to steady retaliatory fire from all weapons in a series of

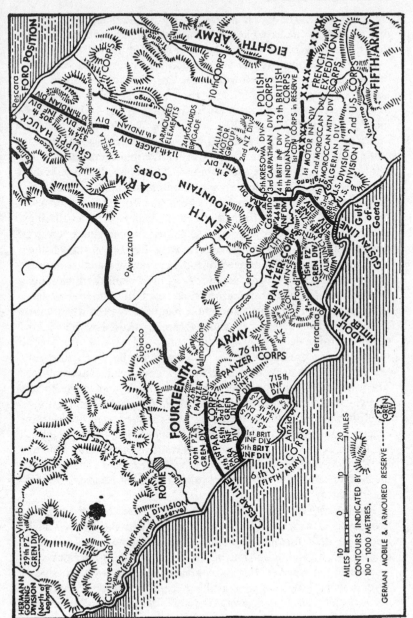

Map 9: The Fourth Battle situation and the Italian Front, 11th May 1944.

efficiently organised German attacks. By nightfall they had been forced back to the east bank, leaving a detachment of little more than a company in isolation on the other side of the river.

General Kirkman appreciated that a strenuous effort to erect bridges across the river was vital if his Corps was to retain the initiative. After desperate efforts by the engineers, which cost them many casualties, bridges were erected so that by the 14th morning men of 4 British Division had seized San Angelo, the objective that had eluded 36 Division in January. 13 Corps was poised to battle a way into the Liri Valley, but the Germans had decided to throw in the last reserves available to Tenth Army. These reserves moved down and were joined by units and sub-units of ancillary corps and services in attempts to check the British Corps on the threshold of the road to Rome through the valley. Reckless daring pilots of the German Air Force tried to press home attacks on the river bridges but their valiant efforts were in vain. Although the Tenth Army infantry continued to resist and delay the efforts of 13 Corps to advance up the valley, their right flank had virtually collapsed under the unceasing pressure exerted by the French and Americans. By 15th May a great hole had been blasted where four days before the German 71 and 94 Infantry Divisions had been manning strong defences.

Only in two areas had the German defenders been able to stand firm and throw back the attackers who suffered heavy losses. These were on the hills behind Monte Cassino and in the town below. Once again General Heidrich's paratroopers were grimly determined to hold on to the death or until they were ordered to evacuate the positions that had defied capture for weeks gone by. By 16th May, D plus five, General Alexander was still not able to let VI Corps begin its breakout from Anzio because the cork in the bottleneck of the Liri Valley had still to be removed by the Eighth Army.

The infantry of both Polish Divisions clambered over their start-lines at 1.00 a.m. on 12th May. Prior to that the soldiers had waited in their forward positions which in many cases were so close as to be within earshot of the Germans. At 11 o'clock the barrage began which a platoon commander described as follows: "Apart from 1100 pieces of artillery there were the mortars and the anti-tank guns blazing away—the noise deafened us. We had no idea how long this artillery bombardment would last, but I for one felt that if it went on for long I would go mad . . . We were confident that no Germans could possibly outlive such a devastating bombardment." General Duch's Carpathian Division had assigned a battalion on to each of the main objectives, one to capture Massa Albaneta, the other to press against Hills 593 and 569. The Second Battalion captured most of Point 593 within twenty minutes and had soldiers fighting on the northern side of Point 569 before an hour had passed. Further progress was checked because on their right flank the First Battalion had been held up by a gorge about four hundred yards short of Massa Albaneta. Severe close quarter fighting, aided by intensive artillery support, had enabled them to reach the northern slopes of the gorge by dawn, but thereafter the infantry were pinned down as daylight revealed their position to the German observers, not only at Massa Albaneta, but on Colle San Angelo. Mines in the gorge disabled tanks that had been sent to support the battalion, and heavy casualties forced the survivors to withdraw to their start-line. Their gallantry had not been sufficient to overcome the defences.

Meanwhile the battle for Points 569 and 593 continued. On 593, the Calvary Mount, casualties to the Second Battalion mounted alarmingly as the hours of 12th May went slowly by. Attacks and counter attacks were inevitably rapid affairs as groups of Germans, armed with hand grenades and sub machine-guns, would suddenly leap out from behind cover and capture one of the Polish positions, then, just as quickly, a handful of Poles would spring up as if from nowhere and drive off the Germans in the same manner. By nightfall the Polish survivors, one officer and seven men, made their way back as the Paratroopers moved in on Hill 593 and captured several prisoners. A platoon commander, who was rescued four days later, stated that the Germans were as exhausted as the Poles themselves: "As I studied the drawn faces of the Germans in the cave, I came to the very obvious conclusion that the defenders of Monte Cassino were already beaten." The platoon commander in temporary captivity took a more optimistic view than his senior commanders. The Carpathian Division's attack had failed: in General Anders' words: "It soon became clear that it was easier to capture some objectives than to hold them," a lesson that had been learnt several times in past battles for the Calvary Mount, Point 593. On the right the story of 5 Kresowa Division brought even gloomier news to the Corps Commander.

The leading brigade, 5 Vilna Brigade, advancing on Colle San Angelo, had captured Phantom Ridge and exploited forward to Point 517, but then disaster struck. Heavy fire from the Second Battalion of 3 Parachute Regiment, supplemented by accurate artillery concentrations, tore holes in the closely packed Poles as they sought shelter. Polish guns in support were unable to silence the opposition as, one by one, the forward observation officers, moving with the assaulting infantry, were killed or wounded. General Anders had no alternative but to withdraw the survivors behind their start-line as soon as darkness fell on the evening of 12th May.

The Germans had won the first round at Monte Cassino, a fact that General Leese was quick to appreciate when he visited Anders in his Headquarters. The Poles had taken a severe knock, but Leese was adamant that without their efforts, 13 British Corps in the valley below could not have succeeded in establishing their bridgehead over the Rapido. The Polish attack had drawn away artillery fire at a crucial period and had tied down reserves, reserves that might have played a vital part in holding the British in their attempt to establish a foothold west of the River Rapido. Nevertheless it was equally clear that further attacks by the Poles would have little influence on the battle being fought by 13 Corps until and unless the efforts of the two Corps were coordinated.

So far, the Polish Corps had not won a yard of ground from General Heidrich and his Paratroopers, who had withstood the onslaught of two divisions. Monte Cassino still seemed impregnable and unconquerable but during the lull in the battle on the hills the Germans could not fail to see that the British were moving into the Liri Valley, as scores of tanks and guns crossed to the west of the bridgehead. The trap behind Monte Cassino was closing and the defenders of the Abbey could but watch—and begin to wonder how they would escape. The Poles also waited before the next and final attack, keeping German nerves taut by carrying out local attacks, by probing forward with strong patrols and by harassing fire, using all available guns on to the key positions. Nevertheless, in spite of the depressing situation on General Heidrich's right flank, it was still clear that no major withdrawal had yet been made by the Parachute Division.

General Anders and his two divisional commanders pondered over the failure of their attack on 12th May. Why, with their superior numbers, had they been unable to defeat the Germans? Experience pointed to three major reasons: the first was that the opening bombardment of artillery concentrations on to known strongpoints did far less damage than optimistic forecasts had indicated. The result was that the Polish infantry soldiers were badly mauled from an early stage in the attack. The second was the lack of detailed local intelligence, which meant that junior commanders had to cope with unforeseen minefields, or were held up by previously undiscovered German outposts. The Poles had not been allowed to send out any patrols before the attack; for security reasons this order was sensible, for tactical purposes it was an error which cost lives. The third reason was a fortunate one from the German point of view, because the Polish attacks on the 12th came at a time when reliefs were taking place. The extra German troops were thus able to help out, to hold firm, and to mount local counter attacks, before the Poles could dig in on their hard won objectives.

The Polish generals were able to alter plans for artillery support in the next battle, and they could and did send out extensive patrols so that the second requirement was met and rectified. As far as the extra defenders were concerned, Allied intelligence stated that the Parachute Division had been substantially weakened after 13th May because it had been ordered to send reinforcements into the valley below, in order to bolster up the sagging Gustav Line. There were solid grounds for cautious optimism in the next battle, which would begin on the orders of the Commander of the Eighth Army, General Leese.

On 16th May General Leese decided that 13 Corps was almost through the Gustav Line defences, and was ready with the Poles for the final assault on the Cassino bastion. 78 Division was attacking northwards to cut Route 6 and isolate the town. By the morning of 17th May, 4 Division had reached the railway at Route 6, so that the Cassino lifeline had been cut. By this time the Polish Corps had begun its second attack, with the main artillery programme being completed by 0720 hours. In spite of careful preparation and better intelligence about the German defences, the assaulting troops had to endure heavy blows from the men of Heidrich's Division: once again the same divisions battled for the focal points, Point 593 (the Calvary Mount) and Colle San Angelo.

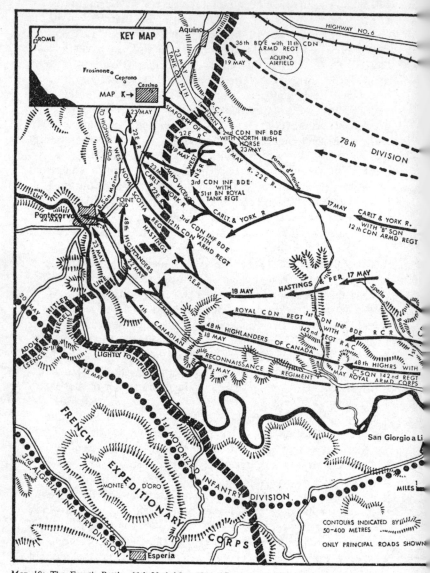

Map 10: The Fourth Battle, 11th-23rd May 1944 (Gustav and Hitler Lines are broken).

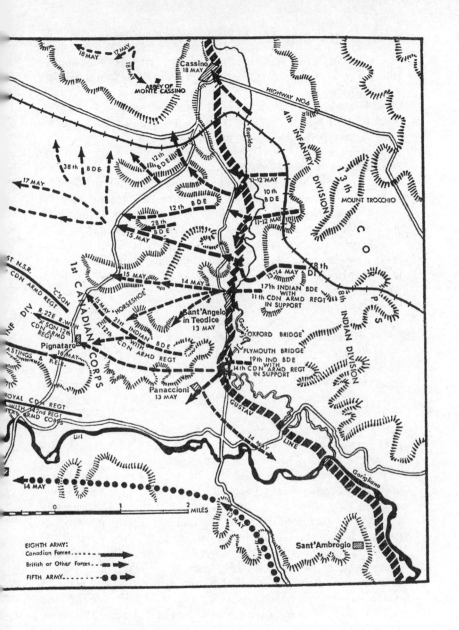

EIGHTH ARMY:
Canadian Forces ....
British or Other Forces ....
FIFTH ARMY ....

The battalions that had not been directly involved in the first attack on 12th May spearheaded the assault which followed up a heavy artillery bombardment. The plan did not differ substantially from General Anders' first one, and again the Poles found the Germans waiting for them. However, at the last moment, circumstances radically changed for 5 Kresowa Division. During the night of 16th May a company from 16 Battalion set out to reconnoitre Phantom Ridge, only to find that one or two positions on the ridge were lightly held. These were captured and the battalion commander, using his initiative to exploit success, moved up his other companies before midnight. A German counter attack failed to remove the intruders so that a firm base was available for the opening attack by 17 Battalion on Colle San Angelo next morning. As a result, men from 17 Battalion managed to penetrate Colle San Angelo within half an hour and, apart from some pill-boxes on the western end, cleared the position. The Germans, however, were past masters at striking before their opponents could consolidate, and this they did with artillery and mortars, followed by heavy small arms fire from Basso Corno, and by determined counter attacks from the south western slopes. For ten hours the fighting continued, with the Polish battalions suffering heavy casualties, and their ammunition supply dwindling at an alarming rate. To save such a desperate situation General Anders was forced to order forward a combined force from 16 and 18 Battalions; German ambitions were checked but, for the time being, such was the limit of success achieved by the 5th Kresowa Division.

The Carpathian Division set off one more against the Massa Albaneta and the Calvary Mount, only this time with tanks from 2 Armoured Brigade in support. The tanks were to neutralise the hamlet of Massa Albaneta and keep the Germans under heavy fire on the western slopes of Point 593 while the men of 5 Division stormed their objectives. 6 Battalion duly advanced and by determined fighting cleared the gorge that had held up the previous attack on 12th May. This enabled some tanks to move forward and give effective support, mostly against 3 Company of the 3rd Parachute Regiment which was all but destroyed; taking advantage of such support, 6 Battalion moved to within two hundred yards of Massa Albaneta where they were held up by expertly constructed and manned defences. It was now the turn of 4 Battalion to tackle Point 593.

For the rest of the day the battle for Points 593 and 569 continued with severe losses to both sides. The fortunes of attacker and defender quickly changed from good to bad as blow and counterblow were delivered by the exhausted contestants. Most of Hill 593 was captured, but the Polish hold on it was tenuous, and Point 569 was still held by the Paratroopers as darkness fell on 17th May. Anders commented: "That critical moment of a battle had come when both sides face each other in a state of exhaustion." The Poles ended the day with some gains, but the Germans had fought with great skill and determination against superior numbers.

Bohmler asserts that at the end of the day's fighting on 17th May the Poles had not captured in battle Colle San Angelo or the whole of Massa Albaneta or the Calvary Mount, Point 593. Allied records show that Hill 593 was captured by the Poles and was in their possession at dusk on the 17th. Be that as it may, it is an indisputable fact that, in the end, events below the Monastery caused the German High Command to make the decision to evacuate Heidrich's Division before their escape route was closed for ever. The Monastery was isolated and such a decision could not be delayed any longer.

The paratroopers who left their position did so with heavy hearts. Their casualties had been so numerous, particularly those suffered by the 1st Battalion 3 Parachute Regiment—its No. 1 Company, who had defended Point 593 to the death, had only three survivors still fit to fight at midnight 17th May. From the town, the 2nd Battalion Parachute Regiment returned up and over the slopes of Monte Cassino. In silence the Germans left Cassino to the Poles, to the dead, and to the few of their wounded who remained behind on the battlefield.

Next day the Poles began clearing and mopping up the remaining parts of Hill 593, Hill 569 and Massa Albaneta. Here and there small groups of Germans fought the Poles in order to cover the withdrawal of the remainder of the Parachute Division. The finale at Cassino was in complete contrast to the main acts of the tragedy that had been enacted over five months. In the place of tough bloody fighting around the Monastery there was peace and silence. One version of the end recorded by the CRA 3rd Carpathian Division: "From my O.P. I saw the white flag hoisted over what was left of the building. Through my artillery regimental commander I telephoned the Brigade commander of the 2nd Brigade to give him the news. At first he refused to believe that the Germans had surrendered. When I had finally convinced him I asked for a patrol to be sent to the Monastery with our national flag, but I was told that the infantry were too exhausted. I then got in touch with our Cavalry Regiment on a ridge nearby and bade them send somebody up to Monte Cassino with the Polish flag."

A patrol of 12 Podolski Lancers made their way up towards the Monastery, but no shots were fired at them by the thirty soldiers, many of them wounded, who waited to surrender. At 1020 hours the Poles raised the red and white standard with the white eagle over the ruins. To achieve this the Polish 2 Corps had suffered nearly 3,000 casualties in less than a week's fighting.

In the moment of triumph there was, for General Anders, time for sober reflection: "The slopes of the hills, particularly where the fire had been less intense, were covered with an incredible number of red flowers, weirdly appropriate to the scene."

The Monastery revealed its secrets to the Poles. They found that the main cellars had not been destroyed, even by the heaviest artillery bombardment and bombing, and in several places the fallen pieces of masonry served to strengthen them. The German paratroopers had constructed loopholes in the ruined walls from which they could fire in several directions. Outside the walls the whole area had been sewn with mines and booby traps. At strategic points innumerable caves and shelters had enabled the Germans to survive the heaviest of bombardments until the Allied guns stopped firing and allowed the paratroopers to emerge and continue the fight. Even in desolation, and in the unnatural silence after so much noise, Monte Cassino looked like an impregnable fortress. So it had been; it did not fall to direct assault, or succumb to the heaviest weapons available to the Allies. Now it was no longer important as the war swirled its way up the Liri Valley and the Poles made contact with 78 Division on Route 6, ready to begin the next phase in Alexander's major offensive.

The Poles deservedly won the worldwide acclaim for their gallantry and sacrifices. To General Anders came messages couched in glowing terms—such as the words used by General Leese: "This notable feat will, I believe, go down in history as a mighty achievement of Polish arms." Even more rewarding was a simple message of congratulations received from the Polish Underground

Army in Warsaw, where men still battled to throw out the Nazis and watched the oncoming advance of the Russians with considerable apprehension.

The Fifth and Eighth Armies continued the advance on Rome. For the moment, Cassino and its Monastery were forgotten. As was pointed out earlier, its capture in the Fourth Battle was to be a phase in 'Operation Diadem', but one of the utmost importance and significance. Alexander in announcing that Cassino had fallen to the British, and the Abbey to the Poles, added: 'After the unique feat of the Fifth Army in penetrating the Gustav Line on 14th May and thanks to the swift advance of French and American troops in the mountains, the enemy has been completely outmanoeuvred by the Allied armies in Italy . . . The 1st Parachute Division, the best fighting unit in the German Army, has lost more than half its strength.' Perhaps the true meaning of the previous abortive attempts by the Allies against Cassino was revealed in a further message by Alexander to Churchill: 'Capture of Cassino means a great deal to me and both my armies. Apart from its Foreign Office value it seems to have great propaganda possibilities.'

With the comfort of over a quarter of a century's retrospection, the tragedy of Cassino can be seen in these words. Cassino meant too much to both sides; to Hitler and the German High Command its defence was a dedicated mission, a chance to show the world that the German Army was still invincible; to Churchill and to Alexander, it was an obsession, a challenge, a fortress that had to be taken before the tide of victory could once again flow in favour of the Allied cause in Italy.

On May 18th a great and overriding victory seemed to be more than a strong possibility in Italy.

18

Rome and the Last Victory

The fall of Cassino brought a radical change in the respective fortunes of war in the Liri valley. No longer was there any reason for the Tenth Army to make a stand south of the Hitler Line, and events were now moving so quickly that the Line itself was in grave danger of being outflanked. It had taken German Intelligence a few days to realise that four of the Allied divisions, which they had stated inaccurately were in base areas or held back in reserve, had been playing a significant part in the opening phases of the 'Diadem' attack. As a consequence, Kesselring had been slow in appreciating that the land battle was indeed the major effort and that a further invasion from the sea could be discounted. Kesselring's unhappy position had been brought about by the speedy advances achieved by the French and American Corps, with startling successes by the French Goumier who threatened to take Pico on the 19th May.

By this time Kesselring had virtually taken personal control of the battle and by timely moves of reserves had stabilised, to a certain extent, the front based on the Adolf Hitler defences. The right wing of the Tenth Army gave him most concern, so that the Fourteenth Army near Anzio was instructed to send one of its reserve divisions, 29 Panzer Grenadier Division, to the assistance of its hard pressed sister Army. Such an order was not carried out without a measure of prevarication by the staff of Fourteenth Army. In the meantime, Eighth Army had massed tanks, guns and vehicles up against the outer defences of the Hitler Line. At no time did the attackers have an easy passage; the Polish Carpathian Division seized Piedimonte on the 20th of May, only to be thrown back by a spirited counterthrust made by a battalion of the indomitable Parachute Regiment. Around Monte Caira the Kresowa Division met determined resistance. Progress on the Eighth Army front continued to be slow until the 23rd May; by that time General Leese's Army had penetrated a distance of less than ten miles beyond the Gustav Line in contrast to the spectacular successes achieved by General Keyes' II Corps (Terracina, twenty-five miles beyond the Gustav Line) and Juin's men assaulting Pico. The conglomeration of vehicles that headed the Eighth Army advance up the Via Cassilina (Route 6) presented grave problems of traffic control to the staff and this was advanced as one of the reasons for the delay.

On the 23rd May General Leese was ready to begin Eighth Army's part in the next phase. Pico, the key to the Hitler Line defences, had been defended with skill and resolution by 26 Panzer Grenadier Division, the Division that had originally been sited as reserve to cover the beach-head at Anzio, but Juin's Corps eventually captured the town by midday on the 22nd May. The moment had come for General Truscott's VI Corps to launch its attack and smash a way out of the beach-head at Anzio. By this time Fourteenth Army had lost both its armoured divisions, 26 and 29, because these were fighting hard in an attempt to save Tenth Army in the south. Alexander's excellent timing of the breakout found the Tenth Army facing defeat and the Fourteenth Army without any immediate armoured support: the climax of Operation 'Diadem' was at hand.

The Canadians advanced towards Monte Corvo and by dawn on the 26th, the First Canadian Division had taken the town. The Poles, once again, took up their attacks against Piedimonte and against Monte Caira and, after heavy losses, these were both captured on the 25th May. The same day witnessed the link of Truscott's VI Corps and the Fifth Army advancing up the coast—the junction that had been sought in January when the first Cassino battles had started and VI Corps had landed on the 25th January on the then peaceful beaches at Anzio. Three hours after the leading elements had made contact the scene was again enacted for posterity, with General Mark Clark beaming his approval in the photographs issued to the world.

Kesselring had still to accept that Fourteenth Army could not hold its own and had moved 334 Infantry Division across from the Adriatic in an attempt to bolster its defences. It is clear that he appreciated that Alexander intended to strike towards Valmontone and thus threaten to cut off Tenth Army which would herald a major disaster. Such indeed was Alexander's intention and it was for this purpose that the landing at Anzio had originally been devised. By the 25th May the capture of Rome was just a matter of days, but still to be decided was how much of Tenth Army would escape to the North before being cut off by Truscott's VI Corps. Alexander had more than the prospects of a great victory; he had the chance to destroy a large part of the Army that had defied him for months gone by, with the trap closing by the evening of the 25th May when General Truscott's leading elements moved within striking distance of Valmontone.

The background to the astonishing change of plan that occurred thereafter has been the subject of much controversy. The arguments will excite the attention of soldiers and historians wherever and whenever the Italian campaign is studied. Once again, the character and personality of Mark Clark had a powerful influence on events that, for a short but critical period, were taken outside Alexander's direct control. What is not easy to decide is whether Alexander could have overridden his subordinate; was it his reluctance to interfere or did the political pressures lie too heavily on him when it came to a direct showdown with the Commander of the Fifth Army? Whatever the reason, there are two indisputable facts that have stood the test of time: firstly, General Mark Clark firmly decided that his Fifth Army and no one else would have the honour of entering Rome; and secondly, the two German armies on the verge of a major debacle, were given the chance to escape the Allied net, to survive, and to fight again before and during the battles of the Gothic Line, later that year.

It may be an over simplification to cast Mark Clark as the sole villain of the piece although he was the leading actor with his strong obsession to be the first to claim the prize of Rome. He wrote: "We not only wanted the honour of capturing Rome, but we felt that we more than deserved it; that it would to a certain extent make up for the buffeting and frustration we had undergone in keeping up with the winter pressure against the Germans. My own feeling was that nothing was going to stop us in our push towards the Italian capital . . . we intended to see that the people back home knew that it was the Fifth Army that did the job and know the price that had been paid for it." These words remain for posterity and no one can doubt what Mark Clark's feelings were about being the first to liberate Rome. In what way and how did he contravene the orders given by his superior commander, General Alexander?

There is no published record of what happened at the highest level of command; accounts written by three American generals have been studied and certain inferences have been made from them. In this connection it is worth noting that Alexander did not give vent to feelings of disappointment or frustration at the time and refused to comment on the controversy after the war. Mark Clark's book 'Calculated Risk' has been mentioned and this reveals how he was irritated and suspicious about Alexander's suggestion that the Fifth Army should swing due north, a move that would not only have helped Eighth Army, but would have made it unnecessary for Leese's Army to attack the Hitler Line. In Clark's eyes such a change in direction meant a delay in capturing Rome. It also meant American lives being risked in order to save British ones. Clark's elation at the speedy advance made by his two Corps added to his irritation at the slow British advance up the Liri valley. Eighth Army had been given the chance to capture Cassino after Fifth Army had borne the stigma of three defeats; in spite of the fact that in Operation 'Diadem' planning, Rome had always been in the Fifth Army sector, Mark Clark found it impossible to trust Alexander at the crucial moment in the Italian campaign, or to resist the lure of the publicity that would reward those who liberated the Italian capital city.

General Lucian Truscott of VI Corps was a commander trusted by Winston Churchill and the British Chiefs-of-Staff, as well as by his own countrymen. His words written in 'Command Missions' show that he was dumbfounded at receiving Clark's orders on 26th May to abandon the drive on to Valmontone: "This was not the time to drive to the north-west, where the enemy was still strong; we should put out maximum power into the Valmontone gap to ensure the destruction of the retreating German Army." Truscott, too, had previously noted that Mark Clark "was fearful that the British were laying devious plans to be the first into Rome." And Truscott remained convinced that the original strategic objective of Anzio would have been fully achieved if Clark had not changed Alexander's instructions.

Major General Fred Walker, whose 36th Division had moved into reserve in Anzio, met Mark Clark on the 23rd May. Clark made uncomplimentary remarks about the British Eighth Army and said that one lone Canadian Division was being used to capture Ponte Corvo at a time when all the stops should have been pulled out by General Leese and his staff. It must be stated that Alexander was not blameless in this matter because he had not yet released Route 6 for use to anyone except the Eighth Army—even though it was his intention that they should bypass to the east of Rome.

It is unfortunate that General Mark Clark's emotional statements in his book have overshadowed one or two sound military reasons for not continuing with the VI Corps thrust on Valmontone. The cutting of Route 6 would not have effectively blocked all the escape routes available to the German Tenth Army. Moreover from a military viewpoint the country beyond Valmontone is not easy going, and Truscott's men would have been advancing against the grain as far as the hill contours were concerned. VI Corps would have been extended and open to counter-attack by an enemy still capable of hitting back whenever grave risks were taken by his opponents. Against these factors, even more powerful arguments can be mustered to show that Alexander's original plan for the Anzio force to seize Valmontone was an inspired one. What is certain, however, is that Clark's reasons for turning towards Rome were not military ones; he was determined to seize the City for his army as a reward for their toil and tribulations since landing at Salerno.

The switch was ordered on the evening of 26th May by Mark Clark. First class staffwork by the experienced VI Corps Headquarters enabled the new offensive towards the north west to be unleashed within twelve hours. Alexander was, in effect, presented with a 'fait accompli' and he accepted the situation in his normal unruffled way by deciding to let Clark continue with the revised plan. The alternative was a direct confrontation with a suspicious and reluctant American Army commander. In the interests of Allied unity, and in the knowledge that Clark's plans might still achieve a victory, Alexander allowed events to take their course. In London, Churchill was not at all satisfied with the new development: "At this distance it seems more important to us to cut the line of retreat than anything else . . . 'a cop' is much more important than Rome, which would anyway come as its consequence." The British Prime Minister's disturbed feelings were again revealed in his next telegram to Alexander: "The glory of this battle, already great, will be measured, not by the capture of Rome or the junction with the beach-head, but by the number of Germans duly cut off." By this time, however, there was no chance of a 'cop' as the Americans had swung towards Rome.

Justice was done when the US 36 Division struck the decisive blow on the night of 30/31 May. Spearheaded by the 142nd Regiment which climbed the steep slopes of Monte Artemiso, the whole Division reached the Velletri road in the rear of the German defences. Great credit must be given to General Walker for the imaginative operation which he had suggested to his Corps Commander, Truscott. On the other hand Kesselring was furious with the inefficient complacency of 14th Army and commented: "This was the last straw which decided me to recommend to Hitler a change in the commander" (Von Mackenson).

36th Division's success exposed the flanks of 1 Parachute Corps and Clark gave orders for a general advance. Now there was nothing between the Americans and the goal they sought, Rome. Fourteenth Army withdrew behind the Tiber and the Commander-in-Chief of the German troops, Kesselring, ordered his men to move out of Rome without any attempt being made to destroy a single one of the many bridges over the Tiber. In that hour of defeat, Kesselring had given strict orders that Rome was to be handed over without any fighting or demolition or destruction. Little credit was given him at his trial after the war; belatedly, therefore, let us remember the humane act of the Commander-in-Chief of the German forces in Italy when he spared the ancient city of Rome from the horrors of war and thus avoided senseless destruction.

Mark Clark drove into Rome on June 5th, following the leading troops of the new 88 Division who had reached the centre of the city on the evening of the 4th of June. The General said to members of the world press and to the Italians gathered round him: 'This is a great day for the Fifth Army and for the French, British and American troops of the Fifth Army who made this victory possible.' For the Eighth Army moving to bypass the city there was no publicity or acclaim. However, the joy and jubilation of the capture of Rome was soon to be eclipsed by news of greater significance, that of the invasion of Normandy. 'Overlord' had begun on the morning of June 6th.

The first chapter of the Italian campaign was over and a victory had been achieved. Was it a total victory? Should the Tenth Army have survived in the face of annihilation to fight again? For there was to be no easy road from Rome into Austria for the Allies. By skilful rearguard actions the Germans continued to delay and hold the British and American advance guards throughout the summer months of 1944. But of even more consequence the strategy of the whole Italian Campaign was once again to suffer from the original decisions made by the Combined Chiefs of Staff. Churchill pleaded that the Italian campaign should be crowned by an advance into the Balkans. Alexander tried to retain all his divisions by pointing out that the withdrawal of experienced commanders and troops, for operations elsewhere, would mean that a glorious opportunity to score a really decisive victory would be lost forever. The British protestations were to be of no avail; once more 'Anvil' and 'Overlord' took first place and the campaign in Italy became one of secondary importance as far as the top American advisers were concerned. At the height of its victory, Fifth Army had to withdraw seven of its best divisions for the invasion of Southern France. The fall of Cassino, the capture of Rome, and the heavy bitter fighting at Anzio and Salerno, seemed to lose much of their point and significance when the Americans insisted on launching 'Anvil'. Alexander was left, once more, with the task of fighting a campaign in difficult country without any marked superiority in infantry. The fruits of the victory south of Rome had been cast away and there was to be no chance of entering Austria before the following Spring.

The role adopted by Alexander and his depleted forces, after the fall of Rome, is outside the scope of a book about the battles of Cassino. Before the Allied soldiers lay another barrier, the Gothic Line, and its battles were to last from late August 1944 into the following Spring. The way from Cassino to the Alps proved to be a long and costly one for the Allied armies. On the other hand events were to show that Operation 'Anvil' contributed little to the defeat of Germany. Alexander's armies at full strength in Italy would surely have made a bigger contribution to victory but what cannot be assessed is, to what extent the cancellation of 'Anvil' might have changed the story of the Italian campaign itself. There are grounds for belief that a political victory would have ensued, as the Anglo-American armies might have reached the Balkans before the Communist forces moved into the vacuum created by the defeat of the German forces in that area. Unfortunately, Churchill's motives for suggesting an advance into the

Balkans were viewed with as much suspicion by his American colleagues as they were distrusted by Stalin.

The Italian campaign continued to be a slow and bitter fight until the end of the war and to this day, official historians still argue about its value to the Allied cause. To pose the question 'Why Italy?' is to invite arguments that do not point to any clearcut conclusions.

Cassino today, over a quarter of a century after the war, is a flourishing town. The post war autostrada passes nearby and so much of the Rome-Naples traffic now by-passes the town. The stark features remain and the Monastery sits in splendour on Monte Cassino, rebuilt as a replica of the former Abbey, bombed and destroyed in 1944. Only the castle on Castle Hill has been left in ruins as a reminder of the devastation of war.

Above the bustling new town stands a monument which already shows the ravages of time. It is a simple, tall staff built on top of fast-crumbling marble blocks and surrounded by an iron chain. It is situated on top of the hill, known as Point 593 to the Allies, and as the Calvary Mount to the Germans. All around is nothing but the scrub and moss-covered rocks of the mountain. The simplicity of the monument and the tragic irony of the inscription are very moving; the words read:

> "We Polish soldiers,
> For our freedom and yours
> Have given our souls to God
> Our bodies to the soil of Italy
> And our hearts to Poland."

Well over 1100 Poles lie among the rocks or in a bleak field not far from the slopes where they fell in battle. Their sacrifice for Poland was to be in vain because the Polish Resistance forces were decimated by the Germans before the Russians moved in and set up a Communist government.

From Point 593 the landscape has not changed very much, as the farmhouses have been rebuilt on the same spots as the ruined shells that gave meagre support and shelter by day and night to soldiers during the bitter 1944 winter. Time has not changed the perfect view from the high ridge over the ground below, the ground over which Americans, British, Indians and Poles hurled

200

themselves against defences manned by the resolute German defenders.

The passing of the years has softened the countryside and farms flourish where death and destruction held sway. Nevertheless the long-abiding impression that remains is that the Italian Military College could not have selected a better example of an impregnable natural defensive barrier than Cassino. It is easy to see how and why the Germans held out against attackers who, although given lavish air and artillery support, could not conquer Monte Cassino. There can be little, if any, argument about the Germans' choice and preparation of defences—and their conduct in fighting the battles thereafter. They knew their way about before the Allied attacks started, their artillery and 'nebelwerfers' were so located that rarely were there any blind spots in the defensive mosaic, while observation posts, sited on excellent vantage points, ensured accurately controlled fire at all times. The Germans evolved and perfected a system of speedy local counter-attacks against key positions which, they appreciated, had to be recaptured before the invader was given a chance to consolidate. Time and again these tactics paid off, particularly in the struggle for Point 593. Americans, Indians, British, Gurkhas and Poles reached its summit but found it impossible to retain a hold on it for long.

There are few who find fault with the German tactics at Cassino or how they carried them out. The majority of Allied soldiers who fought at, and survived, Cassino had an unstinted admiration for their opponents—and lest we forget, a high regard for the 'clean' way the Germans fought. War is too brutal and degrading for the term 'sporting' to be used, but the Parachute Division came as close to earning this appellation as is possible. So much for the German side of the story; the questions arise when Cassino is viewed against the Anglo-American strategy. Why were the battles fought? Were they necessary? Could the Allies have avoided them by outflanking the Monte Cassino defences?

Why were they fought? The simple defence of the First battle is that it was launched to keep the German Tenth Army occupied while VI Corps established a bridgehead at Anzio. If, as originally visualised by Winston Churchill, Anzio had indeed clawed the Germans down from their rear, then the conduct of the First battle could never be questioned. Anzio did not bring the Germans to their knees: within a matter of days the invaders were clinging on to a narrow beach-head and, in desperate straits, sought help from their comrades fighting on the main front.

The First battle was both necessary and inevitable, but need it have relied on a frontal assault? Two alternative attempts were made to outflank Cassino, by the British X Corps, and by the French Corps under Juin. The nature of the mountains that faced X Corps in the drive over the Garigliano and up the Ausente valley did not give rise to optimism during the winter months. Some 15 kilometres of mountainous terrain lay as a barrier before the Liri valley could be reached. Encouraging though the initial gains were by X Corps, a larger force than three divisions would have been necessary to force a way up the Ausenti.

General von Senger und Etterlin rightly criticises the Fifth Army plan of three Corps attacking across the front, thus dissipating any reserve forces available to exploit any opening made in the Gustav Line. Even if there were reasons for such a strategy it was not mandatory to maintain the original plan to the bitter end. No reserves were at hand to exploit the surprising success of X Corps against the right wing of General Vietinghoff's Tenth Army; no reserves were available to the Allies although Kesselring took decisive action to plug the hole before the flank of the Gustav Line was turned. And so we can but pose the question, what might have happened if the Fifth Army had mounted one more concentrated attack over the Garigliano? Would it have been possible with the forces available, for the US 11 Corps to have forced a way forward if it had passed through British X Corps after the Garigliano bridgehead had been established? General Von Senger implies that he would not have had the reserves available to stop such a thrust; the Rapido fiasco would have been avoided and the later battles at Cassino might have taken another form. All is conjecture; certainly we must not under-estimate the uncommon natural strength of the country in the Ausonia defile with its hazards accentuated by a bitter Italian winter like the one experienced in 1944.

No question mark is put against the Rapido River disaster. Evaluation of records, German and Allied, and a personal knowledge of the country, gives rise to grave doubts about Majdalany's version, a version that leans heavily on the excuses advanced by General Mark Clark and the Congress Inquiry that subsequently 'whitewashed' him. An attack by a lone division against San Angelo over the River Rapido, without any real attempt at diverting the attention of the German defenders—never have soldiers been given a more forlorn hope than that given to the American 36th Division. It seems quite irrelevant to mention the battle experiences or otherwise of the divisional staff and the combat troops under command. They had no chance whatever—nor was the risk justified as the German reserves had already been drawn away from the area of Anzio by X Corps' early drive over the River Garigliano.

In defence of the frontal attack made in the First battle by General Keyes' 11 Corps, it must be admitted that 34 Division's spectacular advance over the mountains north of Cassino, which reached a point only one mile from Route 6 and the Liri valley, nearly won the day. Victory was so near that it is possible if 36 Division had not been mauled on the banks of the Rapido, then its full strength, added to 34 Division, might have tipped the balance against General Von Senger's troops. Again this is surmise; we are on more definite grounds when stating that much of the justification for the second direct attack by fresh troops on Monte Cassino lay in the fact that 34 Division, depleted in strength and tired though it was, nearly defeated the Germans by its gallant assault in the early days of February.

In spite of 34 Division's exploits, many believe that General Juin's advocacy of a drive across the mountains into the Atina basin should have been adopted by Generals Alexander and Clark. Juin made such a plea in January 1944 so that, unlike historians, he was not speaking with the comfort of retrospection. He was supported by another astute tactician, General Tuker, who also wrote a paper before the Second Battle started, suggesting that mountain troops with maximum logistic support would be able to isolate Cassino. Subsequently Juin has pointed out that the terrain although difficult was not as inhospitable as the Aurunci mountains through which his Corps forced a spectacular advance in May. To Juin and his adherents we can make one point: there was a way over the mountain and it might not have been impossible, but after the middle of February when Arctic conditions prevailed for over three weeks, logistic problems might have crippled the fighting ability of a large body of troops, trying to operate in the mountains.

Why was the Second battle fought? Primarily, to save Anzio, but additionally because 34 Division's example showed that a breakthrough might depend on the availability of extra infantry, ready to move forward at the crucial moments of an attack. Hence, two full strength divisions were called forward to relieve the understrength Americans. And the other great inducement to try, once more, to battle the quickest and shortest way up to the Abbey was the promised air strike against Cassino.

The lesson that first class troops cannot be driven out of well prepared defences by hundreds of bombs and dozens of shells or by sheer weight of metal, is not peculiar to Cassino alone. Nevertheless there is little doubt that far too much faith was put in the aerial bombardment that preceded the Second and Third battles. Air bombardments had been used before but the number of planes and the weight of bombs used against so small and concentrated a target area, made the Cassino experiment unique in the annals of war. It is difficult to blame the Allied commanders when they agreed to let the Air Force 'whip out Cassino like an old tooth' but, it is more probable that without such a preponderance of air support the Third battle might not have been fought—and possibly, the tactics adopted for the Second battle might have been those advocated by Generals Juin and Tuker, a thrust across the mountains to the north east of Cassino rather than a direct assault on to Monastery Hill. We can conclude, therefore, that overwhelming air superiority clouded the judgement of the senior Allied generals, Alexander, Clark and Freyberg, and that they would never have attempted to attack the Gustav Line at its strongest point unless they had been mesmerised by the destructive capability of the bombers, supplemented by the massive artillery support. Overwhelming fire support did not win the day especially when the terrain favoured defenders who were determined to fight to the last round at the last ditch.

Mention of the Abbey is not to repeat the arguments for and against the bombing or ask why the decision was made. Political and ethical motives in favour of allowing the building to be a neutral zone, surrounded by some of the strongest defences ever seen, were overruled by military necessity and expediency. For the sake of his troops' morale, General Alexander could not have made any other decision. The tragedy was that Fifth Army and New Zealand Corps Headquarters failed to coordinate the devastating bombardment with the ground attacks—and made no real effort to seek a postponement of the Air Force programme until Fourth Indian

Division was ready to attack Point 593 and the Monastery. Consequently, any advantages that could and should have accrued from the bombardment were nullified, so that, in the end, the decision to destroy the Abbey was a pointless one. The ground attacks put in by New Zealand Corps thereafter were gallant ones but never looked like achieving a victory and their task was made doubly difficult when First Parachute Division, under the able commander General Heidrich, was given the responsibility for the defence of Monte Cassino.

If the Third battle is weighed against three questions then it is a task of some magnitude to provide an adequate explanation and answer to the queries. Why was it fought? Conceived in haste against the clock, in an attempt to launch it at the height of the crisis of Anzio, three weeks of bad weather then curtailed and ruled out any idea of aggressive action. During the enforced delay the German efforts to overrun the beaches at Anzio were to be soundly defeated and the moments of acute danger disappeared. Furthermore, Alexander and his staff had already begun to plan Operation 'Diadem' which, with the spring weather, was to open the road to Rome and destroy the German Tenth Army. Was there any military justification for the Third battle when it eventually began on 15 March? There were political reasons for continuing the pressure against the Germans and, rightly or wrongly, Alexander felt that the bad weather precluded any major action being taken anywhere else, other than at Cassino. From start to finish he remained convinced that the Liri valley was the key to Rome and the other routes were of secondary importance only. In my opinion, the Third battle was not necessary and had little, if any, tactical or strategical value. The two fresh Allied divisions in New Zealand Corps lost a thousand men each without any important gains to boast about, or hand over at the conclusion of their abortive attacks. Freyberg's conduct of the battle is open to question, particularly his reluctance to commit more infantry when the Paratroopers were bewildered and reeling immediately after the bombing had ended. All told, this battle was an inexplicable one that did little to help the Allied cause in Italy. It witnessed some of the toughest and most desperate infantry fighting seen in the Second World War—again the bloody infantry 'in fighting' might never have taken place if Alexander had not allowed himself to be swayed by the promised effects of a really heavy bombardment by all the air resources in Italy on to Cassino town.

And so to the final act at Cassino, the Fourth battle. It was an important phase in Operation Diadem, a phase that was to isolate the Monastery and open the Liri valley for Eighth Army's advance on Rome. The final design of the whole offensive was the fruit of weeks and weeks of preparation and the results added lustre to General Alexander's high reputation as a commander in war. At Cassino General Anders and his Polish Corps eventually triumphed where others had failed, but at a cost. Without in any way detracting from their courage, tenacity and determination, it must be remembered that the Poles captured the final objective at a time when the Gustav Line had already been smashed by the Fifth Army—and 13 Corps had moved behind Monte Cassino itself. Therefore, there are grounds for questioning the necessity for the second of the large scale attacks put in by the Poles on 17 May, when the evacuation of the Cassino defences by the Parachute Division had become inevitable. Bohmler has gone further by stating that the Polish attack, launched on 12 May, had little significance and led to unnecessary casualties in attempts to capture objectives which events elsewhere were already forcing the Germans to evacuate. Two points can be produced to refute his statement. Prior to H hour on 12 May no Allied general, except Juin, had foreseen that the French would make such an important thrust into the flank of the Gustav Line with such speed and impetus. No one except Juin had expected the opposition against the Eighth Army to be quite as tough and desperate. If the Liri valley had to be opened, then 13 Corps had to cross the Rapido in the early stages of Operation Diadem. And there are solid grounds for General Leese's assessment when he told Anders that the bridgehead could not have been won without the gallant efforts made by the Polish Corps to capture Point 593, attacks which fully occupied and diverted most of the attention of the German artillery away from events near San Angelo in the valley below.

On balance, it might be fair to judge the attacks made on the 12th May as being justified, but to assert that, afterwards, the Polish Corps should have been asked to probe and harass the Parachute Division without being ordered to undertake the second full scale attack on 17th May. After the 12th May, the Parachute Division was understrength and so exhausted that its attention could have been held by a series of aggressive patrols, supported by generous artillery concentrations and air strikes. Surmise it may be, but there seemed to be a desperate longing in the hearts of the senior Allied generals to capture Cassino and seize the Monastery rather than wait for the prizes to fall into their laps. In the end the Monastery was not stormed. The final act was one of anti-climax and in a sense, mocked the efforts of the Allies to take Monte Cassino during the preceding five months' fighting.

The fall of Cassino, the junction of the Fifth Army with VI Corps from Anzio, the fall of Rome, all these were heady champagne to the Anglo-American forces in Italy. The winter of discontent and attrition was over and a Spring promised victories to end the Italian campaign.

Alas, the Combined Chiefs of Staff decided that the projected invasion of southern France ('Anvil', later called 'Dragoon') was to take priority over the Italian campaign—and some of the 'sharpest teeth' were withdrawn from the Fifth Army. The war in Italy did become a secondary campaign and continued to be treated as such by the Americans until the end of the War in Europe.

Nevertheless, it is tempting to discuss what might have been the result if Alexander had taken Juin's advice and thrust down the Milfi to the Atina basin, instead of battering away at the Liri Valley and the grimly held Cassino features, or if Mark Clark had obeyed Alexander's instructions and closed the gap at Valmontone before the two German armies united. The campaign will always be one for debate and it is wise to realise that each of the alternative courses would have suffered from unexpected snags which no plan, however well furnished, can ever foresee. It is salutary, for any critic, to study Theodore Roosevelt's words, quoted in the preface of this book; in particular, "It is not the critic who counts, nor the man who points out how the strong man stumbled, or where the doer of deeds could have done them better".

Back at Cassino let the words of N. C. Phillips end this story: "Ruins are dismantled and new buildings arise on the sites of the old. Men remember, but their memories fail and finally die with them. And of the deeds bravely done and hardships bravely borne soon nobody will remember but the imperfect record itself." Hence this book—while memory still serves.

Epilogue—The Bombardment of Monte Cassino

It may seem strange that in 1979 controversy over the bombing of Monte Cassino flared up again, thirty-five years after the event. This was largely due to publication of a booklet, *The Bombardment of Monte Cassino*, written by Professor Herbert Bloch and made available for sale on the bookstall at the Abbey of Monte Cassino. Before long, letters began to appear in the correspondence columns of *The Times* and *Daily Telegraph*, all alleging that Herbert Bloch had presented his case unfairly, in particular by pointing the finger of accusation at Generals Freyberg and Tuker. In New Zealand, there was an immediate outcry when Freyberg was singled out for blame by Herbert Bloch. The Prime Minister, R. D. Muldoon, was furious and in a statement made in the New Zealand Parliament, affirmed that he and his countrymen felt slighted by the accusations made in Bloch's booklet.

In Britain, I was introduced to the affair by the 4th Indian Division Officers' Association. Their committee was also incensed by the allegations in the work. Bloch, a German who later became a naturalised American citizen, believed that Major General R. S. Tuker should bear much of the responsibility for the destruction of the Abbey in 1944. His widow, Lady Cynthia Tuker, objected to this and asked me to persuade the Abbot at Monte Cassino to withdraw the offending booklet from the bookstall. Failing that, she hoped he would at least allow one produced under the auspices of the 4th Indian Division, to be sold alongside Bloch's version of events.

It is not a purpose of this epilogue to describe, in detail, my investigation into the background of the Monte Cassino bombardment. Suffice to say that I received a great deal of assistance from the Archbishop of Westminster, Cardinal Hume, and Father Richard Yeo (the Abbot Primate's secretary in the Vatican) which resulted in me going to Monte Cassino in

November 1983 to interview the Abbot. It transpired that he had been a young monk in 1944 and had been inside the Abbey when the bombardment had begun. Not unnaturally, he became very emotional when describing how the once beautiful building had been totally destroyed. He maintained that, to his knowledge, there had been no armed German soldiers within the building before the bombardment began, and therefore the Allies had not been justified in ordering its destruction. I disagreed and pointed out that in fact General von Senger had condemned the Abbey to destruction at the same time as he had decided to defend Monte Cassino to the bitter end. I accepted the Abbot's word that no heavy weapons had been concealed within the Abbey before the bombardment, but explained that from its elevated position near the summit it could be, and was, used as a vantage point by the enemy, who could then use wireless and telephones to direct artillery and mortar fire on to the Allied troops fighting below.

After reading my short paper on the subject, he listened with courtesy to my plea on behalf of Lady Tuker, and assured me that if and when Bloch's booklet was reprinted, all references to General Tuker's alleged guilt would be omitted.

Shortly after my visit, wartime diaries kept by monks during those controversial days of early 1944, were found and examined by two American authors, Donald Hapgood and David Richardson. Their findings appeared in 1985 in a book published by Angus and Robertson, *Monte Cassino*, and their main conclusions were as follows:

1   Although the Germans did declare a three hundred metre 'neutrality zone' around the Abbey, to some extent that edict was forgotten after 5th December 1943. In fact, though they made no military use of the giant building itself, they violated the zone on several occasions. Indeed, General von Senger himself ordered his men to 'make defences right up to the Abbey wall if necessary'. Later, Kesselring issued the instruction: 'the building *alone* is to be spared'.

2   Entries in the monks' diaries indicated that the building was being hit, and damaged, by artillery and mortar fire from both sides, *before* the actual bombardment took place.

3   For reasons of 'military necessity', General von Senger decided to defend Monte Cassino. At the same time he must have realised that his opponents would be forced to assault the Abbey itself if Monte Cassino was to be taken.

4   Well within the three hundred metre zone, the Germans had set up a munitions dump in a cave, as well as a command-post bunker, several machine guns and one or two well sited observation posts.

5   Although Professor Bloch's pamphlet, on sale in the Abbey, specifically accused General 'Gertie' Tuker of being the chief advocate of the bombing, the American authors produced evidence that before he went into hospital, Tuker argued strongly against a direct assault on the Abbey. It was only when General Freyberg overruled him that General Tuker conceded, saying that if they were going to attack the Abbey with his division leading the assault, Freyberg should at least ensure that blockbuster bombs were used in the operation. Hapgood and Richardson claimed that Professor Bloch had quoted Tuker out of context, and thus made him appear to be one of the instigators of the bombing.

Military blunder though it was, the bombing of Monte Cassino was not a war crime. With hindsight it is feasible to claim that the fate of the Abbey helped to save Rome because, subsequently, the Germans decided not to defend the Holy City. The Allies respected this decision. Only later did both sides realise that the destruction of Monte Cassino could have been avoided. General Tuker had been admitted into hospital eleven days before the bombing, and never returned to Cassino. After the bombardment he continued to criticise the decision to attack the German's strongest held position in Italy.

There will always be questions, but for now let us pray that the new and beautiful Benedictine Abbey be the symbol of hope for the future of mankind. Let us hope that the word 'PAX', engraved on the Abbey portals, will conquer mens' hearts and that war will never come again to Monte Cassino.

Index

Adriatic Coast, 31
Aegean Is., 23
Alban Hills, 28, 64, 73
Alexander, Gen. Sir Harold,
    passim
  character, 170
  decisions, 160-161
  directive, 28
  well-matched, 37
Algerian troops, 41
Allied artillery, 20, 97, 100
Allied Conference (Cairo &
    Teheran), 23
Allied Forces:
  Air Force, 92: 15th Army
    Group, 81
  5th Army (US), *passim:*
    Salerno landing, 12
  8th Army (Brit.), 10, 14-15,
    18, 20, 31, 73, 192-193
    Cassino, 171-172
  15th Army Group, 27
  1st Canadian Corps, 172
  II Corps (US), 30, 40, 66, 179
  2nd Polish Corps, 173-190
    passim
  VI Corps (US), 62, 84, 169,
    193-194: position critical,
    108
  10th Corps (Brit.), 29, 30-31,
    49, 173
  13th Corps (Brit.), 40, 155:
    Rapido bridgehead, 184
  French Expeditionary Corps,

31, 32, 40, 41, 47: Algerian
    & Tunisian troops, 63,
    68; startling progress, 180
  N.Z. Corps, 75-123 *passim:*
    junior leaders, 138-139;
    Maori troops, 99-106 *passim*
  1st Armoured Div., 37, 47, 62
  3rd Carpathian Div. (Polish),
    177-178, 189
  4th Div. (Brit.): San Angelo,
    181
  4th Div. (Ind.), 31-32, 72-
    132 *passim*, 158: Gurkha
    & Rajputana troops, 102-
    141 *passim*, withdrawal, 157
  5th Kresowa Div. (Polish),
    177-178, 188, 192
  6th Armoured Div. (Brit.),
    172
  8th Div. (Ind.), 172, 180
  34th Div. (US), 37, 40-41,
    62: Cassino town, 68, 69-
    70; Rapido, 66, 67
  36th Div. (US), 30, 38, 47-
    48, 203: loss of leaders,
    54; Rapido, 49-50, 52-
    58 *passim*
  78th Div. (Brit.), 150, 172:
    Castle Hill, 149, 157-161
    passim
  85th Div. (US), 179
  88th Div. (US), 179
  N.Z. Div.: staff changes, 78

Allied Forces (*cont'd*)
48th Engineer Batt. (US):
Rapido, 131
1/4 Essex Regt., 125: Castle
Hill, 129, 135
1/2 Gurkha Rifles, 102, 105
1/9 Gurkha Rifles, 102, 104-
105, 106
Hangman's Hill, 128-129
2/7 Gurkha Rifles, 102, 146
133rd Inf. Regt. (US): Cassino
town, 69; Rapido, 66
135th Inf. Regt. (US): Monastery Hill, 71; Rapido, 66
141st Inf. Regt. (US):
Rapido, 52
142nd Inf. Regt. (US):
Rapido, 51
143rd Inf. Regt. (US):
Rapido, 52
168th Inf. Regt. (US):
Rapido, 67
2nd King's Regt.: Gari/
Rapido, 180
28th Maori Batt., 99-100, 143
21st N.Z. Batt., 153
24th N.Z. Batt., 131
25th N.Z. Batt., 120
26th N.Z. Batt., 131
12th Podolski Lancers (Polish), 190
4/16 Punjab Regt., 92
1/6 Rajputana Rifles, 127:
Castle Hill, 129
4/6 Rajputana Rifles, 102, 143
1st Royal Sussex Regt., 89
6th Royal West Kent Regt.:
Castle Hill, 150
2nd Somerset Regt., 180
756 Tank Regt. (US):
Rapido, 67
America, 9, 25
Amphibious operations, 22-23

Ancona, 17
Anders, Gen., 33, 63, 173-190
passim
'Anvil', 25, 165, 198, 207
Anzio, 13-115 *passim*
beach-head, 167
breakout, 193
landing at, 62
Rome, battle for, 27
'Shingle', 26
'Approach to Battle' (Tuker),
163
Atina basin, 31

Baade, Gen., 33, 40, 75, 111
Bailey bridge, 57
Balkans, 25, 199
Bateman, Brig., 127, 147
'Battle for Rome', *see* Anzio
Beckett, Maj. D.A., 125, 145,
146, 150
Behr, Col. Baron, 75
Belvedere, *see* Monte
Bohmler, 119, 132, 156, 180,
206
Bond, H.L., 71, 75, 85, 87
Bonifant, Brig., 140
Buckley, C., 70, 118
Burma, 35
Burns, Gen., 173

Caesar Line, 169
Caira, *see* Monte
'Calculated Risk' (Clark), 195
Caserta, 79
Cassino, *passim*
art treasures, 42
Castle Hill, 120-150 *passim*
Continental hotel, 136-150
passim, 153

Cassino (*cont'd*)
  Hangman's Hill, 120-142
    passim, 155-156
  Hotel Des Roses, 139, 141,
    143
  Monastery, 39, 44, 45: con-
    struction of, 86; Monastery
    Hill, 18, 71, 100, 120,
    153; secrets revealed, 190
  Railway Station, 100, 120, 132,
    138
  Snakeshead Ridge, 71, 102
  town, 45, 69, 101, 124, 132
Castelforte, 29
Casualties, 11, 15, 54, 57-58, 59,
    60, 69, 75, 101
  see also: German Forces;
    Rapido
Channon, Gen. John, 81
Churchill, Sir Winston S., 9-10,
    13, 28, 93, 110, 132, 160,
    198
  Anzio, 64, 73, 75-76
  eloquence, 16
  negotiations, 26
Cifalco, *see* Monte
Clark, Gen. Mark, *passim*
  Anzio, 49
  leadership, 170
  Rapido, 47-61 *passim*
  Rome, 197
Colle Abate, 64
'Command Missions' (Truscott),
    28, 48, 195
Committee on Military Affairs,
    59
Conrath, Gen., 43

Dalton, Maj., 96
'Diadem, Operation', 72, 164-
    169 *passim*, 193
Dimare, Abbot Gregario, 42, 93

  see also Cassino
Dimoline, Gen., 90-98 *passim*,
    117
Drinkall, Capt. M., 129, 134

Eisenhower, Gen. Dwight D.,
    20, 23, 35
Evans, Maj., 133, 134

Feuerstein, Gen. Valentine, 166
Flying Fortresses, 81, 93
Foggia airfields, 36
France, 9, 11, 23, 35
Franck, Gen., 40
Freyberg, Gen. Sir Bernard, V.C.
    passim
  background, 78, 79
  monastery attack, 143-144
  Rapido, 63
Frosinone, 28, 167
Fuller, Gen., 9, 11

Galloway, Maj. Gen., 117, 132,
    140
Gari River, 40, 172, 179
Garigliano River, 14, 29, 47, 69
  bridgehead, 60
Geneva Convention, 151
German Forces:
  artillery, 64, 127
  casualties, 60, 69, 108
  High Command, 12, 16, 119,
    124
  10th Army, *passim*
  14th Panzer Corps, 37, 40,
    150: War Diary, 157-158
  LI Mountain Corps: Cassino,
    166
  LXIII Panzer Corps, 114
  Luftwaffe, 16, 142, 164, 182

German Forces (*cont'd*)
1st Parachute Div., 69, 104, 123, 162: holdfast, 184; Railway Station, 142
5th Mountain Div., 20, 40, 63, 111
9th Div., 20
15th Panzer Grenadier Div., 20, 40, 69
Rapido, 56, 57, 111
26th Panzer Grenadier Div., 167, 193
29th Panzer Grenadier Div., 20, 30, 167
Rapido, 49
44th Hoch Und Deutsch-meister Div., 40, 63, 111
71st Inf. Div., 69, 111
90th Panzer Grenadier Div., 40, 111
Rapido, 49, 75, 167
94th Inf. Div., 21, 29, 180
Hermann Goering Panzer Div., 20, 42, 167
Shultz Battle Group, 72
Todt Organisation, 14
71st Mortar Regt., 124
90th Panzer Grenadier Regt., 99
134th Panzer Grenadier Regt., 66
200th Panzer Grenadier Regt., 75
1st Parachute Regt.: Castle Hill, 154
2nd Parachute Regt., 71
4th Parachute Regt., 145
Parachute Machine Gun Batt.: Railway Station, 141
Germany, 9, 18
Glennie, Lt. Col. J., 89, 95, 96
Goebbels, Dr., 44, 94
Goering, Hermann, 44

Goums, 171
Great Britain, 9
Gruenther, Gen., 88
Gurkhas, 7, 78, 83, 102, 139, 162
Gustav Line, *passim*
lynch pin, 45
strong point, 161

Harding, Gen. Sir John: masterly appreciation, 167
plans, 116, 138, 165
Heidrich, Lt. Gen., 33, 111, 135, 166
Hitler, Adolf, 10, 20, 38, 75, 108
Hitler Line, 169, 192

India, 9
'Infantry Brigadier' (Kippen-berger), 83
Italy, *passim*
capitulation, 12
Italian campaign, 37
terrain, 10

Jamrowski, Lt., 119
Japan, 17
Jennings, Lt., 155
Juin, Gen., 31, 39, 109, 171, 178
Rapido, 63

Kesselring, Field Marshal Albert, *passim*
anticipation, 17
decisive action, 30
Rapido, 60
Keyes, Maj. Gen. Geoffrey, 38, 49, 179: Rapido, 55, 63

Kippenberger, Maj. Gen. Howard, 50, 99, 110, 117
  on Freyberg, 83
Kirkman, Gen., 172
Knolls, *see* Points

Leese, Gen. Sir Oliver, 20, 172, 184, 192
Liri, river & valley, 17, 28, 44, 73, 140, 171, 192
Lovett, Brig., 90, 92, 101, 104
Lucas, Gen., 27, 28, 32
  Anzio, 62, 73
Luftwaffe, *see* German Forces
Lungo, *see* Monte

McCreery, Gen., 49
Mackenson, Gen. Von, 72, 77, 89, 107, 197
Majdalany, Fred, 27, 50, 51, 84, 178
Majula Hill, 71
Mallinson, Maj., 155
Maoris, 106-117 *passim*, 143
Masse Albaneta, 74, 183, 188
Mignano Gap, 15
Monte Artemiso, 197
Monte Belvedere, 64
Monte Caira, 19, 41, 109, 173, 192
Monte Castellone, 71, 72, 83, 179
Monte Cifalco, 63
Monte Faito, 179
Monte Lungo, 15, 48
Monte Maio, 180
Monte Trocchio, 20, 28, 47, 117
Montgomery, Gen. Sir Bernard L., 15, 20, 35
Moroccan troops, 41

see also French Corps
Mussolini, 10, 36

Nangle, Lt. Col. G.S., 127, 134, 146, 156
Naples, 86
'Neither Fear nor Hope' (von Senger), 37
Nepal, 9
New Zealand, 35, 39
Normand, Capt., 155
North Africa, 17, 35

Ortona, 16
'Overlord', 11, 23, 25, 108, 170, 197, 198

Parkinson, Maj. Gen., 117, 124, 125, 136, 140, 143, 162
Patton, Gen., 35
Phillips, N.C., 86, 138, 207
Pico, 193
Points (knolls):
  (56), 66
  (165), 120, 127, 133, 145, 150
  (175), 145
  (202), 134, 141
  (213), 66
  (236), 120, 133
  (435-Hangman's Hill), 72, 128, 141
  (445), 72, 106
  (450), 105
  (569), 183, 188
  (593-Calvary Mount), 71, 94, 105, 106, 149, 183, 189
Poland, 9, 33
Pontine Marshes, 18

Rapido River, *passim*
  bridgehead, 101
  casualties, 57, 60
  crossing, 52
  dammed, 19
  description, 50
Ringel, Gen., 40
Rodt, Gen., 40, 56
Rome, 14, 34, 48, 194
  Germans' takeover, 12
Rommel, Field Marshal, 12, 13
Roosevelt, Pres., 23
Route (6), 18, 32, 72, 132
Route (7), 30
Russia, 11, 116
Ryder, Gen., 86

San Angelo, 47-66 *passim*
  see also Rapido
St. Benedict, 42
Salerno, 10, 13, 17, 28
Sangro River, 14
Schlegel, Lt. Col. Julius, 42-45
  passim
Schuster, Lt., 119
Secca Valley, 63
Senger und Etterlin, Gen. von,
  16, 18, 32, 44, 111
  criticisms, 202
  Garigliano, 60
  Rapido, 60
  responsibility, 37
  Rhodes Scholar, 38
  victory, 157

'Shingle', *see* Anzio
Showers, Lt. Col., 105
Sicily, 17, 23, 35
Sonnie, Capt., 151
Stalin, Joseph, 25, 116

Thirty Six Assn., *see* Committee
Tito, 23
Trident conference, 23
Trocchio, *see* Monte
Truscott, Gen., 28, 35, 47, 169,
  195
Tuker, Maj. Gen. F.S. (Gertie),
  31, 72, 117, 158, 163
  experience, 82
  Monastery findings, 86

Vietinghoff, Gen. von, 12, 202
Volturno River, 14, 15

Walker, Maj. Gen. Fred L., 33,
  38, 48
  dilemma, 49
  Rapido, 56, 59
Washington, 23
Wilbur, Gen., 50, 54
Wilson, Gen. Sir Maitland, 168
'Winter Line', 14, 15

Yugoslavia, 23